FILLED WITH
SPIRIT AND POWER

FILLED WITH SPIRIT AND POWER

Protestant Clergy in Politics

LAURA R. OLSON

State University
of New York
Press

Published by
State University of New York Press, Albany

© 2000 State University of New York

All rights reserved

Production by Susan Geraghty
Marketing by Dana Yanulavich

Printed in the United States of America

No part of this book may be used or reproduced in any manner whatsoever without written permission. No part of this book may be stored in a retrieval system or transmitted in any form or by any means including electronic, electrostatic, magnetic tape, mechanical, photocopying, recording, or otherwise without the prior permission in writing of the publisher.

For information, address State University of New York Press, State University Plaza, Albany, N.Y., 12246

Library of Congress Cataloging-in-Publication Data

Olson, Laura R., 1967–
    Filled with spirit and power : Protestant clergy in politics / Laura R. Olson.
        p.   cm.
    Includes bibliographical references and index.
    ISBN 0-7914-4589-5 (hardcover : alk. paper). — ISBN 0-7914-4590-9 (pbk. : alk. paper)
    1. Clergy—Political activity. 2. Protestant churches—Wisconsin--Milwaukee—Clergy Case studies. I. Title.
BV4327.O47 2000
323'.042'0882044—dc21   99-41450
                                                                         CIP

10 9 8 7 6 5 4 3 2 1

For my family

CONTENTS

Tables	*ix*
Acknowledgments	*xi*
Chapter 1 A Tale of Two Pastors	1
Chapter 2 Political Involvement: Choices and Strategies	13
Chapter 3 Personal Resources for Political Involvement	31
Chapter 4 Contextual Resources for Political Involvement	43
Chapter 5 Substantive Political Agendas	61
Chapter 6 Abortion	81
Chapter 7 Crime and Violence	97
Chapter 8 Family Values	111
Chapter 9 Filled with Spirit and Power	127
Appendix	*137*
Notes	*139*
References	*157*
Index	*169*

TABLES

Table 3.1	Attitudes about Propriety of Political Involvement	35
Table 3.2	Feelings of Political Efficacy	37
Table 3.3	Gender	40
Table 3.4	Career Stages	41
Table 4.1	Denominational Traditions	52
Table 4.2	Per Capita Personal Income (in $) of Church Neighborhoods	55
Table 4.3	Unemployment Rates (in %) of Church Neighborhoods	55
Table 4.4	Percent Living Below Poverty Level in Church Neighborhoods	57
Table 4.5	Minority Population (in %) of Church Neighborhoods	57
Table 4.6	Race and Neighborhood Socioeconomic Status	58
Table 5.1	Network News Lead Stories, June–July 1994	63
Table 5.2	Issues of Greatest Concern to Clergy	64
Table 5.3	Concerns about Issues of Immediate Life Circumstances	65
Table 5.4	Concerns about Family and Sexual Morality	71
Table 5.5	Concerns about Discrimination	73
Table 5.6	Concerns about Nonlocal Issues	76
Table 6.1	Salience of Abortion	93
Table 6.2	Positions on Abortion	94
Table 6.3	Abortion Positions by Denomination	94
Table 7.1	Milwaukee Area Crime Rates, 1992–1994	100
Table 7.2	Salience of Crime and Violence	109
Table 7.3	Positions on Crime and Violence	109
Table 8.1	Positions on Family Values	123
Table 8.2	Political Involvement, Family Values, and Denomination	124

ACKNOWLEDGMENTS

I would like to take the opportunity to thank some of the special people who generously supported me through the development of this book. While I bear full responsibility for my work's shortcomings, I could never have completed this study without the help and support of others.

First I must thank the forty-six Milwaukee pastors who kindly consented to be interviewed for this study. They welcomed me into their churches (and in some cases, their homes) and shared freely of their time and energy. They taught me more than I could have ever imagined, both individually and collectively. Each of them is truly filled with spirit and power. It is my hope that I have represented them well, as this story is theirs.

The Department of Political Science at the University of Wisconsin–Madison is a wonderful place to study. I can never sufficiently thank my mentor and friend, Booth Fowler, for his unending support and confidence in me. His enthusiasm has sustained me through good times and bad. Chuck Jones kept me focused on clarity and spent time helping me to improve every chapter of this book substantially. My debt to Gina Sapiro is also great, for she set high standards and offered extremely valuable criticism. I would also like to thank four other individuals at the University of Wisconsin—Murray Edelman, Charles Franklin, Mary Jane Hill, and Graham Wilson—for the many contributions they made to this study and its author.

Later in the process of turning this study into a book, I benefited enormously from helpful reviews offered by Chris Gilbert, Jim Guth, and Stuart Lilie. Several other colleagues from the subfield on religion and politics lent me considerable support throughout the preparation of this manuscript, especially my friends and co-authors Sue Crawford, Allen Hertzke, and Ted Jelen. I would also like to express my thanks to Melissa Deckman, John Green, Lyman Kellstedt, Matt Moen, and Corwin Smidt. Moreover, Zina Lawrence and Susan Geraghty at the State University of New York Press have both been extremely helpful during the publication process.

My colleagues in the Department of Political Science at Clemson University provided a collegial working environment as I completed this manuscript. And my students at Clemson and the University of Wisconsin have inspired me with their energy and ideas. Now that I am a teacher, I value even more highly the wonderful education I received as an undergraduate at Northwestern University, and before that, in the public schools of Racine, Wisconsin. I am also blessed with many wonderful friends who contributed in a variety of ways to the process of writing this book, especially Pam Christopherson, Sue Hullin, Andy Murphy, Lara Schrader, and Dave Siemers.

Finally, I cannot explain in words the importance of my family in this work and in my life. To list the contributions they have made to this book and its author would be impossible. All I can say is that I simply would not *be* without them, and that I love them more than anything in the world. It is to my family—my parents, my brother, and the memory of my grandparents—that I dedicate this work.

But as for me, the Lord fills me with his spirit and power,
and gives me a sense of justice
and the courage to tell the people of Israel
what their sins are.

—Micah 3:8

CHAPTER 1

A Tale of Two Pastors

To begin to understand the choices clergy make about becoming involved in politics, it is helpful to consider an average day in their lives. Where, on a typical weekday afternoon, might they be found? Perhaps they are visiting elderly members of their congregations, or leading Bible study groups in their churches. Perhaps they are preparing sermons about the relationship between the week's scriptural lessons and current politics. Or perhaps they are at city hall, lobbying public officials to pass gun control legislation. Religious leaders make a wide variety of choices when it comes to managing their time and other resources. Some of them choose to include some form of political involvement in their busy schedules, while others shun politics.

All clergy would likely consider themselves to be, as the Book of Micah encourages, *filled with spirit and power*, but they express the presence of these forces in their lives in many different ways. What impulses guide them toward, or away from, the political realm? Under what circumstances do clergy decide to act as links between the people they serve and the American political system? It is of great importance to understand clergy's orientations toward political involvement. Clergy have the potential to mobilize hundreds of people, should they choose to do so, and to make significant contributions to the political agendas of the communities in which they serve. Little is known about what drives some clergy to become deeply involved in politics, or what leads others to avoid the political realm altogether. This study adds to the overall understanding of the choices religious leaders make about political involvement by telling the stories of forty-six clergy and their political decisions.

Just as the religious traditions over which they preside are characterized by great diversity, so too the political involvement of religious leaders varies tremendously. All clergy must reconcile the institutional rules and expectations of the organizations they serve with their own goals and preferences when they decide whether to include political involvement as an element of their official roles as clergy. Some reject the idea of translating their religious authority into political authority. Others opt to present an agenda of important issues for their congregations to consider. Still others have both the desire and the opportunity to lead their congregations in political endeavors. This book is an exploration of the variety of orientations urban Protestant clergy display regarding political involvement, as well as the many factors that shape their activity. I show that in an urban setting, the choices pastors make about political involvement are shaped in a profound way not only by their specific religious traditions, but also by the socioeconomic status of the neighborhoods in which they serve.

The setting for the study is Milwaukee, Wisconsin and its suburbs: a metropolitan area with a population of over one million people. Milwaukee is a city of much more than its trademark beer, bratwurst, and cheese. It is also home to hundreds of religious communities. Since its founding, Milwaukee has been an ethnic melting pot, and this fact is clearly reflected in its organized religious life. The clergy who lead Milwaukee's congregations have traditionally played a visible role in both the culture and politics of their city. The diversity of Milwaukee's religious leadership is reflected in myriad ways among its pastors, but a brief tale of two Protestant clergy illustrates this variety particularly well.

A casual observer might expect that of the hundreds of Protestant pastors in Milwaukee, Louis Bound and Alan Rickover[1] should be among the most similar. Both are middle-aged, with thinning hair and wrinkled brows. Like many Milwaukeeans, both are of German descent. The Protestant denomination in which they both serve claims the upper Midwest as a stronghold, yet both Reverend Bound and Reverend Rickover were born and raised in other regions. Both share what could be considered a moderately liberal theological outlook, and both identify with the Democratic Party. In 1964 both participated in the pro–civil rights Freedom Summer in Mississippi. Since these two pastors seem to share so much in common, it would be very easy to assume that their orientations to political involvement would be similar too.

Their tale, however, tells as much of difference as it does of similarity. It took Reverend Bound an hour in an interview setting to provide a mere thumbnail sketch of his political activities in the past week. He was particularly proud of the fact that because of the efforts of a coalition in which he is active, a tavern in his church's immediate neighborhood had recently been stripped of its liquor license.[2] On many occasions police had discovered drugs, weapons, and underage patrons in this tavern. He said that "The city attorney told us it couldn't be done, but we worked hard and we shut down that tavern. I personally lobbied four of the city alderpersons" (M4).[3] Reverend Rickover, however, said of his lack of political involvement: "I have decided that it isn't working. I don't know what works. I don't know what's right" (M14).

Bound was proud that people join his church specifically because of its political agenda: "They know that we take very strong justice stands on social issues" (M4). Rickover, though, expressed a belief that "The purpose of a sermon is not to advocate political action or to push a certain political agenda" (M14).

This tale of two pastors, along with that of forty-four of their counterparts, forms the basis of this study. I explain the circumstances under which some leaders (clergy) of "nonpolitical," and certainly extragovernmental, social institutions (churches) choose to extend their spheres of influence into the political realm while others do not. What is responsible for the dissimilarity between Bound and Rickover, each of whom asserted that he was typical of the denomination in which they both serve? As it turns out, one important element of this divergence lies in the fact that Bound serves a congregation located in one of Milwaukee's most economically stressed neighborhoods, while Rickover is employed by a church situated in one of the city's wealthiest suburbs.

Pastors face a variety of demands on their time and energy. They must balance these demands in such a way as to maximize their ability to meet the externally defined expectations of their position, as well as to implement their own agendas. Among the goals of some pastors is political involvement, either in their community or on a larger scale. Others prefer to steer themselves and their congregations away from the political realm. In either event, it is crucial that clergy present their preferences to their congregations in such a way as to rally support for these goals. Some clergy *value* such activity more than others, and some are *more successful* at it than others. Erving Goffman has argued that "When an individual appears before others his actions will influence the definition of the situation which they come to have."[4] Some who define social realities do so in a conscious, calculating fashion, while others are less aware of their ability to shape their group's circumstances. Clergy have the capability to shape their congregations in many ways. Some pastors are able to present themselves as *political* leaders for their congregations, while others are not—or choose not to try.

In an urban setting, the choices pastors make about political involvement are shaped in a profound way by the socioeconomic characteristics of the neighborhoods in which they serve. The type and frequency of pastors' political activities differ depending on whether they serve in economically challenged central city congregations or wealthy suburban churches. Moreover, pastors who work in central city neighborhoods embrace different issue agendas and ideological orientations than their counterparts in outlying areas, regardless of denominational affiliation. A pastor in the central city may look out of his or her office window and see drug houses, the scenes of violent crimes, and homeless people. As one of the central city pastors I interviewed pointed out, "I'm sure you've noticed the poor living conditions we have here in Milwaukee's inner city. Some of the people around here live in awful rat holes" (A9). The same would not be true for a pastor in an affluent outlying area. He or she would see a large parking lot, expensive homes, and attractive scenery. These circumstances have important ramifications for the political choices such clergy make.

THE UNBREAKABLE LINK BETWEEN RELIGION AND POLITICS

Despite the constitutional maintenance of "separation of church and state" in the United States, religious groups have not avoided political involvement. After all, as Alexis de Tocqueville observed, "By the side of every religion is a political opinion, which is connected with it by affinity."[5] This observation is perhaps more true today than it was when de Tocqueville visited the United States in the 1830s. The constant presence of religious voices in debates about such issues as abortion, prayer in school, and capital punishment provides plenty of evidence that religion and politics are profoundly intertwined in the American political culture. The political visibility of religious leaders as different as Jerry Falwell and Jesse Jackson highlights the broad sweep of organized religion's role in American politics.

The 1940s brought about a blurring of legal boundaries between church and state as the Supreme Court incorporated the First Amendment's religion clauses.[6] From the 1950s through the 1970s, churches served as rallying points for history-making social movements.[7] By the 1980s, previously inactive evangelical Protestants began to emerge as a potent electoral force,[8] and in 1988, two major presidential contenders were ordained Protestant clergy.[9] Most recently, politically active Christian groups have been important players in the political struggle to define American morality.[10] Thus it should come as no surprise that clergy often find themselves under pressure to participate in politics. As the tale of two pastors illustrates, however, widely divergent views about both the desirability and scope of pastoral political involvement coexist within the world of American clergy.

Several important studies of clergy involvement in politics were undertaken in the late 1960s and early 1970s. Harold Quinley, Jeffrey Hadden, and Rodney Stark and his colleagues were all concerned with documenting and exploring the radicalization of mainline Protestant clergy during the civil rights movement.[11] Taken together, their studies came to represent the benchmark of scholarship in the area of clergy and politics for two decades. Only recently has scholarly attention again been paid to the political involvement of clergy. James Guth and his colleagues have amassed and analyzed the results of thousands of surveys about clergy and their political beliefs and practices, and Ted Jelen has undertaken pioneering ethnographic work by interviewing clergy and visiting their churches.[12] Before these studies appeared, though, much was being made of the political mobilization of religious people, yet there was little discussion of the role of the pastor in this process. In their path-breaking studies of political mobilization in churches, for example, Kenneth Wald and his colleagues discussed the "political tenor" of various religious communities at length, but they did not focus much attention on the roles clergy play in shaping political context for their congregations.[13] This is surprising given that religiopolitical activism is really an example of the broader phenomenon of political involvement by the leaders of nonpolitical social institutions. It has, however, never been treated as such. Nowhere are the motivations of nonpolitical leaders to take on political roles analyzed in detail.

The recent large-scale study of the political involvement of clergy by Guth and his colleagues represents a major step forward. Guth in particular has been a pioneer of the recent study of clergy involvement in politics; his work on Southern Baptist clergy has paved the way for other research.[14] In their body of work, Guth and his colleagues argue that "social theology" is the central determinant of political activism among clergy. They have compiled an enormous amount of data in the course of their research, but they have not written the final theoretical chapter on the subject of clergy and politics.[15] Jelen's work on clergy and politics is also valuable because it provides some rich contextual detail of the circumstances under which clergy make political choices, but its generalizability to urban settings is limited because it is based on research in rural Indiana. Moreover, Jelen's study is tightly organized around the various denominational groupings to which the clergy belong. As a result, the study is primarily descriptive, carrying with it normative conclusions.[16]

THE SETTING: METROPOLITAN MILWAUKEE

Milwaukee is located in the southeastern corner of Wisconsin on the west shore of Lake Michigan. The city is divided geographically by the industrial valley of the Menomonee River. This geographical division corresponds to strong patterns of de facto racial segregation.[17] While Caucasians reside in all parts of the metropolitan area, residents of the near north side are predominantly African American, and Hispanic Americans are most likely to live on the near south side.[18] Suburban sprawl has proceeded to the north, west, and south; Milwaukee's wealthiest residents live in suburbs on the far north side. The downtown area has enjoyed a renaissance in the late twentieth century, and during the summer months a host of ethnic festivals celebrate the city's cultural diversity. For this reason residents of "the city of festivals" are often said to be filled with *Gemütlichkeit:* a spirit of social friendliness.

As the twin nineteenth-century impulses of immigration and westward expansion progressed, so too Milwaukee grew.[19] In 1818, the French Canadian Laurent Solomon Juneau arrived in the Northwest Territory and established a trading outpost on the southwestern banks of Lake Michigan. By 1834, Native Americans had ceded all lands in and around the Milwaukee River, and European Americans, particularly German immigrants, began moving into the area. The impact of German immigration on Milwaukee's history cannot be understated. Milwaukee's economic base grew rapidly thanks to the beer industry, which was spurred by such notable German Americans as Jacob Best, Frederick Pabst, and Joseph Schlitz. To this day the culture of Milwaukee retains a distinctly German American flavor.

At the same time, Milwaukee has been a melting pot for various ethnic groups. Polish immigration began in force around 1850 and continued into the twentieth century. Polish Americans settled on the south side of the city, while German-born residents lived on the north side. Over time, the arrival of more ethnic groups, together with assimilation and intermarriage, resulted in more mixed housing patterns among European Americans. Some neighborhoods, however, retain their distinct ethnic character to this day. African Americans began moving to Milwaukee in the mid-1850s, some making their way north through the Underground Railroad. Following emancipation and well into the twentieth century, African Americans continued to move north to urban centers like Milwaukee in search of employment. Peter Eisinger argues that the great speed with which African Americans moved into the metropolitan area created a stress on the city. Milwaukee, says Eisinger, was not prepared to face this rapid demographic shift, and has suffered from difficult race relations for decades as a result.[20]

Religion and politics have been intimately interconnected in Milwaukee throughout its history. Solomon Juneau was Catholic, and the Roman Catholic Church retains a strong presence and influence in Milwaukee. However, Juneau also encouraged the growth of Protestant churches. Ground was broken by Presbyterians for the city's first church on April 13, 1837, and the Milwaukee Catholic Archdiocese was established in 1844. The first clash between religion and politics in Milwaukee sprang from tensions between Catholics and Protestants. During a period of labor unrest in the mid-nineteenth century, a lecturer and former monk named E. M. Leahy gave a talk that was highly critical of the Catholic Church at the Spring Street Methodist Episcopal Church. This incited a riot between Methodists and Catholics, causing a great deal of damage to the church building. Pew railings were broken off and used as clubs. As a result of this melee, the Milwaukee Common Council, in its first documented entanglement with religion, voted to award the Methodists $150 to repair their church.

More recent and far more significant were the political efforts of the late Father James Groppi, a Catholic priest and civil rights activist who led African Americans in demanding fair and equitable housing policy. In the wake of bloody riots in Watts, California, and Newark, New Jersey, a similar crisis began in Milwaukee on July 31, 1967. Father Groppi and his followers defiantly violated curfews imposed by the city government, and Mayor Henry Maier was soon forced to the bargaining table with the Conference on Religion and Race, a group of clergy organized by Groppi. Later Groppi led a series of marches and protests designed to force the issue of fair housing continually before the eyes of the city government. Groppi encouraged a spirit of cooperation between Catholics and Protestants, and perhaps more significantly, between white and black clergy.

Cooperation between white and black clergy was also in evidence in the early 1980s in Milwaukee under the auspices of the Coalition for Justice for Ernest Lacy.[21] Ernest Lacy was an African American man who died in police custody, raising serious questions in the community about police brutality. Laura Woliver demonstrates that "the religious element in the Coalition grew, becoming more than the personal faith of the [Lacy] family, [and took] on a dimension of its own as more and more clergy and religious activists joined the Coalition."[22] These legacies live on today.

THE CLERGY AND THEIR CHURCHES

I considered only Protestants in this study to establish a baseline; all interviewees, at a minimum, shared in common the fact that they were clergy in Protestant churches. The largely white mainline Protestant denominations, which advocate a nonliteral approach to Scripture, have long-standing roots in the United States. Mainline churches were indisputably the most socially influential through the nineteenth century of American history, but they began adapting to religious pluralism—and thus lost their position of social hegemony—when the Catholic Church expanded during the second great wave of European immigration from 1890 to 1920.[23] While mainline clergy tend to endorse a liberal political agenda, their laity have often been characterized as politically conservative.[24] This has created a political "gap" between mainline clergy and their laity that has stifled the mainline's potential for mass political activism.[25] Many mainline clergy embrace the "social gospel," which is a politicized interpretation of Scripture that emphasizes extensive welfare programs, world peace, and human rights. I interviewed sixteen mainline clergy who represented the United Church of Christ, the United Methodist Church, the Presbyterian Church (U.S.A.), the Evangelical Lutheran Church in America, the Episcopal Church, and the American Baptist Church.

Evangelical Protestants are predominantly white, and they strictly interpret Scripture as the word of God—and in some cases, the *literal* word of God. They also stress the importance of each individual's personal salvation experience with Jesus Christ. The evangelical sector of Protestantism encompasses fundamentalists, who interpret the Bible literally and often adopt a separatist stance toward society; evangelicals, who are less literal in their interpretation of Scripture and focus a great deal of energy on spreading the word of God; and Pentecostals, who believe in "gifts of the spirit" such as speaking in tongues and miracles. The evangelical sector encompasses a large number of denominations, and some evangelical churches operate independently of super-church organizations. The source of evangelicals' national political strength lies in the strong grassroots networks they developed for political activism in the late 1970s. The political organizations that arose to represent evangelical Protestants, such as Jerry Falwell's now-defunct Moral Majority and Pat Robertson's Christian Coalition, advocate Christian activity to combat what they perceive as the advanced moral decay of American society. They seek to place politicians in office who share this goal. The issues on their agenda reflect an underlying concern for the moral fiber of America: they oppose abortion, support prayer in public schools, and deplore pornography and violence on television. I interviewed sixteen evangelical clergy who represented the Assemblies of God, the Southern Baptist Convention, the Evangelical Free Church, the Wisconsin Evangelical Lutheran Synod, the Lutheran Church-Missouri Synod, the Church of the Nazarene, the Church of God, and several churches with no denominational affiliations.

African Americans constitute a separate category within Protestantism. African American Protestantism has had its own unique experience and as such stands apart from predominantly white Protestant traditions. Many African American clergy share a commitment to a strict interpretation of Scripture with white evangelicals, but the two groups are politically dissimilar. On some issues African American Protestants adopt conservative positions, but they are politically liberal on other matters.[26] African American clergy enjoy a great deal of social—and often political—influence, particularly because of the traditional centrality of the church in the black community. African American Protestants have long been politically active, and historically black churches have been an important locus of mobilization for civil rights protests. At the same time, there is great diversity within African American Protestantism, which presents challenges for political cohesion and effectiveness. While most African American Protestants belong to traditionally black denominations, there are some black or multiracial congregations in urban areas like Milwaukee that are affiliated with traditionally white denominations. Such congregations and their clergy are often distinctly African American, or even Afrocentric, in nature. I interviewed fourteen African American clergy who represented the National Baptist Convention (U.S.A.), which is by far the largest black church body in the Milwaukee area, the Church of God in Christ, the African Methodist Episcopal Church, and three traditionally white denominations.[27]

LOOKING AHEAD

This book is an exploration of the choices religious leaders make about involving themselves in politics. I will argue that in an urban setting, the choices pastors make about political involvement are shaped not only by their religious traditions but also by the socioeconomic realities of the neighborhoods in which they serve. In chapter 2, I explain the variety of strategies Protestant clergy employ in approaching political involvement. Just as the religious groups over which these clergy preside are characterized by great diversity, so too their own political involvement varies tremendously. Ultimately all pastors must reconcile the expectations of others with their own personal goals and preferences when they decide whether to include political involvement among their official roles. Pastors who become involved in politics do so in different ways and with varying intensities.

In chapters 3 and 4, I explore several possible explanations for the choices pastors make about becoming politically involved. These explanations are rooted in personal and contextual factors that shape the political involvement of clergy. Chapter 3 focuses on a set of personal resources, including attitudes about the normative propriety of political involvement by clergy; feelings of political efficacy; gender; and career stage. In chapter 4, I turn to two central contextual factors: denomination and the socioeconomic status of church neighborhoods. The principal theme that emerges from these two chapters is the complex interplay between personal convictions and political context that marks the decision-making process clergy undertake with regard to political involvement.

The focus of chapter 3 is the importance of personal resources for the facilitation of political action. Pastors' attitudes about the propriety of political involvement by clergy constitute a definitive and central element of their overall orientation to politics. It would be highly unusual, for instance, to find clergy who believe that they ought to steer clear of the political realm leading marches or organizing protests. Moreover, clergy who are positively oriented to political involvement may be expected to feel a strong sense of political efficacy, while pastors who believe that they have little effect on politics and policy may limit their own political involvement as a result. Personal circumstances may also be expected to structure the choices clergy make about becoming politically involved. It is more difficult for women clergy, for example, to establish themselves as political leaders. Career stage is also important; clergy who are at mid-career enjoy certain advantages if they choose to become politically involved.

Chapter 4 contains the heart of my argument: neighborhood circumstances play a crucial role in structuring the choices clergy make about political involvement. I consider two contextual factors, one—denominational tradition—that has been stressed heavily in previous studies of clergy involvement in politics, and another—church neighborhood socioeconomic status—that has not received such attention. Because tremendous attitudinal differences exist along denominational, theological, and racial lines, it is important to explore the ramifications of these factors for pastors' political involvement. Some Protestant traditions encourage political leadership while others scorn it. Neighborhood context, however, also matters. The socioeconomic status of a church's neighborhood is actually much more indicative than its denominational affiliation of the choices its pastor will make about political involvement. Differences in neighborhood political context translate into differences in the political involvement levels of the clergy whose churches are located within them. Members of churches in affluent areas are often active in their communities on their own or through secular organizations. Their clergy often have little incentive to provide them with a stimulus for political involvement. On the other hand, members of central city churches may spend proportionately more time concerning themselves with basic survival needs. Thus their pastors may have an incentive to engage in political activity on their behalf. Political leadership is in fact *imperative* for some pastors regardless of their denomination, their theology, or even their race, as politically active pastors tend to be those whose congregants face the most trying economic circumstances.

Political activity must be motivated by some issue or set of issues. In chapter 5, I consider the specific issues the pastors identified as most important to them and discuss the extent to which their political agendas are related to the choices they make about political involvement. Among the most frequently mentioned issues were abortion and racism. Less frequently mentioned issues included gambling and the environment. These issues, which they identified "off the top of their heads," are a good indication of the pastors' political agendas. Specifically, clergy who were less politically involved focused most heavily on issues concerning morality, family, and the human body, while clergy who were deeply involved in politics displayed most concern about issues affecting Milwaukee's immediate economic situation and the issues of crime and violence that plague it. Again this illustrates the importance of the context provided by pastors' neighborhoods in structuring their orientations to politics.

In chapters 6, 7, and 8, I explore the relationship between pastors' political involvement and their views on three front-burner issues of the 1990s: abortion, crime and violence, and "family values." Surprisingly, neither the degree of importance the pastors assigned to the issue of abortion nor the substantive content of their comments about it was related to their level of political involvement. Consistent with the argument that neighborhood socioeconomic status matters, however, the ways in which pastors framed the issue of crime and violence were related to their level of political involvement. Clergy who were least directly critical of those who commit crimes were the most politically involved. The pastors did not agree about the importance of family values in American political discourse. The pastors' comments on the subject of family values were especially diverse and colorful. Many pastors perceived this debate as a fabrication of the political Right, while others were quite sure that the fabric of the family needed to be strengthened through stiffer discipline.

In chapter 9, I summarize the findings of the study and consider the directions future research ought to take. Specifically, I discuss the need to incorporate measures of external political context into all explanations of the choices clergy—or any other nonpolitical social elites—make about translating their authority into the political realm.

CHAPTER 2

Political Involvement: Choices and Strategies

What exactly do clergy *do* if and when they become involved in the political realm? What sorts of activities do they define as being political? Over the years, political involvement has been subject to a wide variety of conceptualizations and definitions. In their classic work on the subject, Sidney Verba and Norman Nie argue that "political participation refers to those activities by private citizens that are more or less directly aimed at influencing the selection of governmental personnel and/or the actions they take."[1] Political participation, though, has come to mean many things; distinctions have been drawn, for example, between conventional and unconventional participation[2] and between symbolic and instrumental participation.[3] Activities as varied as voting, working for candidates and political parties, writing to public officials, demonstrating, and even rioting have been included in various definitions of participation. Recently, in fact, Steven Rosenstone and John Mark Hansen have defined political participation so broadly as to say that it is "action directed explicitly toward influencing the distribution of social goods and social values."[4] The wealth of attention that has been paid to this topic is not surprising given the central importance of political participation in a democratic polity.

Recently, Verba and his colleagues stressed that individuals who participate in politics must possess specific resources—time, money, and civic skills—in order to do so.[5] They have argued that religious organizations are an important source of these crucial political resources,[6] particularly the development of civic skills, which they define as "the communications and organizational skills that facilitate effective participation."[7] It is reasonable, therefore, to expect that many pastors would be involved in politics in some capacity. To some extent, all pastors possess the resources of which Verba and his colleagues speak, which taken together represent potential energy for political participation *as part of their official roles as clergy*. The degree to which pastors choose to use these resources in the pursuit of political goals defines their orientations to the political realm, or their *political involvement*.

13

My notion of political involvement involves a more specific conceptualization of participation. Political involvement here refers to the engagement by pastors in politics as part of their institutional roles as clergy. I am not concerned with whether or not clergy, as private citizens, vote in elections. Nor am I interested in whether they display bumper stickers on their vehicles, campaign buttons on their jackets, or signs in their yards, because these are *personal* actions. The critical definitional step lies in the fact that the subject of interest is neither participation by private citizens nor mobilization efforts by leaders of interest groups or political parties. Instead, it falls between these two poles. The question here was when and why elites of nonpolitical institutions choose to extend their influence into the political sphere.

The Verba group has distinguished between "skill-producing churches" and "politically mobilizing churches."[8] These two distinct types of churches are both thought to enhance their congregations' potential for political participation, but in different ways. Skill-producing churches provide people with opportunities to practice civic skills in ways that need not be explicitly political (such as organizing a rummage sale). Politically mobilizing churches expose their congregations directly to political messages or activity. Certainly clergy play an important role in shaping the political context of their churches in directions such as these. Therefore, I am specifically interested in the political efforts that clergy undertake on behalf of the groups they serve (their congregations, the neighborhoods surrounding their churches, their denominations). Clergy may have clear personal political beliefs, or they may even be active in interest groups or political parties, but if they do not bring their politics directly to bear on their congregations, they do not act as political leaders on behalf of, or even in reference to, those whom they lead.

A word about terminology is in order. V. O. Key differentiated between "political participation" and "political involvement." He thought specifically of political involvement as being one's degree of psychological investment in the political process, rather than the specific actions one takes toward political ends.[9] I will employ the term "political involvement" rather than "political participation" because I am principally interested in distinguishing among pastors' various *orientations* to the political realm. The term "political" means different things to different clergy. For some, no activity they undertake under the auspices of their job description is political. For others, every aspect of their work has political implications. The main issue here is one of the degree to which pastors *choose* to utilize the resources they have available for political participation.

Some scholars, most notably Sue Crawford, have made important strides toward delineating the different types of activities clergy pursue that *may* be political, from running soup kitchens to carrying out electoral activity and advocacy.[10] Here, however, I explore political involvement from the definitional perspective of the clergy themselves. In this study, definitions of political activity are derived directly from the pastors. An action is political when the pastors *themselves* label it as political. Because I did not want to lead them in any way, I did not want to impose a definition of politics upon the clergy I interviewed. To distinguish the differences between their personal political views and the sort of political involvement discussed above, I asked the pastors to describe any (self-defined) political activities that they and their congregations had recently undertaken. The result was their presentation of a strikingly wide range of roles they play in their congregations' political endeavors. Some pastors defended a disengaged stance toward political involvement. Others carefully defined specific boundaries for their limited political involvement and the agendas they set for their congregations. Finally, some explained that they actively lead their congregations into political endeavors and consider themselves to be political activists.

Each pastor was asked "What specific political projects have you and your congregation been involved with lately?" Their responses varied widely in scope and content, and each pastor had a unique story to tell. Their general levels of political involvement, however, fell into three categories. The categories may be thought of as ideal types into which no two pastors will ever fit in exactly the same way.[11]

First are those sixteen clergy who were disengaged from political involvement. The *disengaged,* as I call them, were most often very deliberate about being apolitical. Twelve of them focused exclusively on evangelism and other pastoral responsibilities that kept them outside of the political fray. Disengagement from politics does not imply a lack of information, interest or awareness on their part, though. Rather, these clergy simply chose to avoid direct involvement in politics. The second type of clergy are what I call *agenda setters:* pastors who described themselves as playing a number of political roles without personally confronting public officials (or becoming these officials themselves). They said they frequently set a general tone for their congregations' political engagement and provided concrete suggestions to members of their congregations who were interested in politics. Most of the seventeen agenda setters took it upon themselves to inform their congregations about pertinent political issues and events, often from the pulpit. They did not, however, take part with their congregations in any political battles. Finally, there were thirteen clergy who were overt and active *political leaders*. They include pastors who were also activists and public officials. They reported that they could not conceive of their roles as clergy in the absence of political involvement.

DISENGAGEMENT FROM POLITICS

"My approach, my belief is that when a person makes a commitment to the Lord, their philosophical base will change. Their life will change" (E1). So said Rev. Andrew Cunningham,[12] one of Milwaukee's pastors, who, when asked to describe the partisan orientation of his congregation, replied that he had no idea. Politics was very low on his list of priorities. He believed that the government could never solve the country's problems. Instead, he waits with great faith for the spiritual revival that he is sure will come one day soon. Cunningham stated emphatically that abortion is murder, but he also said that he had neither the time nor the inclination to lead, or even to join, protests at abortion clinics. Most of his working hours were devoted to rebuilding a congregation that had been in steep decline when he took its helm. He claimed to spend his days helping members of his congregation solve their personal problems. His principal commitment was to evangelism, not politics.

> I believe I should be a responsible citizen but I don't believe God put me here to be an activist. I don't think that's why I'm here. . . . I believe the most important thing that we have to do is to lead people to know and to make a personal commitment to Jesus Christ. That's why I'm here. (E1)

Reverend Cunningham typified sixteen of the forty-six Protestant clergy I interviewed: he was politically "disengaged."

Disengaged pastors do not translate their institutional power into the realm of politics. Again, this is not to say that they do not care about politics, or that they isolate themselves from their communities. Instead, they see neither themselves nor their positions as being political in any way. As one disengaged pastor succinctly stated, "I am just not a very political person" (E4).

Even though many clergy made it clear that they were not involved in politics at all, I asked them nonetheless to describe any "social" or "community" involvement in which they and their congregations had recently participated. Responses to this question varied, but no one *claimed* that their activities were political. Some disengaged pastors were involved in activities sponsored by their denominations or other large para-church organizations, in which the pastors themselves seemed to function mainly as fund-raisers. Their congregations often contributed money to general funds used by the denomination for a variety of purposes, such as (on occasion) political lobbying. Other disengaged pastors were involved in local efforts to build and strengthen their communities, such as meal and clothing programs for the less fortunate. For example, several reported being involved with The Gathering, a meal program serving poor and homeless people in downtown Milwaukee. The key here, however, is that the disengaged clergy did not categorize their activities as being political. For them, participating in a soup kitchen was not inherently political, although it may very well be for pastors who are also involved in other forms of political activism.

Some of the disengaged pastors reported that their congregations were involved in other sorts of community activities that they did not see as being political. Several indicated that their churches had "food pantries": stores of nonperishable food items contributed by members of the congregation on which people in poverty and other crisis situations may rely. Several admitted, though, that these food pantries were not often used; some were only available to the members of the congregations themselves. Many of these pastors' churches also supported "clothing banks." In fact, one church was the center of a citywide clothing bank effort: "They give us a lot of clothes, and we just give them away" (E7). But this pastor did not see any political meaning in the clothing bank.

Offerings of money and letters were also common in the congregations of disengaged clergy. Some of the disengaged pastors reported encouraging their congregations to provide financial support for politically active central city churches. In addition to providing funding, members of some of these congregations were also encouraged to volunteer their time for causes such as after-school tutoring programs in the central city. Some of the disengaged also said they tolerate limited discussion and letter writing about specific issues, and a few mentioned that they remind their congregations to vote at election time. The letter writing efforts were not clergy-led, congregation-wide campaigns; rather several pastors simply volunteered the fact that they tell congregants who are upset about specific issues to write to their representatives. While he does not encourage it himself, one pastor reported that "our people have written petitions to the FCC. . . . They want to remove all religious programming and we think that's wrong. . . . It's the nonbeliever who wants to push that religion off" (A1). Overall, while some of these actions may be said to touch the hem of politics, their proponents did not call them political.

Disengaged clergy provided a number of reasons for their noninvolvement in politics. Some called it a matter of personal choice: a lack of personal inclination to pursue political involvement. Others cited an array of factors that prevented them from entering the political fray. A few pastors stated that they simply did not have the time for politics. As one said, "If you take care of your spiritual duties and try to maintain your flock and tend to the needs of the sick, you don't have the time" (A8). This particular pastor was residing outside of the Milwaukee metropolitan area and was therefore truly pressed for time because of his long commute and other commitments. Moreover, some clergy must hold down secular jobs for financial reasons, which cuts into the time they are able to spend on their pastoral activities.

Others attributed their disengaged stance to the fact that they just did not see themselves as "political" people. Often they were shy and reticent about becoming involved in something as public as politics. As one pastor put it, "I haven't made politics my main emphasis. I do believe in the conservative issues, but I don't believe it's my calling to be a politician, but if people in the church feel called to do it, I allow them to do it, but I am not going to be there" (E12).

Another pastor shared the similar sentiment that "I've got to be honest and say that I've grown up in a background where I've not been aggressively involved in political issues" (E6). Particularly illustrative of the power of personal preference to remain disengaged from politics was the story of a pastor who, despite presiding over a congregation whose laity were themselves quite involved in conservative political activism, does not join in any political ventures. He stated that "I keep myself busy with other things [and] don't really think about politics much other than when it's time to vote. . . . I kind of steer clear of politics, personally" (E16). His congregation was politically mobilized *despite* his own disengagement.

Other pastors wished they could be more politically active but faced barriers that prevented them from doing so. Two were women pastors; one in particular characterized her congregation as very unwilling to become involved in politics, which she found to be a limitation on what she could do on her own. She was hesitant to push her congregation toward political involvement because of her goal of serving the congregation for many years: "As the new kid on the block, I'm certainly not going to get into that" (M15). Therefore, her community endeavors on behalf of her congregation had to come in areas "that don't have a strong political element" (M15). In the absence of these special constraints, these women would in all likelihood be much more politically involved.

Others cited the Bible as the key source of constraint on their political involvement. They argued that political involvement would detract from the task of preaching. In the eyes of one pastor, "I see the real solution to society's problems as evangelism and personal holiness in the lives of individuals rather than social activism" (E4). For such clergy, these solutions must be sought by preaching the gospel, not politics. "When we get involved in something in the community, or we take a stand on something, it has to do with how we interpret theology" (E14). This pastor, whose own father was a career politician, said that for him political activism did not mean protesting or rallying but rather "it means speaking and living out God's word" (E14).

A final factor that disengaged clergy faced was the tradition and norms of the specific church or denomination in which they serve. One disengaged pastor pointed out that clergy serving his congregation had been historically apolitical, so he was expected to conform to this model. He speculated that this historical disengagement from politics was rooted in the fact that "the political issues that one would get involved with, probably the folk here have been on the side where it didn't bother them that much. I think that's because their nose wasn't being pushed to the side at any point" (M2). More general denominational constraints were also significant. One pastor traced his denomination's political disengagement to the days of German immigration to Milwaukee: "They were immigrants and German-speaking and so really kind of felt isolated from political life, which of course was all in English, and which was dominated by Yankees" (E7). This tradition of standing apart from the rest of society persisted, and he had been socialized into it.

To summarize, the disengaged clergy did not see themselves as politically involved on behalf of, or even in reference to, their congregations. This is not to say that they were not aware of politics. They simply did not translate their leadership into political action. Their congregations were involved in some community activities, but the clergy did not label these endeavors as political. A variety of factors prevented disengaged clergy from becoming politically involved. Some simply chose to avoid politics, while others felt structurally inhibited.

SETTING AN AGENDA FOR OTHERS

"The whole arena of the world seems to be fair game for what the church is about. You open the newspaper in one hand and the Bible in the other, and you keep the two in conversation" (M7). So said Rev. Gordon Kane, the long-tenured pastor of one of Milwaukee's most historic Protestant churches. He reported that he was called by this church in the late 1960s when it was facing a serious membership crisis, and he brought experience working toward racial integration in another major urban area. Reverend Kane reinvigorated the dying church by redirecting its energy outward. He inspired the congregation to address problems such as drug abuse in their neighborhood, and later to write letters of protest about American foreign policy in Central America. He said he regularly addresses political issues from the pulpit, but does not involve himself personally in political action. Reverend Kane may be called an "agenda setter."

How might agenda setters differ from the disengaged? Pastors who remain disengaged from politics usually do not involve themselves in activities that they would label as political. They do not use their pulpits as political forums, nor do they mobilize their congregations for political activism. They do not use their institutional power as religious leaders to frame political issues for their congregations. They are not involved in political action on behalf of or with their congregations. They are very careful about how they present their agendas:

> I suspect that when clergy preach on social issues, if the congregation perceives that they are grinding an ideological ax, you really generate hostility. But when the clergy address issues of conscience . . . from a perspective of Christian responsibility, then that generates a response that I think transcends political agendas and ultimately is more effective. (M12)

Agenda setters define important issues, encourage their congregations to think about these issues, and set the tone for political involvement in their churches.

Clergy classified as agenda setters encouraged political participation among members of their congregations in several ways. Three pastors mentioned that they sometimes spoke to their congregations about certain political issues, but they did not urge church members to undertake political activity in relation to these issues. These three clergy differed from their disengaged counterparts in that they did articulate a clear political vision—an agenda—for their congregations. Eight other agenda setters said that they identify important issues but also encourage each individual church member to devise his or her own personal course of action. Finally, six agenda setters said they present both specific issues and specific strategies to their congregations. Generally speaking, all of the agenda setters defined important issues for their congregations, but they differed in the extent to which they were also willing to suggest specific political strategies.

Three of the agenda setters were opposed to the idea of their congregations taking political action. One pastor who set an agenda of noninvolvement presided over a congregation whose pastors had been visibly involved in politics before he arrived. He scorned leaders of the church who had "jumped on the Father Groppi bandwagon" (M5) in the 1960s in support of his fair housing protests "after the real battles had been fought" (M5) over the issue. "They figured that as a matter of principle they had to stand with the liberals, the blacks, the Father Groppi movement, at the expense of being pastoral to the long-standing members of the church who were finding it very difficult to accept this new reality" (M5). His church paid a high cost in terms of membership for the former clergy's political stance. This pastor felt comfortable talking about issues with his congregation, but he had steered clear of personal political involvement because of this precedent.

It is ironic that another pastor who discouraged political involvement was herself a very political person. She reported extensive personal involvement in local groups working on behalf of the rights of African Americans, and she was also quite knowledgeable about both political issues and political theory. Her endeavors, however, were not part of her official role as a pastor. The church she was serving is located in one of the most troubled neighborhoods in Milwaukee; her main concern as a pastor was the day-to-day survival of the members of her congregation. "Political activism is based on the premise of money. A lot of [the members of] our congregation are of indigent status. The pastoral staff here are God's servants. We are not prepared to lead them on a political agenda" (A3). She made it very clear that she finds American society to be racist and unfair. While she acknowledged that the path to addressing such inequalities is political, she also felt that no progress could come from trying to mobilize her congregation, particularly because of their daily survival challenges. She felt that her church should follow in what C. Eric Lincoln and Lawrence Mamiya have labeled the survival tradition, wherein theological focus cannot be placed on liberation because survival needs are more immediate.[13]

Another agenda setter was the pastor of a rapidly growing fundamentalist church with no denominational ties. Fundamentalists are distinct from other evangelical Protestants in that they assume a highly separatist stance toward the broader culture. Nowhere was this fact more evident than in this pastor's attitude toward his congregation's potential political involvement. Despite strong opposition to abortion, he was steering his congregation away from involvement in the abortion debate.

> You know, there's churches that really go out and push the abortion protests. We don't do that. We go downtown. We walk right past the protests. We've even stopped and sung a few hymns, but we go on our way and hand out, downtown, several thousand pieces of gospel literature. (E8)

While the act of joining in the singing of hymns suggests a tacit approval of the abortion protests, this pastor maintained that his congregation's sole outreach to the community lay in its ongoing effort to convert people to Christianity. He felt no pressure to conform to anyone else's political expectations of him: "I answer to no one and we're independent. No one tells us what to do. We report to no one" (E8). He was an agenda setter because he made it clear to his congregation that politics is *not* a priority—while at the same time making it clear to them where they *ought* to stand on issues.

An additional group of agenda setters was comprised almost exclusively of evangelical pastors, all of whom were concerned about what they saw as the moral decline of American society. They were particularly troubled by the issue of abortion. Abortion has been on the political front-burner in Milwaukee since the summer of 1992, when the anti-abortion group Operation Rescue targeted Milwaukee as one of the centers of its nationwide protest.[14] Since that time, a prominent Christian radio station has also focused a great deal of attention on the issue. The station has encouraged Christian laity to join anti-abortion protests—regardless of their pastors' views on the value of protesting—and asked them to implore their clergy to do the same. One pastor reported that

> To serve as sort of a clearing house, the congregation formed a community impact committee and that was because in the last three years . . . people have struggled with all sorts of political concerns, especially abortion . . . stimulated by ultraconservative radio here in Milwaukee. (E16)

A common misconception about evangelical clergy who oppose abortion is that they are all on the front lines at clinic protests, or even that they encourage their congregations to attend such protests. It is true that many clergy care about the issue, and many said they preach sermons about it. They tend to support members of their congregations who choose to become involved in the pro-life movement, but most felt that such involvement must be a matter of personal choice. Several of them mentioned that people had left their congregations when the pastoral staff refused to embrace the firm anti-abortion stance encouraged by the Christian radio station. These clergy were also almost uniformly opposed to groups such as Operation Rescue and the Milwaukee-based Missionaries to the Preborn: "My feeling is that those kind of activities are too political, . . . and the attitude and the militancy that's purveyed by those organizations does not really match up to the attitudes we have in the church" (E9).

Of all the agenda setters, the most explicitly political were the six who clearly articulated important issues and played a vital role in developing potential strategies of action with their congregations. One congregation in particular had grown progressively more involved in politics due to the positive orientation of its pastor toward political involvement:

> Years ago, our people were not inclined to be real, you might say, politically conscious. . . . But as time went on they began to realize that if you're going to permit people who have no regard for God to make the laws, you're going to have to live by those laws, and so they became more concerned, more interested. (E15)

Within this church there was an active pro-life group involved with literature distribution and "talking to people about the sin of abortion" (E15).

Many of the agenda setters who were most explicitly political, however, tended to focus on a liberal political agenda that they put into action by focusing their congregations on "Christian responsibility to our neighbors" (M12). As one pastor put it, "We have a real strong tradition of being involved . . . with those who might be defined as underprivileged or who have experienced tragedy or misfortune in their lives . . . both locally and internationally" (M3). One pastor and his congregation were in the process of developing a community outreach center. Another was busy organizing discussion groups about specific issues; he had also involved his suburban congregation in an "immersion project" of shared worship and discussion with a central city congregation. Management was the special skill of another agenda setter, who designed a wide variety of committees to study and discuss world hunger, environmental concerns, and "peace and justice" issues. He said his aim was to inspire voluntarism in members after they had established patterns of faithful attendance and gotten their own spiritual needs met. In his view, people cannot be expected to help others before their own needs have been met, so he liked to direct his political messages toward more established members of the congregation.

To summarize, agenda setters were politically involved, but only in a limited sense. They defined issues of importance for their congregations, and to varying degrees, they encouraged political involvement in their churches. They stopped short, however, of engaging in personal political involvement on behalf of their congregations. None reported making the critical leap of translating their leadership roles into the political realm outside the church walls. Some encouraged their congregations to avoid politics, while others felt more comfortable providing suggestions for political strategy to members. What binds them together, however, is the fact that each defined a clear issue agenda for his or her congregation.

POLITICAL LEADERSHIP

Rev. Kenrod Garvey may be seen from time to time on Milwaukee television not only because of his prominent status as the pastor of one of the fastest growing churches in the metropolitan area, but also because he is himself a public official. He was so busy with pastoral and political activities that it took four attempts to schedule his interview. He expressed pride in his successful track record of endorsing political candidates: "I think that one of the areas that made [us] one of the notable, leading congregations is, as Mayor [John] Norquist says, [we] pick winners" (A2). Reverend Garvey saw no division between religion and politics; in his view, one cannot exist independently of the other. In fact, he called his church a "holistic unit." He said he literally seeks to meet all of the needs of his congregation. "If there's any area or situation that comes to us, we like to feel that we either are equipped or must equip ourselves to deal with the challenges of our community" (A2). Spiritual regeneration, he said, is the source of all political change. For Reverend Garvey, though, encouraging spiritual growth is just the beginning of inspiring broad-based social change.

Garvey is an example of the thirteen pastors I interviewed who lived out the connection between religion and politics every day in word and deed. These "political leaders" included coalition builders, activists, and a few public officials. Not only did they speak about politics regularly from the pulpit, many also said they invite political elites to speak from the pulpit during their services. Most significantly, politics was centrally important in their own lives. They perceived their political involvement as an integral part of their calling as clergy. One political leader referred to his life's work as "a ministry for systemic change" (M1). Another said that people frequently joined his church specifically because it gives them an opportunity to work for social change: "They know that we take very strong justice stands on social issues" (M4). In the words of one politically involved pastor:

> From the Swahili word *mutu*, meaning god-conscious, we understand that everything is interconnected. We encourage being involved politically, but we understand that's one piece of the puzzle. Foundationally we must connect spiritually, and also politically, economically, socially, and educationally. (A11)

In Milwaukee there exists an ecumenical political group called Milwaukee Innercity Congregations Allied for Hope (MICAH). MICAH was founded in 1985 as a multiracial and interfaith coalition of clergy and laity dedicated to addressing the challenges of life in Milwaukee's central city though political means.

> Our motto is "TO DO WHAT IS JUST!" and our tools are education, advocacy and action. Our goal is the empowerment of our people so that together we may identify, protect and promote the individual and collective interest of our congregations and of the inner city of Milwaukee.[15]

In the summer of 1994, thirty-seven churches belonged to MICAH. While it is an organization of both clergy and laity, clergy form MICAH's leadership team. Among the group's stated goals is to empower laity, who in turn work for the improvement of the community in cooperation with the clergy. As one MICAH pastor stated, "My style is instead of being an authoritarian or [building] a hierarchy ladder, I empower people" (M11). Each MICAH congregation has a "core team" of laity who work with clergy to identify issues and plan strategies for MICAH's multifaceted political agenda. An "Educational Task Force" is concerned with educational reform. A "Crime and Drugs Task Force" deals with issues as diverse as drug rehabilitation and police misconduct.[16] MICAH also organizes pickets of drug houses and prayer vigils at murder scenes.[17] The "Housing and Economic Development Task Force" is perhaps the most ambitious of all; by 1994 it had secured nearly $500 million in guaranteed low-interest loans from over a dozen lending institutions. These loans were earmarked for residents of the central city who wish to build dwelling units or businesses.[18]

One of the MICAH clergy, whose own political involvement began in the 1950s when he was a civil rights activist in the South, was proud of the personal role he played in the group's efforts, but he gave the ultimate credit to MICAH: "I think I have made a real difference, . . . [but] it is not just my persona and my [long pastorate]. . . . MICAH is a power organization. We confront elites, hold them accountable. We are a force that has to be reckoned with" (M4). A similar story of the pride these pastors took in what MICAH accomplishes involves its encounters with the legal system.

> We're having problems with drug houses in this neighborhood, and MICAH is very forceful working against [them]. . . . Instead of the pastor attempting to get rid of the drug house on his own in his neighborhood, what happens is the organization will meet at that church and strategize. . . . There was a drug house down here on the corner, and now we got rid of it. . . . [The drug dealers] had [control of] the telephone booth down there. . . . You'd go in the telephone booth and take the top off the receiver and get your drugs out. So we attempted to get rid of that and we did, . . . and then we found one realty company that all they did was sell to drug dealers, . . . and we [are going] after the company. (A9)[19]

The most striking fact about MICAH is that it is ecumenical and multiracial. Even though Milwaukee is one of the most racially divided of all American cities, black and white pastors work side-by-side in MICAH for what they see as the benefit of all Milwaukeeans. The energy that African American clergy reported bringing to MICAH was a testament to its true ecumenical strength. After all, there is a great deal of theological disagreement between mainline and African American churches. According to the clergy, though, congregational mobilization efforts for MICAH activities appeared to be equally effective in both African American and mainline churches. Like their white colleagues, African American MICAH clergy exhibited a very strong sense of efficacy about the organization: "We have the right people in place with MICAH" (A5). In fact, the experience of becoming involved with MICAH actually changed one pastor's entire attitude about political activism: "I never have really just reached out into the community like we are doing now" (A4). At first, he "said no, I don't want to be part of nothing like these organizations that say a lot and take up a lot of time" (A4), but later he changed his mind and became an integral part of MICAH's leadership team. Another pastor's dedication to MICAH and its mission was clear in his declaration that "MICAH meets all the time, at all hours, . . . but when they call, I come running" (A9).

MICAH, of course, was not the only manifestation of political involvement among the political leaders. In fact, the variety of their political endeavors was remarkable. As one pastor explained,

> I've tried to lift up that Biblical vision of Shalom, that love and justice approach, peace with justice. . . . What we try to promote is . . . being rooted and grounded in the spirit so that you're going out into the world and trying to make a difference wherever you are. (M10)

Another pastor told of his congregation's long-standing tradition of involvement with political refugees, which dates back to the church's days as a station in the Underground Railroad. "The congregation really operated a station, . . . but that was not merely an incident in the early life of the church. It was a very fundamental thing that has carried on in the self-perception of the church to a remarkable extent" (M13). The congregation continued in this vein of political involvement through efforts such as the resettlement of international war refugees. Another pastor, who was even more dramatically involved in such efforts, offered a similar story. During what he called "the communist bugaboo" (M4) of the 1980s, his congregation provided shelter and other forms of assistance for people seeking refuge from war-torn El Salvador. He took pride in the fact that this effort stood "directly in violation of the policies of the Reagan administration and the [Immigration and Naturalization Service]" (M4).

Others felt called to address the problems of their own neighborhoods through smaller scale groups than MICAH. As one pastor stated, "I have recognized the Gospel as a command to defend and protect the oppressed here in Milwaukee, and especially in my neighborhood" (M1). Some pastors actually founded neighborhood organizations; Milwaukee is made up of many historic neighborhoods, and these neighborhood organizations are designed to build upon the historic roots and to foster community within them. One neighborhood organization, for example, was in the process of implementing a plan to open a medical clinic and a community center in one of its local churches. The pastors who reported being involved in such groups conceived of their churches as organic parts of these neighborhoods. As such, they felt a strong obligation to help preserve the neighborhoods. They argued that neighborhood organizations were often even more effective than MICAH at solving specific local problems. One pastor characterized his neighborhood organization as "our local political community organization that helps us actualize things in our own neighborhood. And then MICAH helps us with how we can help others throughout the city" (M1). Scholars have shown that neighborhood organizations such as these can work to restore "urban democracy" in American cities.[20]

Neighborhood organizations were a source of great pride in these pastors' versions of their political efforts. Several pastors, for example, reported implementing job training programs in their churches under the auspices of neighborhood organizations. These programs were designed to provide instruction and work experience in such areas as construction and landscaping for both teenagers and unemployed adults. One pastor worked to create special opportunities for unemployed women, many of whom had been sexually victimized, to end their need for public assistance by providing them with job training. In the interim, he paid them for their efforts. "The persons are receiving a small stipend. In a way that's civil disobedience because if you report that, then if you're on public assistance that's subtracted, so we give it as a gift and in a cash way" (M11). Another pastor said he had worked to establish his church as a center for weapons collection in one of the most crime-ridden neighborhoods in the state of Wisconsin. Still others reported being involved in efforts to bring about a handgun ban in Milwaukee (these efforts, however, had been unsuccessful). Some had been involved in programs to combat racism and injustice in Milwaukee. "Beyond Racism," for example, is a program that pairs black and white people for the purpose of developing friendships. The theory behind this program is that personal interracial relationships sensitize people to the problems of racism and can thus lead to a more harmonious community.

Three of the pastors served in various capacities as public officials: one at the county level and two on city commissions.[21] Not all politically involved clergy, however, thought seeking public office was necessary or even desirable. One pastor shared the story of his own candidacy for public office, which he aborted when he realized he had no chance to win due to a lack of resources: "I found that pastoring and running for public office is too much" (A9). Some of the political leaders who were not themselves public officials frequently invited politicians to visit their churches. Politicians were not only welcomed at services, they were sometimes allowed to speak from the pulpit about their political views and aspirations. One pastor, whose office walls were decorated with photographs of himself posing with prominent elected officials, said that he found it very helpful to have candidates visit his church because "we learn from politicians. . . . I want an informed congregation. It makes my job much easier when they're concerned about what's going on in the community" (A7). And these clergy believed that they are taken seriously by political elites:

> There are times when as a pastor I talk to politicians, [U.S. Representative] Tom Barrett, [U.S.] Senator [Russ] Feingold. . . . We have a pastors' conference and we invite them to come. . . . There are times when they like to come to the office and just sit and talk about some of the things that I am concerned about as an African American pastor. (A7)

Moreover, these pastors felt that they are taken seriously by their congregations, and that they could not truly serve God without being politically involved in their community.

To summarize, political leaders are clergy who extend their roles as institutional elites into the political realm. They are political coalition builders, activists, and a few are themselves public officials. They conceive of their roles as clergy as inextricably linked with politics. Most expressed the opinion that they must be involved in politics in order to fulfill their divine calling. They were involved in a wide variety of efforts, the widest reaching of which were organized by MICAH.

LOOKING AHEAD

The forty-six Milwaukee clergy fall into three general categories of political involvement. The disengaged chose to focus on evangelism and other pastoral responsibilities rather than pursuing direct involvement in politics. Agenda setters were pastors who did things like issue definition and strategy building but stopped short of involving themselves personally in the political process as representatives of their congregations. Those clergy who chose to act as political leaders included pastors who reported serving as political coalition builders, activists, and public officials. It is important to keep in mind the fact that these three categories are designed to be useful organizational devices rather than determinist classifications. In the chapters that follow, this organizational framework will come in handy in exploring potential explanations for the variation that the typology captures. In the pages ahead it will be interesting to consider whether these three distinct orientations to political involvement help structure the "skill-producing churches" and "politically mobilizing churches" of which Verba and his colleagues speak.[22] In the next two chapters, I explore the personal and contextual resources that may contribute to the choices clergy make about becoming politically involved.

CHAPTER 3

Personal Resources for Political Involvement

The choices Protestant clergy make about political involvement are invariably influenced by the ways they conceptualize their roles and responsibilities as pastors. Several factors have the potential either to encourage pastors to include political involvement among their official activities or to inhibit them from taking such action. Such factors serve either to keep pastors' attention focused primarily on their own congregations or to direct it beyond the walls of their churches and into their neighborhoods and the rest of the world. Because clergy are elites who are tied to a specific social institution (the church), it is reasonable to assume that both personal and contextual factors influence the choices they make about becoming involved in politics. Some clergy become involved in politics simply because they wish to do so; they are interested in politics or feel a personal calling to become politically involved. Factors related to pastors' personal circumstances also structure the choices they make about political involvement. Specifically, a pastor's gender and career stage may be expected to influence his or her likelihood of engaging in politics. Furthermore, because resources for political involvement flow from the context within which a pastor works, the traditional characteristics of pastors' congregations and denominations may either advance or inhibit their opportunities for political involvement. The more resources pastors have available for the facilitation of political involvement, the more likely they will be to include some form of political action as an element of their official responsibilities.

This chapter is an exploration of four personal resources that may either facilitate or prevent political involvement among clergy. Personal beliefs about whether clergy ought to be involved in politics in the first place, coupled with the presence or absence of feelings of political efficacy, have a strong and perhaps obvious effect on the choices individual pastors make about politics. Moreover, there are aspects of pastors' personal situations that also structure their decision-making processes when it comes to political activism. Because of their minority status in the profession, women clergy may be expected to have a more difficult time becoming politically involved (should they wish to do so). The stage of a pastor's career also bears a relationship to the likelihood that he or she will pursue political involvement; early and late career clergy may not have as much time or energy for politics as their colleagues who are at mid-career.

ATTITUDES TOWARD POLITICAL INVOLVEMENT

Attitudes toward the propriety of political involvement among clergy vary widely within American Protestantism. As Ted Jelen has argued, "It is an open question whether ministers can attempt to convey political meanings to their congregations without damaging their other clerical functions."[1] Some denominational traditions strongly discourage political involvement among clergy, while other traditions enthusiastically support it. White evangelicals, for example, have traditionally held that politics is the realm of the devil, and should therefore be avoided. There has long been a norm among African American Protestants, however, that pastors should be politically involved. And there is a great deal of diversity within denominational traditions on such matters. As the tale of two pastors in chapter 1 illustrates, some clergy simply believe that there is no place within their institutional roles for political involvement, while others vehemently disagree. A pastor's attitude about the general propriety of political involvement among clergy is a definitive and central element of his or her overall orientation to politics. It would be highly unusual, for instance, to find clergy leading marches or organizing protests who believe that they should stay out of the political realm.

I asked each pastor "in general, how involved do you think clergy ought to be in politics?" Twenty-seven of the pastors believed that clergy should be involved in politics, while the remaining nineteen felt they should not. The words of two of these clergy, both of whom draw explicitly on Scripture, clearly illustrate the contrast between these two positions. On the one hand, Scripture may guide those who favor political involvement by clergy. A pastor who holds this opinion explained that

> David was the king of Israel, and was a man after God's own heart. Daniel was a great prophet and was also a statesman. Hezekiah was a prophet as well as a king. The Bible, the Scripture is replete with instances where religious people, spiritual leadership, has been in authority. It is extremely important for religious individuals to play a political role. (A2)

Another pastor offered his own biblical argument against the political involvement of clergy: "In the Book of Acts . . . Paul and the other disciples were confronted with a lot of people from a lot of different areas in need of different social things, [but Paul] said we are to be about spiritual things" (A3).

Some pastors felt that politics does not constitute a worthwhile endeavor for clergy because it diverts them from the mission of serving God. As one said, "I understand the Old Testament to be telling us in part that when we are in power, we need to bend over backwards to put aside that power and not use it" (M15). She also believed that clergy abuse their institutional power when they allow it to spill over into the political realm. Another argument put forward by pastors who opposed political engagement was that politics dirties the church and reduces it to just another voice in an increasingly crowded pluralist society: "The church's voice needs to be one beyond politics, not a political voice.... When the church becomes too politicized, the churches [lose] their prophetic voice" (E9).

Some pastors felt that clergy as a group lack the qualifications for political involvement. "I don't think clergy necessarily are heads above everybody else in terms of political awareness and judgment" (M5). One pastor spoke specifically of his distaste for "headline seeking pastors." In his view clergy ought to be facilitators, not agitators. "You are ordained to put your people into ministry.... You're the person that's enabling them" (M5). He felt that political involvement hinders pastors from this task because it distracts their attention and "makes them feel too self-important" (M5). Similarly, another pastor shared that "my personal feeling is that a pastor who gets deeply involved in politics... is going to diminish his effectiveness. I think that one of the great roles of the pastor is to be able to bring together widely divergent people around the person of Christ" (E2). He saw politics as a divisive and potentially destructive force. This feeling that politics is negative and polarizing was common among the nineteen clergy who opposed political involvement.

Of the twenty-seven pastors who favored clergy involvement in politics, ten saw it as a necessary part of their role. Seventeen others felt it is acceptable, but not an absolute necessity. These seventeen pastors were supportive of the general notion of political involvement by clergy, but they expressed a belief that specific circumstantial and situational limitations ought to apply to such involvement. The most typical concern here flowed from a perceived need to avoid allowing politics to interfere with other pastoral duties. First, there is the limiting issue of time. Some clergy felt that they should only pursue politics to the extent that time permits: "I think we ought to be involved in the community, in the moral debate and the discussions, but the way ministry has gone in the last quarter century, the demands of the congregational life are so strong that you don't have a lot of time to be out in other organizations" (M7). As another pastor said, "I do think that all clergy need to be involved, . . . [but] we are called to preach first. . . . Most everything we do involves politics. There are always some political tentacles that are going to touch us somewhere" (A14). Some, of course, did not personally desire political involvement, but they were glad to see other pastors in the political realm: "Some clergy have the vision and the call to be on the forefront of moral and political leadership. . . . God bless them and let them be out there" (M8). Others expressed a similar sentiment: that clergy who avoid political involvement should not disparage their colleagues who are active. "I don't think everyone is called to make that their main thing, but I don't think clergy should be attacking those who are standing up" (E12).

There were some pastors, however, who said they supported the general notion of clergy involvement in politics, but were nonetheless somewhat suspicious of politicized colleagues who claim to speak for everyone: "If a particular person feels called to take leadership on a particular issue, that's great, but I think the clergy need to be wary of speaking in the name of the church or the name of God" (M1). Some believed that political involvement by clergy is warranted only in specific situations. This sentiment is typified by the view that "It depends on the congregation. . . . A congregation that is more politically attuned should have a pastor who is more politically active" (M3). Clergy sharing this view suggested that it is acceptable, and perhaps desirable, for a pastor to reflect the congregation's own organic orientation to politics; trying to change the congregation's political outlook or to mobilize its members, however, may be inappropriate. For example, pastors may deem certain issues important enough to be presented to the congregation, but they should not "tell their congregation how to vote" (E15).

Not surprisingly, clergy who conceptualized political involvement as a necessary part of their role spoke of it as a vital element of the divine calling to which clergy must respond. In the eyes of one pastor,

> Clergy . . . have a responsibility to work with each other. . . . It bothers me that so many do not, and I think it's irresponsible for a pastor to create his or her own kingdom and special relationships with City Hall. . . . The idea of just trying to create a large church . . . [without] being involved politically is . . . *a violation of the faith*. (M6)

As another said, "I don't think pastors should be limited to just inside the congregation. I think that . . . our ministries should take us beyond the walls of the church to deal with issues, because the people are not going to *live* in the church" (A6).

Most of the pastors who expressed a positive attitude about political involvement provided very specific reasons why clergy must be involved. "Unless the pastor becomes involved with the issues outside his congregation, I don't think that any of these issues in the community will really ever be brought under control" (A4). Similarly, "If you keep the church over here in a pen, it can't help. . . . Their values can and should impact the community" (A5). Other pastors suggested that without the political leadership of clergy, society would become morally adrift: "Sometimes if the clergy don't lead and . . . stand up for what's right, the people have no one to follow" (E14). One suggested that "clergy should be knowledgeable of what the government is about, and they should facilitate various forums" (A11). Another argued that "we ought to be working for community and political change. I believe that the clergy can cause policy change within our state level as well as the national. . . . We want it to the point that the mayor can't even make a decision without asking us. And that's the way it should be" (A9).

Table 3.1 reveals that all pastors classified as political leaders felt that political involvement by clergy is acceptable. Agenda setters, however, were quite evenly divided on the issue. Perhaps the belief that pastors should not be politically involved is what prevented some of them from becoming political leaders. Finally, very few (only five) of the disengaged expressed the view that political involvement by clergy is acceptable.

POLITICAL EFFICACY

Political efficacy refers to the degree to which an individual believes in his or her personal power to influence political outcomes. Clergy who are positively oriented to political involvement may be expected to feel a strong sense of political efficacy.[2] They ought to believe that clergy *can* be politically effective. On the other hand, pastors who believe that they have little effect on politics and policy may plausibly limit their political involvement as a result. The pastors were split in their feelings of polit-

TABLE 3.1
Attitudes about Propriety of Political Involvement

	Politically Disengaged	Agenda Setters	Political Leaders
Acceptable	5 (45%)	9 (53%)	13 (100%)
Not Acceptable	11 (55%)	8 (47%)	0

Source: Compiled by author from interviews. Percentages are column percents. $N = 46$.

ical efficacy. Nearly half answered the question "Do you think clergy have a lot of influence when it comes to politics?" in such a way as to suggest that they do possess strong feelings of political efficacy. The other half, however, responded negatively.

Twenty-two pastors expressed feelings of political efficacy. They stood in sharp contrast to those who lacked efficacious feelings. Most efficacious pastors had confidence in their own political effectiveness as well as that of clergy in general. As one pastor asserted, "Our involvement in politics can make a great difference, and what is really lacking in any community is that the church is not involved. . . . We can really be a power force when we speak" (A4). This efficacy appeared to be rooted in a number of factors, not the least of which was the notion that when clergy work together, they have the potential to make a real difference. In particular, the clergy who were involved in MICAH embodied this sense of efficacy. "I think we're most effective when we encourage people to participate in the process" (A5). Quite simply, "When pastors join together as a whole, then there's power. There's power" (A8).

Some of the pastors felt that both political elites and the general public respect clergy because of their status as moral leaders: "When spiritual leaders are in authority, they make a difference. . . . Attention is directed to them, they become the leaders, they set the policy. . . . There's an integrity that comes with the clergy. . . . People trust religious leaders" (A2). At the same time, political elites are both strategic and observant: "They know where the masses of people are, and that's in our churches" (A7).

The most efficacious pastors believed strongly in their power to shape the political opinions of members of their congregations. As one suggested, "Many people who have a high regard for their pastor, . . . if he's strong on a particular topic, . . . you'll find that most of his congregation will kind of line up" (E15). Perhaps the most telling comment of all was "at times . . . I am amazed with the amount of influence I can have" (M2). Finally, one pastor argued that American society is trying to play down the political influence of clergy.

> Political agencies separate church and state . . . [especially] because of the power of the black church. . . . They saw strongly in the civil rights movement what the church can do. . . . Now there is a strong drive against the church because there's a perception of "if we can make the church appear like a cloak of hypocrites then we can deflate and we can disempower." (A2)

Twenty-four pastors reported feeling that political efforts undertaken by clergy are largely ineffective. They felt that the voices of religious leaders in today's society are muffled at best and ignored at worst. This was attributed in part to changing times: "Two centuries ago, on the frontiers, when the clergy were often the only educated people in the community . . . you have a totally different role" (M8). In today's society, however, "I don't think religion is taken seriously any more" (M9). A similar sentiment involved the belief that clergy cannot reach those who might need their help politically: "People who need convincing aren't coming to hear us, so I'm not sure we have that much influence on anything" (E1). Several pastors argued that politically involved clergy are ineffective because "when clergy become politicized they lose their prophetic voice. . . . We must turn to God first and with that bring mission to the country" (E9). Others suggested a more theological explanation for political ineffectiveness among clergy: "They aren't going to change society because there's got to be a divine intervention" (E6).

When pastors do not agree with the endeavors of politically active clergy, it may be because they do not feel efficacious themselves. For example, one pastor suggested that unlike him, "the clergymen . . . in the political arena tend to be theologically liberal. . . . Their moral standards are not the Biblical standards. . . . They would tend to ally themselves with the homosexuals and other things that God is very much against" (A10). Another pastor argued that clergy's

> political clout is not what it should be. I mean you can get some gay leader up there and he may represent a hundred people and he'll get up and he'll call a rally and they'll have news coverage. . . . You get a clergy group together, and they represent thousands, and the news media pays no attention. (E4)

Others called for the Christian community to unite so that clergy might have more influence, and one even argued that "the government wants to break church groups up into camps, to prevent them from having influence" (E11).

In summary, the pastors were nearly evenly split on the matter of political efficacy. Half felt that clergy can be politically effective; the other half disagreed. As table 3.2 shows, only one pastor who is classi-

TABLE 3.2
Feelings of Political Efficacy

	Politically Disengaged	Agenda Setters	Political Leaders
Efficacious	6 (38%)	4 (24%)	12 (92%)
Not Efficacious	10 (62%)	13 (76%)	1 (8%)

Source: Compiled by author from interviews. Percentages are column percents. N = 46.

fied as a political leader did not report feeling efficacious, while the agenda setters and politically disengaged clergy tended not to share these feelings. Some of the pastors who are less politically involved simply do not believe political activism will have any effect. On the other hand, perhaps those who are deeply involved in politics are kidding themselves about how effective they can be, or really are.

GENDER

Lester Milbrath showed that people who do not feel effective in their everyday tasks are relatively unlikely to participate in politics.[3] Scholars used to report that women were somewhat less likely than men to participate in politics.[4] More recent studies, however, have noted that women are, in fact, substantially involved in a variety of forms of political action, though their involvement is not always recognized by society at large as much as men's participation.[5] Kay Schlozman and her colleagues have reported that differences between men's and women's participation are due to disparities in important political resources, particularly money.[6] If women are even slightly less likely to participate in politics than men, then female clergy may be expected to participate much less than their male colleagues. It has been very difficult for women to break into the heavily male-dominated ranks of the clergy, and in some religious traditions, they are not permitted to serve in any capacity.[7] Despite the finding of Jackson Carroll and his colleagues, who reported that women clergy are more likely to feel that their churches ought to become politically involved in their communities,[8] it is reasonable to expect that female clergy will be less politically involved than their male counterparts because it may be harder for women to be accepted in such leadership roles.

Gender is an important personal factor that influences the extent to which clergy pursue political involvement. The ministry has traditionally been, and continues to be, a heavily male-dominated field; women rarely pursued careers as ordained clergy until the 1970s.[9] In fact, there were relatively few female pastors in the Milwaukee metropolitan area available to be interviewed for this study. Thus, although I made every attempt to secure interviews with women clergy, it is perhaps not surprising that in the end only four of the forty-six were female. Due to their minority status in their profession, it stands to reason that women face significantly higher barriers to political involvement than their male counterparts, particularly given that women pastors have to work much harder than men to establish legitimacy as religious leaders.[10] Unfortunately, the small size of the sample of women makes it very difficult to draw conclusions about women clergy in general. Despite the fact that the female pastors said they were willing and eager to become politically involved, they felt that their congregations would not approve.

There is great diversity among Protestant denominational traditions in terms of their views on the acceptable roles of women in ministry. Women are welcome in the leadership structures of most mainline denominations.[11] Evangelical churches, however, are far less enthusiastic about women who aspire to positions of religious leadership. While evangelical women are encouraged to serve as Sunday school teachers and to participate in a wide variety of other activities, in 1994 there were no women in ordained ministerial roles in evangelical churches in the Milwaukee metropolitan area. One fundamentalist pastor's opinion was that "good Christian ladies . . . are supposed to dress modestly and stay home with their children" (E8), and they were definitely not welcome on the church's board of trustees. While attitudes toward the participation of women are somewhat different in other evangelical churches, the fact remains that nearly all evangelical clergy in the United States are male.[12] Women are similarly situated in many African American churches. They are often highly revered (senior women church members are often referred to as "mother"), but few churches permit women to serve as clergy.[13] As stated in the membership handbook of an African American pastor's congregation, "We recognize the Scriptural importance of women in the Christian ministries . . . but nowhere can we find a mandate to ordain women to be an elder, bishop, or pastor. . . . Paul styled the women who labored with him as servants or helpers, not elders, bishops, or pastors" (A2).

Three of the four women clergy I interviewed were serving in mainline congregations, and the other one worked in a traditionally African American denomination. Only one of the women was the senior member of her pastoral staff. This is not unusual, as relatively few women clergy attain prestigious appointments.[14] The three mainline women pastors were all politically disengaged. Two of them expressed a desire to be more politically involved, but they felt they lacked the legitimacy to do so. As one of them said, "I would love to be more politically involved" (M16), but she believed she was at a disadvantage because of her gender. She continued that "I'm sure there are some members of this congregation who don't think I should be at the altar because of the shape of my skin" (M16). Another female pastor shared that while she personally espoused a leftist political agenda—"I'm pretty far to the Left" (M15)—she did not feel comfortable putting her beliefs into action with her congregation. Previous studies suggest that women clergy tend to be quite liberal, but that like this woman, often have trouble putting their agenda into motion.[15] Despite the fact that her book shelves were filled with volumes on feminist, liberation, and environmentalist theology, she felt certain that members of her congregation were not even sure about her position on issues such as abortion. To protect her legitimacy as a pastor with her congregation, she kept her political views to herself.

The women clergy cited a variety of specific obstacles that prevented them from becoming politically involved. One of the mainline women clergy recounted a defining moment in her professional life when, before she attended the seminary, she sat on a committee to call a new pastor to her congregation, and a male committee member voiced the opinion that "we can't have a woman pastor. We need a leader, not a mother" (M9). She stated that she would not engage in politics even if she felt empowered to do so. She described herself as "a country girl, and not very political" (M9), and she reported being offended when a male colleague assumed that she "was a feminist and totally pro-choice . . . well, that's not exactly true" (M9). The African American woman pastor was serving a church in one of the most disadvantaged and crime-ridden neighborhoods of all the clergy in the study. She was an agenda setter, but she avoided further political involvement because the senior pastor of her church stressed day-to-day survival issues, rather than politics, as the top priority for his staff.

Table 3.3 summarizes the findings regarding gender. In general, the expectation that women clergy would be less politically involved than their male colleagues holds true. This cannot be confirmed statistically, however, because of the very small number of women in the study.

CAREER STAGE

A final personal factor that shapes the political involvement of clergy is the stage of their careers. As is the case with professionals in other sectors, pastors grow into their institutional roles over time. As they

TABLE 3.3
Gender

	Politically Disengaged	*Agenda Setters*	*Political Leaders*
Male	13 (81%)	16 (94%)	13 (100%)
Female	3 (19%)	1 (6%)	0

Source: Compiled by author from interviews. Percentages are column percents. N = 46.

advance in experience they gain more seniority and respect. Senior clergy enjoy more authority than their more junior colleagues to control the agendas of their congregations and to define the missions of their churches. As they near retirement, however, pastors may begin to relinquish some of this control to the younger clergy who will succeed them. A variety of political scientists have also shown that political participation in general peaks at mid-life and drops off among the elderly.[16] It stands to reason, then, that mid-career clergy might be most likely to become politically involved. Younger pastors must grapple with adjusting to a myriad of day-to-day operational procedures, and may feel overwhelmed, while older pastors may be slowing down as they reach retirement.

I asked the pastors how long they had been in the ministry and whether they had plans to retire soon. Those clergy who had been in the ministry for five years or less were classified in the early career stage; those who planned to retire within five years' time were classified in the late career stage. All others are classified as mid-career. Table 3.4 indicates that fifteen of the forty-six pastors interviewed were at the early stage of their careers; twenty-one were at mid-career; and the remaining ten were nearing retirement.

Younger, less established pastors, as well as those approaching retirement, were less politically involved than those in mid-career. Of the fifteen pastors in the early career stage, ten were disengaged and four were agenda setters. Only one was a political leader, and he actually held the formal position of "pastor for social concerns" at a church with a large pastoral staff. The data show that of the ten pastors nearing retirement, three were disengaged, five were agenda setters, and only two were political leaders. This trend is reversed for those at mid-career, though, with only three disengaged, eight agenda setters, and ten political leaders.

The size of the gamma statistic reported in Table 3.4 means that there is a relatively large correlation between political involvement and

TABLE 3.4
Career Stages

	Politically Disengaged	Agenda Setters	Political Leaders
Early career	10 (66%)	4 (27%)	1 (7%)
Mid-career	3 (14%)	8 (38%)	10 (48%)
Late career	3 (30%)	5 (50%)	2 (20%)

Source: Compiled by author from interviews. Percentages are row percents.
Gamma = 0.39; *chi-square* = 13.38; p = 0.01; N = 46.

career stage (*gamma* = 0.39), and that the relationship is statistically significant (*chi-square* = 13.38; p = 0.01). It is also interesting to note the counter-hypothetical cases of the two late career political leaders. They were both African American pastors who said they had more time for political involvement since they retired from their secular jobs. They reported feeling more invigorated in their ministries; they were pursuing more political involvement than ever before. In summary, though, clergy at mid-career were much more likely to be politically involved than their younger colleagues and those nearing retirement.

LOOKING AHEAD

Four personal factors—attitudes about the propriety of clergy involvement in politics, political efficacy, gender, and career stage—shape pastors' political involvement. Not surprisingly, pastors who said they believed that clergy ought to be politically involved, as well as those who reported strong feelings of political efficacy, were more likely to be politically involved than their counterparts who did not share these perspectives. Gender plays an important role too; female clergy, because they are less accepted as ordained pastors than males, were less politically involved than their male counterparts. Finally, career stage influenced the political involvement of these pastors; those who were at mid-career were significantly more politically involved than their younger colleagues and those nearing retirement.

The variety in clergy orientations to political involvement, then, may be attributed in part to resources that emanate from pastors' own personal circumstances. It is also important to explore the effects of contextual factors on political involvement; clergy themselves have far less control over context than they do over their own personal circumstances. Specifically, the denominational traditions within which the clergy work provide institutional rules and norms about the acceptability of political activity. Evangelical denominations have traditionally taken a relatively separatist stance toward worldly affairs such as politics, so their clergy tend not to be very politically involved. By contrast, African American clergy historically have served as political leaders in their communities. The next chapter shows that another important contextual factor shaping the decisions clergy make about political involvement is the socioeconomic status of the neighborhoods within which they serve. Clergy serving in economically challenged central city neighborhoods may actually encounter more opportunities to become involved politically than their counterparts who serve in areas that are more stable economically.

CHAPTER 4

Contextual Resources for Political Involvement

Like elites in other social settings, pastors face a variety of different demands on their time and energy. They must balance the demands upon them in such a way as to maximize their ability to meet the externally defined expectations of their position, as well as to implement their own agendas. As Sue Crawford has observed, political activity is by definition a secondary pursuit for clergy, because they must first fulfill their explicitly religious duties.[1] The choices clergy make about including politics in their busy schedules is structured in part by their personal beliefs, priorities, and circumstances. Such personal factors, however, do not begin to tell the entire story of the decision-making process clergy undergo with regard to political involvement. Two central contextual factors exert a profound impact on the choices clergy make about political activity: the denominational traditions within which they serve and the socioeconomic characteristics of the neighborhoods where they work.

It is impossible to ignore the contextual factors that structure political participation, particularly that of social elites (such as clergy) who must make choices on behalf of the groups they lead. Scholars, however, have traditionally turned to individual-level explanations to account for varying degrees of political participation, specifically education and income. These explanations, taken together, have been labeled the "standard socioeconomic model" of political participation.[2] According to this model, groups of citizens who lack socioeconomic resources tend to be less likely to participate in politics unless they are able to develop "group consciousness," or a shared belief that they are oppressed by American society and that they ought to take collective political action to seek justice.[3] However, one of the most frequent criticisms of the literature on political participation has been that it does not adequately account for "political context": an individual's social circumstances.

Robert Huckfeldt and John Sprague have addressed this problem by giving substantial attention to the effects of people's surroundings, particularly the neighborhoods within which they reside and work, on their political participation.[4] Furthermore, Sidney Verba and his colleagues have recently reconceptualized political participation as contingent upon the possession of a sufficient amount of three key resources: money, time, and civic skills.[5] In doing so, the Verba group has joined Huckfeldt and Sprague in acknowledging the importance of social context in determining who participates in politics. To some extent, all pastors possess a combination of the resources Verba and his colleagues cite. Taken together, money, time, and civic skills represent potential energy for political participation by clergy as part of their official roles. The degree to which pastors choose to use these resources in the pursuit of political goals defines their orientations to the political realm, or their *political involvement*.

CONTEXTUAL RESOURCES

Charles Glock and Rodney Stark reported in 1965 that American religion had moved to a "new denominationalism" that separated liberals, moderates, conservatives, and fundamentalists.[6] These groups have been shown to have distinct and different political attitudes.[7] James Guth and his colleagues have shown that evangelical clergy place primary emphasis on salvation and evangelism, which means spreading the word of God on an individual basis.[8] They are also sometimes not as heavily bound by traditional denominational structures as are mainline and African American churches.

For these reasons, we might expect that evangelical pastors would possess a wealth of resources for political involvement. Evangelizing should provide them with valuable experience interacting with others, and the freedom some of them enjoy from denominational expectations should allow them the latitude to do as they please politically. However, many scholars have found that the conservative theology of evangelical clergy does not translate well into the political realm.[9] In fact, the classic studies of clergy in politics showed that sustained political action historically has been much more common among religious liberals than religious conservatives.[10]

African American churches have long served as one of the most significant political mobilizers of African Americans.[11] Sidney Verba and his colleagues specifically identified African American churches as being most likely to stimulate political participation among their members.[12] It is also important to bear in mind that African Americans have had a tendency to participate more in politics in general than whites.[13]

Except for the work of David Roozen and his colleagues,[14] existing studies of the political involvement of clergy are weakened by the absence within them of a key variable that is central to the study of political participation: social class. Most scholars who do address this subject operationalize social class in an individual, rather than contextual, manner.[15] A related problem is that so much of the extant literature on religion and politics focuses on the political efforts of a relatively small subset of evangelical Protestants (the so-called "Christian Right") to the exclusion of most other religious groups. Evangelical churches tend to be suburban and predominantly white, so the literature accordingly gives a great deal of attention to the efforts of suburban whites. While this is an important piece of the puzzle, there are other pieces that must also be filled in. Similarly, there have been no studies of the political involvement of clergy that take into account in any systematic manner the socioeconomic status of the neighborhoods within which pastors serve, despite the fact that neighborhood socioeconomic status is one of the key determinants of the political context that shapes the day-to-day existence of a local organization like a church.[16] The socioeconomic status of the neighborhoods within which pastors' churches are situated must also be expected to influence the choices they make about political involvement.

Pastors who serve in economically depressed neighborhoods may have special incentives to lead their congregations politically, because they may be among the few people in the central city with the resources to do so. Clergy who serve in wealthier areas, on the other hand, may encounter disincentives for political participation, because their congregations may not need them to take the political lead. It may be easier for middle- to upper-class citizens to find and finance their own avenues for political participation if they so desire. By contrast, central city residents, who are relatively lacking in many important resources (particularly money), may be more likely to be supportive of a pastor who attempts to engage in politics on their behalf.

As compared with residents of economically stable areas, central city residents may in fact have a greater need to depend on clergy for political leadership. In middle- to upper-class areas, though, efforts by clergy to extend their authority into the political realm may be more likely to be seen as illegitimate; there may be less need, and therefore less expectation, for clergy in wealthier areas to be politically active as part of their official roles. In any case, no complete analysis of the political involvement of clergy can proceed without a careful consideration of neighborhood socioeconomic status. The socioeconomic and demographic characteristics of the neighborhood help to define the political context pastors face, and it is within this context that they make their choices about political involvement.

DENOMINATIONAL TRADITION

Perhaps the most immediate and important of all the contextual factors that influence pastors' political choices is the denominational tradition within which they serve. Each Protestant denomination carries with it a set of time-honored practices, traditions, and institutional rules, all of which have their roots in the denomination's historical and theological foundations. To some extent, these assumptions govern all congregations within a given denomination. American Protestantism is divided into hundreds of separate denominations that fall into three broad traditions: evangelical, mainline, and African American churches. These three traditions, while all existing under the umbrella of Protestantism, are very different and carry with them widely divergent assumptions about the desirability and appropriateness of political involvement among clergy.

I interviewed evangelical pastors from the Assemblies of God, the Southern Baptist Convention, the Evangelical Free Church, the Church of the Nazarene, the Church of God (Anderson, Indiana), and the Lutheran Church-Missouri Synod. Each of these denominations features a national-level organization. Other evangelical churches represented here include the Wisconsin Evangelical Lutheran Synod and the North American Baptist Conference, which are not nationally organized and serve only some regions of the country. Finally, some of the evangelical pastors served churches that exist independently of any super-church structure. Such churches sometimes form loose associations with other evangelical groups, but are not governed by any outside entity.

The mainline pastors interviewed represented the Episcopal Church, the United Methodist Church, the Presbyterian Church (U.S.A.), the Evangelical Lutheran Church in America (ELCA), the American Baptist Church, and the United Church of Christ. Each of these has a strong national denominational structure with deep historical roots. Each also has a national headquarters and regional offices responsible for monitoring local congregations' adherence to denominational policies. Mainline denominations organize their member churches in a rather tightly hierarchical fashion, and the mainline churches I visited were no exception.

The African American clergy came from the African Methodist Episcopal Church (AME), the Church of God in Christ (COGIC), and the National Baptist Convention, U.S.A., Inc. (Missionary Baptists). While other historically black denominations exist, these represent the three main branches of African American Protestantism. These three denominations have national level organizations that are similar in structure and function to mainline denominational organization.

The Evangelical Denominations

The term "evangelical" refers to a sector of American Protestants that has undergone a tremendous expansion in size and visibility during the latter part of the twentieth century. There are three principal branches of evangelicalism. Fundamentalists interpret the Bible literally and tend to assume a separatist stance toward the broader society. Evangelicals are a bit less literal in their interpretation of Scripture and focus a great deal of energy on spreading the gospel to people outside of their church communities. Pentecostals believe in "gifts of the spirit" such as miracles and speaking in tongues. All evangelical Protestants emphasize the centrality of the personal conversion experience, in which each individual acknowledges Jesus Christ as his or her personal savior. The political involvement of evangelicals is a multifaceted phenomenon. Southern Baptist clergy, for example, have been hesitant to embrace the goals of the "Christian Right" political movement, a development that James Guth predicted.[17] Nancy Ammerman has shown that many fundamentalists, while shunning political involvement, believe that America is God's "chosen country."[18] Pentecostals are divided politically. Margaret Poloma has argued that many Pentecostals feel most comfortable when they remain outside of the political fray, but visible exceptions to this rule exist, such as former presidential candidate Rev. Pat Robertson.[19]

Piety and fundamentalism have accompanied some manifestations of American Protestantism since the arrival of Europeans in North America. The great revivals of the nineteenth century highlight the significance of the evangelical impulse throughout American history. American Protestantism has always included evangelical expressions of faith juxtaposed with the traditional, socially dominant mainline, but the differences between these two groups became politically relevant in the 1960s. When representatives of the newly radicalized mainline joined with African Americans in their struggle for civil rights and stood with opponents to the Vietnam War, evangelicals became skeptical because they did not see such political pursuits as appropriate endeavors for religious groups. Nor did they agree with the liberal nature of the political agenda that was being pursued.[20]

After playing a key role in the Prohibition movement of the 1920s, evangelicals did not organize politically again until the late 1970s. Before that time, evangelical clergy commonly judged political involvement beyond ordinary civic duties like voting to be a pursuit of "this world" that detracted from the inward, other-worldly focus of evangelical faith. In reaction to the social changes of the 1960s, however, the tide began to turn. Fear that their traditional social and moral values would be swept away led evangelicals to mobilize politically. The substantive focus of these mobilization efforts was directed at many different targets. Grassroots networks of politicized evangelicals began to emerge during the Carter administration, when the Internal Revenue Service moved to deny tax exemptions for church-sponsored schools that engaged in documented admissions policies of racial discrimination.[21] This policy, in combination with two key Supreme Court decisions,[22] the Panama Canal and SALT II Treaties, and liberal welfare policy, led to an abandonment by many evangelical leaders of their traditional stance against political involvement.

In the late 1970s the fundamentalist Rev. Jerry Falwell made history by founding the Moral Majority. In 1980 Falwell said:

> Americans must no longer linger in ignorance and apathy. We cannot be silent about the sins that are destroying this nation. The choice is ours. We must turn America around or prepare for inevitable destruction. I am listening to the sounds that threaten to take away our liberties in America. And I have listened to God's admonitions and His direction—the only hopes of saving America.[23]

Falwell toured the country organizing patriotic shows, leading marches, and registering unprecedented numbers of evangelical voters. Ultimately the Moral Majority did not meet with much concrete policy success because of the political inexperience and naiveté of its leadership. Moreover, despite the group's name, a majority of Americans disagreed with Falwell's agenda. The Moral Majority did, however, bring such issues as abortion, religious tax exemptions, and "family values" to the forefront of American political debate.[24]

The 1988 presidential race brought a new face to the political realm: the Pentecostal Rev. Pat Robertson. Robertson had already built a career around religious broadcasting, and his bid for the Republican presidential nomination served to augment his power dramatically within the evangelical world. Though he eventually withdrew from the race, Robertson's campaign organization formed the basis for the Christian Coalition, which went on to become one of the most visible grassroots political organizations in the United States. His Christian Coalition took over where the Moral Majority (which folded in 1986) left off. It now assists evangelicals across the country who are running for state and local office. The Christian Coalition has also developed close and controversial ties with the Republican Party. It engages heavily in lobbying on various issues and prepares "voter guides" that rate the degree of correspondence between political candidates' issue positions and those of the Christian Coalition. The specific roles played by local clergy in these efforts are unclear, though there is no doubt that the Christian Coalition has been successful in direct appeals to evangelical laity.

Political involvement among evangelical clergy, while it may seem natural in the context of the overall national movement, actually stands at odds with the historic focus of evangelicalism. As Ted Jelen shows in his study of Protestant clergy, a long-standing tradition in the evangelical world has imposed a strict separation between spiritual and political matters.[25] Evangelical clergy, therefore, should not be expected to be predisposed to overt political involvement. On the other hand, many scholars have suggested that Protestantism may have bifurcated during the twentieth century into two camps: the "orthodox" and the "modernists." Some, especially James Guth and his colleagues, argue that evangelicals embrace a "social theology" that is simply different from that of mainline Protestants. So it may not be that evangelicals are less politically involved; they might just express their political interest differently than their mainline counterparts.[26]

The evangelical clergy I interviewed were generally not very involved in politics. Exactly half of them were disengaged, while forty-four percent were agenda setters. Only one evangelical pastor was a political leader, and this was because his actual title was "pastor for social concerns." Additional variety is evident among the evangelical clergy along the dividing lines of fundamentalism, evangelicalism, and Pentecostalism. Three of the evangelical clergy may be called fundamentalist, and two of them were disengaged. The Pentecostals were more involved: three out of four were agenda setters.

The Mainline Denominations

Mainline Protestant denominations encourage a liberal, open approach to Scripture. Western Europeans who immigrated to North America brought their religious traditions with them, and these religious traditions took hold as the dominant Protestant churches in the United States.[27] Mainline churches in the late twentieth century accept many more alternative interpretations of scripture than do evangelical churches. Evangelical pastors proclaim the absolute inerrancy and infallibility of scripture, but mainline clergy encourage their congregations to derive their own interpretations.

In the 1960s, many mainline seminaries became radicalized, and clergy increasingly came to approach politics guided by what has been called the "social gospel." The notion of the social gospel is a generalized approach to theology that stresses the imperative to help the disadvantaged. The social gospel, at its very core, implies a need for pastors to become politically involved in order to assist the less fortunate. Other factors, however, may make this difficult. Mainline denominations have been suffering from ever-declining memberships while evangelical denominations have been growing ever since the 1960s.[28] Because Americans have been searching for more concrete worldviews and social systems, they have been leaving mainline churches for the evangelical sector. Robert Bellah has argued that Americans have been searching for ways to simplify their lives.[29] Evangelical churches attempt to offer concrete answers to life's problems, while mainline denominations have faltered on this count.[30] Since American churches must compete with each other for members in a free market–like atmosphere, those that are equipped to give people what they are looking for will thrive.[31] Again, the mainline churches have done poorly on this count. As a result, it has become difficult for mainline clergy to mobilize their congregations toward political involvement. Laity who remain in the pews of mainline churches often disagree with their clergy politically.[32] Therefore, mainline clergy who wish to be politically involved often face significant institutional barriers.[33]

Nonetheless, mainline clergy may be expected to have a positive *orientation* toward political involvement, whether or not they actually do anything. I found no consensus among the mainline clergy I interviewed. In nearly equal numbers, they were disengaged (five), agenda setters (five), and political leaders (six). This result shows that there is a tremendous amount of variety within the mainline regarding clergy political involvement. It also shows that the political involvement of religious leaders cannot be predicted by denominational affiliation alone. Evangelical clergy, though, were still less politically involved than mainline clergy as a group. While 56 percent of evangelical clergy were disengaged, the same was true of only 31 percent of mainline clergy.

The African American Denominations

Organized religion in America has a long tradition of being racially segregated. Because of slavery and the systematic discrimination that succeeded it, African American Protestant denominations have had distinct experiences and stand apart from white Protestant denominations. In the days of slavery, one of the only matters over which African Americans had any significant measure of control was their religious belief. Religion became an extremely significant focus of African American social life, particularly as compared with its significance for European Americans. Old Testament accounts of liberation from bondage were particularly powerful for slaves. Oppression after emancipation only solidified the position of religion in the African American community as a bastion of hope and refuge in a sometimes hostile culture. To this day, many African Americans find some comfort in the face of discrimination and inequality, assured of heavenly peace and salvation by a fervent and celebratory belief in God.

African American clergy have been active in politics for decades. Black Protestant churches historically have been an important locus of mobilization for civil rights protest. Whatever success the civil rights movement had can be traced at least to some degree to the mobilization efforts of black Protestant clergy. During the 1950s and 1960s, African Americans were comforted by their churches, but at the same time they were mobilized for protests, marches, and sit-ins. Many of the most prominent civil rights leaders were, in fact, black Protestant pastors.[34]

Some of the African American clergy with whom I spoke were politically involved, but others preferred to avoid the political realm. Of the fourteen African American pastors I interviewed, three were disengaged, five were agenda setters, and six were political leaders. More than half, then, did not lead their congregations in political endeavors. It is noteworthy, however, that the disengaged African American clergy all held secular jobs in addition to their pastoral responsibilities. This fact served to limit the amount of time they had available for anything other than maintaining the basic functioning of their churches.

It is also interesting to compare clergy serving in the different branches of African American Protestantism. Baptists, who represent the largest proportion of African American clergy in Milwaukee, were evenly divided between agenda setting and political leadership, and none was disengaged. On the other hand, both of the African Methodist Episcopal (AME) pastors were disengaged. This may be because there are very few AME churches in Milwaukee. Also, both of the AME clergy indicated that they felt excluded from collaborative work with the African American Baptist churches and the Church of God in Christ (COGIC). Two of the three COGIC clergy were political leaders, while the other one was disengaged. It is interesting to note that neither of the COGIC political leaders was a MICAH member. Finally, two of the three African American pastors who served in denominations that are not historically black were agenda setters, while one was a political leader.

Denomination is certainly an important contextual factor influencing pastors' decisions about whether to engage in politics as part of their institutional roles. Because of the theological differences that accompany denominational categories, it would be easy to expect that denomination would explain most, if not all, of the variation in involvement. The hypothesis, which is rooted in the existing literature on clergy in politics,[35] is easily generated: Because of theological and historical differences among their denominational traditions, evangelical clergy should be less politically involved than their mainline and African American counterparts.

However, table 4.1 illustrates the breakdown of involvement level by denominational tradition. Cramér's V is small in magnitude, and the

TABLE 4.1
Denominational Traditions

	Politically Disengaged	Agenda Setters	Political Leaders
Mainline	5 (31%)	5 (31%)	6 (38%)
Evangelical	8 (50%)	7 (44%)	1 (6%)
African American	3 (21%)	5 (36%)	6 (43%)
Total	35%	37%	28%

Source: Compiled by author from interviews. Percentages are row percents. *Cramér's* $V = 0.27$; *chi-square* $= 6.47$ $p = 0.17$; $N = 46$.

chi-square test of association produces a result that is not statistically significant. This means that denominational tradition may explain some, but by no means all, of the variation in political involvement among Protestant clergy in Milwaukee. Consequently, political involvement must be related to other contextual factors in addition to denomination. Among these other contextual factors, the most important is the socioeconomic status of the neighborhoods within which clergy serve.

THE IMPACT OF NEIGHBORHOOD SOCIOECONOMIC STATUS

The choices Protestant clergy make about political involvement are influenced by the ways they approach their institutional roles and their professional lives as pastors. These factors act as incentives or disincentives as they decide whether to include political involvement among their official activities. They either keep pastors' attention focused primarily on their own congregations or direct it beyond the walls of their churches and into their neighborhoods and the rest of the world. One of the most significant factors that shapes the political contexts within which different pastors find themselves, and that therefore influences their choices about political involvement, is the socioeconomic status of the neighborhoods in which their churches are located.

According to the standard socioeconomic model of political participation, citizens with the fewest material resources may be expected to participate the least in the political process. Central city neighborhoods, such as those in Milwaukee, simply lack resources. The suburbanization of business since the 1960s has had devastating effects on central city neighborhoods, which have been left without an economic base or many meaningful employment opportunities.[36] Central city residents, therefore, are less likely than people who live in economically stable neighborhoods to have the financial resources to engage in conventional political participation. Furthermore, studies have shown that denizens of economically distressed central city neighborhoods experience profound social isolation.[37] Making matters worse, there are more problems stemming from economic hardship that may necessitate political action in central city neighborhoods than there are in outlying areas. It is possible, therefore, that clergy whose churches are located in central city neighborhoods may have more immediate incentives to become involved in politics than those who work in outer city and suburban neighborhoods, where there are higher per capita incomes, lower unemployment rates, and fewer people living below the poverty level.

Low-income citizens may also be easier to mobilize politically than those who are more comfortable financially. To be sure, central city neighborhoods such as those in Milwaukee are plagued by low per capita income, high unemployment rates, and high poverty rates. Recent studies, however, have shown that civic skills developed through membership in voluntary organizations (such as churches) may actually compel low-income citizens to take part in other forms of political activity.[38] The potential for pastors serving in depressed central city neighborhoods to mobilize their congregations for political involvement, then, may be quite substantial.

Race is another important variable in this mix. Oftentimes, residents of disadvantaged neighborhoods belong to racial and ethnic minority groups. Milwaukee is, according to some observers, among the most segregated of all American cities.[39] I analyzed 1990 United States census data for the neighborhoods where the pastors' churches were located and found that the correlation between the percentages of citizens living below poverty and those who belong to racial minority groups is indeed quite high in Milwaukee ($R^2 = 0.553$; $p < 0.000$). Given that African Americans who live in all-black neighborhoods have been found to experience the highest levels of "racial solidarity,"[40] it is particularly plausible that pastors of black congregations in economically distressed neighborhoods would be most likely to become politically involved. Nearly all studies of political participation have shown that those who lack resources remain relatively inactive politically unless they are somehow empowered.[41] In fact, African Americans who are mobilized by community leaders participate substantially more than whites.[42] Economically stressed neighborhoods also provide qualitatively different political contexts than wealthier neighborhoods. Cathy Cohen and Michael Dawson have observed that "living in a neighborhood with high levels of economic devastation leads to greater isolation from social institutions that are most involved in . . . politics."[43] Among the potential mobilizers of economically disadvantaged African Americans are their clergy. Therefore, clergy who serve in economically distressed African American neighborhoods should be most likely to become politically involved.

Every day pastors in the central city come face to face with the symptoms and effects of poverty, crime, and drug addiction. This is unlikely to be true for pastors who serve in economically stable outlying areas; they confront an entirely different array of problems and forms of human suffering. The vast differences that exist between these contexts ought to translate into differences between the political involvement levels of the clergy whose churches are located within them. Members of churches in affluent areas are often politically involved on their own, so clergy may have little incentive to provide them with stimuli for political involvement. On the other hand, central city pastors may have to spend a significant portion of their time concerning themselves with the basic survival needs of people in their immediate neighborhoods, so they may have substantially more incentive to engage in political activity.[44]

As such, even though members of their congregations are often quite politically active, it is reasonable to expect that clergy serving in middle-to-upper-class or suburban neighborhoods will be less likely to become politically involved than those serving in depressed neighborhoods of the central city. If they so choose, central city pastors may have the easiest time finding support in their congregations for their own political involvement, as well as in mobilizing them politically.[45] Suburban pastors' congregations are likely to be made up of citizens "who are best educated and most organizationally active . . . [Such citizens] escape the boundaries of tightly constructed social groups . . . [and] expose themselves to a larger climate of opinion."[46] Residents of the central city are less likely to have this sort of flexibility. As a result, pastors serving in economically disadvantaged neighborhoods ought to have been the most politically involved.

I use data from the 1990 U. S. Census to evaluate this possibility. The forty-six clergy who were interviewed serve in neighborhoods that cover forty-one different census tracts in the Milwaukee metropolitan area. Measures of the relative socioeconomic health of these census tracts include per capita personal income, unemployment rate, percent living below the poverty level, and percent minority population. I use these measures to assess the relationship between the political involvement of the clergy and the socioeconomic status of the neighborhoods where they serve.

One measure of the socioeconomic health of a neighborhood is per capita personal income. In 1990, the average per capita income in the Milwaukee metropolitan area was $19,817, as table 4.2 indicates. This table also shows that the most politically involved clergy served in the most economically depressed areas. The mean per capita income of political leaders' neighborhoods ($9,413) was more than $10,000 below the average for the Milwaukee metropolitan area. The means and medians for the disengaged and agenda setters were quite similar. While they were still somewhat below the average for the metropolitan area, they were significantly higher than those for political leaders. Analysis of variance, which tests for statistically significant differences among three or more means, reveals that the differences among the three groups are nearly significant ($F = 2.80$; $p = 0.07$).

More compelling evidence is provided by the census data on unemployment rates. The problem of inadequate jobs, particularly in the central city, is extremely complex and troubling for many clergy. As one pastor stated, "I get calls every week from people like employment agencies that want people, and the myth is that there's some kind of corps of trained people just waiting for jobs. In this community that is simply totally not true" (M11). Table 4.3 indicates that in 1990, the overall unemployment rate in the Milwaukee metropolitan area was 4.7 per-

TABLE 4.2
Per Capita Personal Income (in $) of Church Neighborhoods

	Politically Disengaged	Agenda Setters	Political Leaders	Milwaukee Area
Range	4,422–26,160	4,086–37,542	4,016–22,968	
Median	14,990	14,304	6,826	
Mean[a]	14,342	16,161	9,413	19,817

Source: U.S. Bureau of the Census, *1990 Census of Population and Housing.*
[a]$F (2,43) = 2.80$; $p = 0.07$.

TABLE 4.3
Unemployment Rates (in %) of Church Neighborhoods

	Politically Disengaged	Agenda Setters	Political Leaders	Milwaukee Area
Range	0.8–37.9	0.9–50.9	0.6–43.6	
Median	4.0	3.6	16.9	
Mean[a]	7.8	8.8	17.5	4.7

Source: U.S. Bureau of the Census, *1990 Census of Population and Housing.*
[a]$F (2,43) = 3.04$; $p = 0.05$.

cent. The corresponding unemployment rates for the neighborhoods served by the most politically involved pastors were by far the highest. The mean unemployment rate for neighborhoods served by pastors classified as political leaders was 17.5 percent, while the mean rates for the disengaged and agenda setters were only 7.8 percent and 8.8 percent respectively. Analysis of variance indicates that the differences among these means are in fact statistically significant ($F = 3.04$; $p = 0.05$). It should be noted that the pastor whose neighborhood had the highest unemployment rate of all (50.9 percent) was an agenda setter who contended that the struggles for daily survival were so intense that there was little time left for political involvement by clergy.

A third measure of the socioeconomic health of a neighborhood is the percentage of residents living below the poverty level. This, too, reveals a similar pattern. As table 4.4 demonstrates, political leaders served in neighborhoods that are much more economically stressed than those served by the disengaged and agenda setters. On average, fully one-third of the residents of political leaders' neighborhoods were living below the poverty level, while the corresponding proportions for the disengaged and agenda setters were far smaller (the means are 13.6 percent and 16.8 percent respectively). Analysis of variance shows that again the differences among the means are significant ($F = 3.56$; $p = 0.04$). The differences among the groups appear even more striking upon comparison of the medians. In neighborhoods served by disengaged clergy, the median poverty rate was 3.9 percent. It was slightly higher (7.5 percent) in the neighborhoods of agenda setters, but the poverty rate for political leaders was 27.9 percent.

Finally, while it is not a measure of socioeconomic health on its own, the minority percentage of a community's population (defined as nonwhite residents) can act as a component of socioeconomic status. Table 4.5 reveals that 17.0 percent of the overall population of the Milwaukee metropolitan area are members of racial or ethnic minority groups. The minority populations of neighborhoods that were being served by clergy classified as political leaders, however, were much more sizable. A comparison of the means for the three categories of pastors' political involvement clearly reveals that the neighborhoods of political leaders were populated quite heavily by members of minority groups (mean = 72.3 percent), while the minority populations of neighborhoods served by the politically disengaged and agenda setters were far smaller: For the disengaged the mean was 19.1 percent, and for agenda setters it was 27.3 percent. Furthermore, analysis of variance reveals a highly significant difference in these means ($F = 9.22$; $p = 0.00$). It is clear that pastors who acted as political leaders served much more sizable minority communities than the disengaged and agenda setters.

TABLE 4.4
Percent Living Below Poverty Level in Church Neighborhoods

	Politically Disengaged	Agenda Setters	Political Leaders	Milwaukee Area
Range	0.9–63.4	0.3–65.9	0.9–62.5	
Median	3.9	7.5	27.9	
Mean[a]	13.6	16.8	33.0	N/A

Source: U.S. Bureau of the Census, *1990 Census of Population and Housing*.
[a] $F_{(2,43)} = 3.56$; $p = 0.04$.

TABLE 4.5
Minority Population (in %) of Church Neighborhoods

	Politically Disengaged	Agenda Setters	Political Leaders	Milwaukee Area
Range	0.5–95.7	0.0–98.4	0.0–99.7	
Median	2.9	5.0	92.3	
Mean[a]	19.1	27.3	72.3	17.0

Source: U.S. Bureau of the Census, *1990 Census of Population and Housing*.
[a] $F_{(2,43)} = 9.22$; $p = 0.00$.

It is important to note that white and black clergy were represented in all three of the involvement categories. It is also true that white, black, and multiracial congregations were all represented by clergy in each involvement category. While clergy serving congregations located in neighborhoods populated by large proportions of members of minority groups were quite politically active, it would be incorrect to conclude that only African American clergy were heavily involved in politics. In fact, a chi-square test of association reveals that there is no significant relationship between the pastors' race and their level of political involvement. This is despite findings (reported in table 4.6) that neighborhoods served by African American clergy were significantly more economically stressed than those served by white pastors.

The overall relationship between clergy political involvement and the socioeconomic health of the neighborhoods where churches are located is quite clear. The notion that clergy serving in middle-to-upper-class neighborhoods are less likely to be politically involved than those in depressed neighborhoods of the central city is strongly supported by the census data. Analysis of variance reveals significant differences in

TABLE 4.6
Race and Neighborhood Socioeconomic Status

	Black Clergy	White Clergy	t (44)	p
Per capita personal income	$7,297	$16,391	4.01	0.000
Unemployment rate	18.7	7.5	-3.24	0.002
Percent living below poverty	36.0	13.4	-3.65	0.001
Percent minority population	83.4	16.9	-7.53	0.000

Source: U.S. Bureau of the Census, *1990 Census of Population and Housing.*

means for unemployment rate, percent living below the poverty level, and percent minority population. Even in the absence of statistical support, however, mere examination of tables 4.2 through 4.5 would reveal that clergy classified as political leaders were serving congregations situated in economically stressed areas, particularly in comparison with the disengaged and agenda setters. The socioeconomic health of the neighborhoods, however, did little to distinguish between the disengaged and agenda setters.

It is important to keep in mind that the sample size here is quite small. Furthermore, these results must not be interpreted to mean that neighborhood socioeconomic status is *predictive* of the extent to which clergy will take on explicitly political roles as part of their official activities. Neighborhood socioeconomic status is one of several factors that shape the political contexts within which different clergy work. Specific incentives or disincentives for political involvement may stem in part from the characteristics of the neighborhood within which a pastor serves, but I do not wish to argue that this alone determines whether they will choose to extend their authority into the political realm. Moreover, it is important to consider the possibility that clergy may self-select into congregations of particular socioeconomic status or be placed there by their denominations.

LOOKING AHEAD

It is clear that contextual factors structure the choices clergy make about political involvement. These contextual factors may actually work together to create incentives or disincentives for clergy to become politically active. Denomination may influence the political involvement of clergy most profoundly in conjunction with the socioeconomic characteristics of the neighborhoods where their churches are located. The clergy classified as political leaders were, without a doubt, serving in some of the most economically distressed neighborhoods in Milwaukee. Central city clergy may in fact find themselves in positions that allow them easily to translate their status as religious elites into the political realm. The mainline clergy who were most politically involved were in fact those who served central city congregations. While the social gospel agenda may not be well accepted by people who attend affluent mainline churches, it resonates well in lower-income mainline churches, particularly when the congregations are racially diverse. The much-touted "clergy-laity gap," which acts as a hedge against religiopolitical activism by clergy, is not a factor in central city mainline congregations.

It may at first seem surprising that evangelical clergy were so unlikely to be politically involved, given the immense amount of attention that has been focused on the political activities of the organized Christian Right since the early 1980s. However, this finding is actually consistent with a variety of previous studies.[47] Nor should it be surprising; most evangelical churches are located in outer city and suburban locations, not in the central city. Evangelical clergy, then, may face an additional disincentive for political involvement because they do not directly serve neighborhoods mired in immediate economic crisis. Pastors who serve congregations in more economically stable neighborhoods may simply have fewer demands placed upon them for their political leadership. This is because citizens who have access to a wide variety of political stimuli come to rely less on any one source than people with fewer resources.[48] It may therefore be that it is simply incumbent upon pastors who serve in economically stressed neighborhoods to enter the political realm. As one of the clergy put it, "I don't think pastors should be limited to just inside the congregation. I think that . . . our ministries should take us beyond the walls of the church to deal with issues, because the people are not going to live in the church" (A8).

Clergy serving congregations in poor central city neighborhoods, then, were more politically involved than pastors serving in wealthier areas. Since these central city neighborhoods are predominantly populated by African Americans, it would appear that clergy serving black congregations are most involved in politics. Perhaps African Americans who are economically disadvantaged are most easily mobilized. Perhaps there are just more immediate needs to be addressed through political avenues in these neighborhoods. Or perhaps clergy with a strong interest in politics self-select into these contexts. In any case, further research on this point is warranted. In the chapters that follow, I explore the relationships between the political agendas the pastors espoused and their political involvement levels, as well as their views on abortion, crime and violence, and "family values."

CHAPTER 5

Substantive Political Agendas

As the previous two chapters demonstrate, both personal and contextual factors structure the degree to which clergy become politically involved. Attitudes about the propriety of clergy political involvement, feelings of political efficacy, gender, career stage, denominational tradition, and especially the socioeconomic health of the neighborhood surrounding each pastor's church all contribute to the decisions they make about political involvement. These factors do not take into account, however, the substantive political agendas clergy espouse. The political issues that pastors say are most important to them also affect their level of political activity. If you profess to care about something, then it follows that your actions should reflect this concern. Moreover, if central city clergy are more politically involved than their suburban counterparts, it is important to understand the substantive nature of their political concerns.

Like other citizens, clergy have views and preferences about various political issues. Pastors who are politically involved either as agenda setters or as political leaders may very well act as what Elihu Katz calls "opinion leaders" for their congregations. In articulating their own positions on issues, and in the simple act of stressing certain issues more than others, they may shape the political attitudes of members of their congregations.[1] The agendas of pastors who are politically disengaged, by definition, will be much less likely to reach the ears of their congregations. As Robert Huckfeldt and his colleagues have pointed out, "People hold many opinions on many important topics, but opinions that are not publicly communicated might better be understood as private opinions."[2] This chapter is an exploration of the various political agendas espoused by the clergy I interviewed. In order to develop a picture of each pastor's substantive political agenda, I asked "What political issue or set of issues concerns you most as a clergy member in this day and age?"

Before turning to pastors' responses to this query, it is helpful to consider briefly the events and issues that were most heavily discussed in the media during the summer of 1994. While I certainly did not expect the clergy to parrot exactly what the media were covering, they do not live in a vacuum. Consequently, their agendas may have been influenced by the most widely discussed "issues of the day." Shanto Iyengar and

Donald Kinder have shown that the American public identifies issues that are frequently discussed in network news broadcasts as more important than all other political issues.[3] This "agenda-setting" effect of the media is most powerful for "those who rarely get caught up in the world of politics. . . . Activists . . . are less apt to be swept away. The more removed the viewer is from the world of public affairs, the stronger the agenda-setting power of television news."[4] Therefore, it is possible that the political agendas of the least politically involved clergy—particularly those who work outside of the central city—would be comprised of issues that were reported heavily by the media. Clergy who distance themselves from politics may also be more influenced by the agenda-setting effect of the media than their colleagues who are politically active. They may therefore also be more likely to identify issues that are frequently discussed in the media as being most important. Alternatively, it is possible that the issues clergy identified as most important reflect the concerns of the groups they lead; studies have shown that group identification has an influence on political attitudes.[5]

One way to assess which events and issues were most heavily covered by the media during the summer of 1994 is to determine the distribution of lead story topics on nightly network news broadcasts. Lead stories create a particularly powerful agenda-setting effect.[6] As table 5.1 shows, the most common lead stories on national network news broadcasts during June and July of 1994 dealt with the O. J. Simpson murder case, genocide in Rwanda, North Korea's nuclear weapons program, U.S. policy toward Haiti, the fiftieth anniversary of D-Day, and health care reform.[7] While I am unable to report whether the pastors were watching network news broadcasts, it is safe to assume that they would have had some contact with the media and would have been familiar with these events and issues. It is also interesting to consider public opinion data from the same time period. A *New York Times*/CBS News Poll for July 14–17, 1994 ($N = 1,339$) revealed that the American public felt that "the most important problems facing this country today" were, among others, health care and health insurance (19 percent), crime and violence (19 percent), unemployment and jobs (9 percent), the economy (7 percent), and foreign policy (6 percent).[8]

Local news may also have had an impact on the pastors' political agendas.[9] For the first time in three years, local news in Milwaukee was not dominated by any one story in 1994. In 1991, the case of serial killer Jeffrey Dahmer[10] and its ramifications dominated local headlines. In 1992, a series of anti-abortion protests captured the city's attention.[11] Finally, 1993 found Milwaukee in the midst of a health crisis for which many attributed blame to the city government as thousands became ill when the parasite *cryptosporidium* infected the water supply.[12] The clos-

TABLE 5.1
Network News Lead Stories, June–July 1994

Issue	Frequency	Issue	Frequency
O.J. Simpson murder case	42	Breast implants	2
Genocide in Rwanda	24	Crime bill	2
Haiti—Sanctions and unrest	21	Exxon Valdez oil spill	2
N. Korean nuclear program	21	Terrorist bombing in London	2
D-Day anniversary	10	Wildfires in western states	2
Health care reform	9	Air crash in Spokane, Wash.	1
Middle East peace process	6	Clinton trip to Oxford	1
Smoking/nicotine hearings	5	Colombian drug smuggling	1
Abortion doctor murder	4	Comet crashes on Jupiter	1
Death of Kim Il Sung	4	Floods in southern states	1
Indictment of Rostenkowski	4	Illegal immigration	1
USAir crash, Charlotte, N.C.	4	Investigation of Mike Espy	1
Carter trip to North Korea	3	Rodney King civil suit	1
Clinton staff changes	3	Soccer player murder	1
Clinton trip to France	3	Stonewall riot anniversary	1
G-7 economic summit	3	Taxes—Earned Income Credit	1
War in Bosnia-Herzegovina	3	Welfare reform	1
Arafat's return to Gaza	2	Whitewater hearings	1

Source: The content of nightly news broadcasts on the three major networks (ABC, CBS, and NBC) is recorded by Vanderbilt University in their *Television News Index and Abstracts,* June–July 1994 (Nashville, Tenn.: Vanderbilt Television News Archive).

est Milwaukee links to nationally prominent news during the summer of 1994 were the Milwaukee roots of Brian "Kato" Kaelin, the house guest of accused murderer O. J. Simpson,[13] and Milwaukee Brewers baseball team owner Allan H. "Bud" Selig's role as acting baseball commissioner while a major league baseball strike loomed.[14] The absence of any major local news stories in Milwaukee during the summer of 1994 may actually have had the effect of broadening the range of issues the pastors included in their political agendas.

Sidney Verba and Norman Nie have observed that "The first . . . question may not be 'where does one stand on the issues?' but 'what *are* the issues?'"[15] What are the substantive political agendas of Protestant clergy, and what significance do they have for pastors' willingness to become politically involved? When people respond to survey questions, they rely on "top of the head" information processing; they provide survey responses based on the considerations that are immediately on their minds.[16] By extension, the issues on the top of the pastors' heads (so to speak) ought to have provided a rough measure of their political agendas from their perspectives as clergy. With the exception of just one pastor, who initially responded "Well, I haven't really given it much thought" (E16), all of the pastors mentioned at least one issue that concerned them, and the average pastor mentioned three or four. The substantive variety and frequencies of discussion for these issues appear in table 5.2.

Comparing tables 5.1 and 5.2, the most striking difference is the virtual absence in table 5.2 of discussion by the clergy of foreign affairs, particularly at a time when crises and conflicts in Rwanda, Haiti, North Korea, and Bosnia-Herzegovina were in the news. Evidently, foreign affairs were not on the minds of the clergy I interviewed. The issue most commonly mentioned by the pastors was abortion, followed by racism, morality and "family values," and religious discrimination. Of these, only abortion was in the news with any regularity in the summer of 1994, and that was due to the murder of an abortion doctor and the debate over reforming the health care system.

The great variety of the pastors' responses may be organized into several broad categories. The most frequently mentioned issues revolve around the immediate life circumstances of others. Pastors who were concerned with such issues focused on the economic situation, physical

TABLE 5.2
Issues of Greatest Concern to Clergy

Issue	Frequency	Issue	Frequency
Abortion	18	Gun control	3
Racism	13	Hunger	3
Morality & "family values"	11	Ineffective laws	3
Religious discrimination	10	NAFTA & trade	3
Crime and violence	9	School prayer	3
Economic inequality	9	Social justice	3
Jobs	9	Societal polarization	3
Drugs	7	Police	2
Gay rights	7	Pornography	2
Health care	7	Welfare reform	2
Foreign affairs	5	AIDS	1
Housing	5	Environment	1
Litigiousness	4	Gambling	1
Bill Clinton as president	3	Gender	1
Discipline in society	3	Mass media	1
Education	3	Representation	1

Source: Compiled by author from interviews.

well-being, education, and safety of their fellow Milwaukeeans. Morality and family values constitute the second most frequently mentioned issue set. A third category of issues includes discrimination against both Christians and minorities. Finally, nonlocal topics including political institutions and foreign affairs make up the fourth category.

THE IMMEDIATE LIFE CIRCUMSTANCES OF MILWAUKEEANS

The first, and most commonly mentioned, of the four types of issues that concerned these clergy deals with people's immediate life circumstances. Among these are economic issues including welfare reform, gambling, jobs, and the general concept of economic inequality. Other issues in this category concern physical well-being; they include health care, housing, and hunger. Education constitutes a third broad focus. Finally, many pastors mentioned safety issues such as crime and violence, drugs, and gun control. Table 5.3 shows the frequency of pastors' responses in this category of issues.

Table 5.3 shows that over half of all the concern about these issues came from clergy who were classified as political leaders. Economic issues and safety issues were the categories most responsible for this divergence between political leaders and their less involved colleagues. Political leaders were more than three times as likely to mention economic issues, and more than twice as likely to mention safety issues, than both disengaged clergy and agenda setters. Political leaders and agenda setters were twice as likely to discuss issues of physical well-

TABLE 5.3
Concerns about Issues of Immediate Life Circumstances

	Politically Disengaged	Agenda Setters	Political Leaders
Economic issues[a]	4 (19%)	4 (19%)	13 (62%)
Physical issues[b]	3 (20%)	6 (40%)	6 (40%)
Education	0	2 (67%)	1 (33%)
Safety concerns[c]	5 (23%)	5 (23%)	12 (54%)
Total	12 (20%)	17 (28%)	32 (52%)

Source: Compiled by author from interviews. Percentages are row percents.
[a] Economic inequality; gambling; jobs; welfare reform.
[b] Health care; housing; hunger.
[c] Crime and violence; drugs; gun control; police.

being compared with the disengaged. Finally, education appeared to be the domain of agenda setters. The pattern here is clear: the more politically involved the pastors were, the more they incorporated issues regarding the immediate life circumstances of others into their agendas.

On twenty-one occasions, clergy identified local economic issues as most troubling for them. Pastors who mentioned these issues discussed specific policy areas, such as welfare reform, as well as more general concepts, such as economic inequality. To a person, though, they were critical of what one labeled "the unfair, unjust economic system that we have in our country" (A4). Two pastors criticized Republican Governor Tommy Thompson's endeavor to reform Wisconsin's welfare system, a policy that had already focused substantial national attention on the state by 1994.[17] One pastor was particularly dismayed at the lack of understanding he perceived in political elites about welfare recipients: "There's a lot of welfare bashing. . . . I bet Thompson doesn't even know anybody on welfare, . . . and Milwaukee, under the governor's policies, has not fared very well" (A5). Another pastor expressed a similar concern about welfare reform because in his congregation,

> There are a lot of people who are really dependent, who are sick and can't work. If they bring about complete welfare reform, how are they going to take care of the people who can't work? Or the people who are in a bad situation and maybe can't find jobs? There'll have to be a lot of job training and a lot of jobs available. (A7)

Another issue that affects poor people more than the wealthy is gambling. Casino gambling began in Wisconsin in the late 1980s. By August 1994, seventeen Native American casinos were in operation,[18] including a high-stakes bingo hall in the city of Milwaukee itself. According to one pastor, "Gambling is my biggest concern, because of the undercutting of the work ethic and people thinking they can get something for nothing. Gambling is a symbol of the growing lack of responsibility in our society" (M8).

Some pastors expressed concern over a perceived shortage of sufficient employment opportunities in the Milwaukee area. Nine identified a lack of good jobs as the root economic problem in Milwaukee. As one stated, "The only jobs around here are jobs that don't pay a living wage" (A5). Another called out for "economic redevelopment in the inner city. These people need jobs" (M6). The government does not take sufficient steps to solve such problems, according to one pastor: "Most of the good stuff goes to the people that already have the good stuff" (E10). Issues related to the job shortage also caused concern; in one pastor's opinion, "The breakup of families is really a job problem" (A4).

Substantive Political Agendas   67

When discussing economic issues, some clergy took a general approach: they lamented the polarization of American society between rich and poor. In the words of one pastor, "I'm very aware of the differences between the rich and the poor, and the harm it does to both.... It destroys human souls on both sides" (M9). Economic inequality and spiritual decline are intertwined, in the opinion of another pastor, and must be addressed together. It was for this reason that he felt clergy must be politically involved. As he illustrated it,

> You can take a pig, wash him up, put a beautiful ribbon around him, make him a number-one prize, but if you have not dealt with the interior, the inner workings, as soon as that pig sees muddy water, there he goes. That is because you have only dealt with the shell, and the appearance. (A2)

In another equation of economic strife and spiritual life, one evangelical pastor expressed dissatisfaction with the Christian Right for failing to pay attention to needy Americans, because they "blow a beautiful opportunity to preach the Gospel in word and deed" (E13). In his opinion, poverty is cast as a "Left issue," so Christian conservatives steer clear of it. This raises the interesting possibility that evangelical clergy feel they should avoid concerning themselves with issues of immediate life circumstance for ideological reasons. If this is so, the "culture war" that is said to separate liberals and conservatives in America may be to blame.[19]

Pastors who were concerned about economic inequality addressed its nonspiritual causes and effects too. Six of them argued that only systemic social change could solve the interrelated symptoms of poverty. Investment by residents of the central city in their own community was a great need in the eyes of one pastor, who asked, "Why clean up a neighborhood where you know you don't own the house? You don't own the corner grocery store. You never expect to have anything" (A4). Another was disturbed, however, by "white upper-middle-class renovation in the inner city" (A3), which in her opinion trivializes residents and puts a glaring spotlight on their lack of ownership.

On fifteen occasions, pastors mentioned issues that concern people's physical well-being. Reflecting its prominence on the American policy agenda during the summer of 1994, health care was among the concerns of seven pastors. Two in particular were quite knowledgeable about the health care debate and discussed various policy proposals and their ramifications. As one argued, health care reform must precede all other social change: "You absolutely cannot reform until you have a basic health care package for everybody" (M2). President Bill Clinton received one pastor's praise for his initiative to reform the system, because "that's one of the most challenging questions that I come into contact with"

(A13). Another pastor expressed dislike for Clinton yet complimented his push for health care reform, because "to deny those less fortunate is totally wrong" (A14). Congress, however, was the target of some ire: with regard to their apparent hesitance to pass health care reform legislation, one pastor wondered "why Congress won't just let it pass" (A8).

Five pastors were concerned about a perceived lack of adequate housing in Milwaukee. One expressed frustration with "the poor living conditions we have here in Milwaukee's inner city" (A4). Another was critical of "Milwaukee's history of racial segregation. . . . It looked like Father Groppi would really change things, but I think he'd be ashamed to see that things today really aren't all that different" (M13). Interestingly, no one mentioned homelessness in this context. Three pastors were concerned about hunger, particularly in the Milwaukee area. "We have been very interested in helping to address the problem of hunger in our city. . . . Many people don't realize just how bad the problem really is" (E13). One expressed concern about hunger in terms that were far more critical of the priorities of Milwaukee's social elite: "I can't believe how groups with money in this city can seek help and put up signs for the environment and ducks when there are people starving to death right here" (A3).

Given that Milwaukee became a hotbed of debate about the policy of "school choice" during the 1990s,[20] it is somewhat surprising that only three pastors mentioned education when listing their greatest concerns. Those who did discuss it were highly critical of Milwaukee's public schools. One argued that school choice was essential so Christian schools and "home schooling"[21] could "work hand in hand with the public schools for the good of all children" (E2). Another pastor was critical of an educational philosophy known as "outcome-based education," which involves bolstering students' self-esteem rather than stressing discipline and accountability.[22] He argued that "outcome-based education is an example of too much government intervention and overbureaucratization, particularly if it means that kids have to provide politically correct responses in school" (E9). Not all clergy shared this view, however: "Our school system would be better off if at least half of the teachers and administrators were Afro-American" (A5).

Finally, safety issues including crime and violence, drugs, and gun control were mentioned on twenty-two occasions. This may be due to the fact that central city pastors have to deal first-hand with violence and its ramifications in their own neighborhoods. One had recently been faced with tragedy when a young man in his congregation was accidentally shot by his own parent. "You hear about somebody getting shot every night, . . . at least two killings a night . . . with a gun" (A9). His deep concern about violence also stemmed from the fact that "here I am right across the street from [a central city] high school. I used to go over there some mornings and just talk to people. And you'd be surprised at the young people that carry guns" (A9). Another pastor shared the fact that his church is located in "the most violent community in Wisconsin" (M11). This makes his job difficult because "you really can't build potentiality or a promise of possibility within people if they're going to be killing each other" (M11). Some of the clergy approached crime and violence with an eye toward solutions. One advocated stiffer criminal penalties. Citing the case of Michael Fay, an American youth who had recently been caned in Singapore, he suggested that public caning should be considered as a serious alternative in the United States. Despite his statement that "I'm not a big fan of capital punishment," he advocated the death penalty for "drug dealers, child molesters, and confirmed rapists" (A5).

Other pastors, particularly those who were members of MICAH, were concerned about the rights of the criminally accused. Several of them were involved through MICAH with ongoing political protest about police negligence and brutality. This issue has especially deep roots in one pastor's congregation, which had organized protests after the 1982 death of an African American man (Ernest Lacy) in police custody.[23] Another pastor expressed particular outrage about the fact that two Milwaukee police officers who had failed to rescue a youth attempting to flee from serial killer Jeffrey Dahmer had been reinstated on the police force.[24] Black-on-black crime was also a major concern. As one pastor said, it "will just tear you to your heart, when you walk in the hospital, and you see the thirteen-year-old shot down over drugs, and sixteen-year-olds walking around with guns in their pockets" (A8). Another equated black-on-black crime to genocide:

> Actually, we as black people, we don't own guns, neither do we own the factories that make guns, but our young boys . . . have all kinds of guns. Where do they get it from? They must have got it from someone else, so we feel it is genocide. We think that the dope in our community is not an incidental problem. We think it was actually put there for a reason. (A4)

Six pastors mentioned the related problem of drug addiction. "I counsel men on drugs, and I encourage them to give their lives to the lord and savior Jesus Christ. The drugs are just a plague upon these men" (A10). Another pastor's church had been involved in fighting the problem of drug abuse since the 1960s, when the congregation operated a van in "the center of the counter-cultural neighborhood, to get people help, to therapy, and to inspire understanding" (M7). The drug problem may be blamed on the media, according to another pastor, as "the media creates a negative culture, a selfish society, and drug use is a result of that" (M6).

Gun control was the final safety issue that caused concern among these clergy, three of whom discussed it as one of their issues of greatest concern. A pastor who called himself "a crusader for gun control in the Milwaukee area" (A9) lamented that he had made little progress in his efforts. As he said, "Small guns, not Uzis, are the problem. The people and the government are not very willing to ban handguns. We need to encourage the buy-back programs, at least" (A9). One pastor had arranged for his church to serve as a center for weapons collection, and another reported lobbying some of his congregation members to support proposed handgun bans.

Chapter 3 shows that clergy who served in the most economically distressed neighborhoods were more politically involved than their counterparts who worked in wealthier areas. The same pastors who were most politically involved were also those who were most concerned about the immediate life circumstances of others. This is yet another reason to believe that clergy in poor neighborhoods may be compelled into the political realm out of necessity. The problems they discussed clearly affect poor people more than the middle class, and it is poor people with whom central city clergy interact on a daily basis.

FAMILY AND SEXUAL MORALITY

The second largest area of great concern for the pastors was morality and family values, including school prayer, the decline of the American family, abortion, gay rights, and AIDS. These are issues that cut to the very core of the sanctity of life. Nearly all of the clergy who mentioned these issues also said they believed that American society has become too permissive. They lamented what they saw as an increase in moral relativism and a decline of the ethic of personal responsibility. Table 5.4 shows the frequency of pastors' responses to this category of issues.

The table shows that agenda setters accounted for exactly half of all discussion about these issues; political leaders were much less interested. This pattern is reflected in all three sub-categories, with the exception of the general discussion of family decline, about which the disengaged and agenda setters were equally concerned. The Christian Right, however, has historically placed precisely these "family issues" at the centerpiece of its political agenda, yet nearly all of the evangelical pastors were either disengaged or agenda setters. Evidently clergy who espoused the agenda of the Christian Right and those who were most politically involved were not one and the same.

Fourteen clergy expressed dissatisfaction with the moral decline they perceived among the American people. They discussed this view-

TABLE 5.4
Concerns about Family and Sexual Morality

	Politically Disengaged	Agenda Setters	Political Leaders
Family decline[a]	6 (43%)	6 (43%)	2 (14%)
Sexual morality[b]	3 (30%)	5 (50%)	2 (20%)
Abortion	7 (39%)	10 (56%)	1 (5%)
Total	16 (38%)	21 (50%)	5 (12%)

Source: Compiled by author from interviews. Percentages are row percents.
[a] Morality and "family values"; school prayer.
[b] AIDS; gay rights; pornography.

point either through the specific frame of prayer in public schools or by expressing regret about moral decline in general terms. Three pastors were especially upset about the absence of prayer in public schools. As one asserted, "Many political leaders are not in touch with religion. That's why they took prayer and the Ten Commandments out of school" (E16). Another argued that "the secular elites who have done away with school prayer want no mention of Christ in society, but we were at one time a Christian nation. The founders saw a need for Christian leaders, and even back to the 1950s Christ was accepted and portrayed positively" (E11).

Others stated their concern in more global terms. "I think that our society has giant, festering sores and wounds from men and women who have given up, or who have lost confidence in marriage and that it's desirable and it works, and they fear it, and they avoid it too much, and it is killing us" (E7), as one said. Another pastor pointed directly to family dysfunction in explaining society's problems: "Some of the ills of society, as we define them, look to me to be a reflection of what's going on in our homes, . . . no parenting, no role models, chemical abuse" (E9). This view was summarized clearly by a pastor who said: "I'm asking you, what's missing? Disregard for life in all its forms" (E5). Still another pastor cast family decline as the root cause of a variety of other problems that concerned him: "I look to the destruction and the moral demise of F-A-M-I-L-Y as the real source of the radical feminist movement, the rise of the homosexual agenda, sexual immorality, and the distribution of condoms. Marriage is now just a flippant thing" (A10).

Not surprisingly, the most frequently mentioned issue in this category was abortion. All of those who brought up abortion described themselves as "pro-life." Amazingly, though, *none* had been involved in sustained political efforts pursuant to this position. Most discussion about abortion began with a categorical statement that "abortion is murder." A typical comment was that "I see it as the taking of an innocent life, and I believe that it is the one issue that will bring God's judgment upon this land" (E3). Another commented that he and his congregation were pro-life because

> There's a biblical basis for that. . . . I've heard all the arguments presented by doctors and psychologists and philosophers, . . . [but] what does God say? There's an account in the Book of Exodus that gives us a clear picture. . . . [If] a woman is with child . . . [and] her fruit departs, . . . if the child does not survive, the Scripture says, a life for a life, meaning that God sees that child in the womb of that mother as a life. (E15)

One pro-life pastor worried that "within the church and outside the church, those that are taking a stand against abortion are getting a bad label right now" (E12). As a frequent target of these pastors' ire, the Clinton administration was accused of "promoting" abortion: "Our present administration has a political agenda to appease a certain segment of our society that wants abortions, and they feel it is a sign of power, or women's rights, or something, that a woman needs to have this choice, this power over her own body, to have an abortion" (E4). There were several pastors, however, who were most troubled by social divisions that they felt the abortion issue tends to create. In fact, one pastor was specifically concerned about "the protest against abortion. . . . Those folks trouble me so much with their pickets. . . . I'm not really for abortion, but sometimes I feel that abortion might be the best alternative. . . . I feel that should be up to the mother and the doctor" (A8).

The pastors also worried about other issues dealing with sexual morality, especially homosexuality. Most who mentioned it viewed homosexuality as unconditionally sinful. "Judges on the bench, even clergy, condoning homosexual behavior, it is frightening" (A10), said one. While AIDS is by no means a "gay disease," some pastors expressed concern about it when they mentioned homosexuality. "I wonder just how truthful the medical profession has been with us about AIDS" (E5), mused a pastor who believed that AIDS patients get special treatment as compared with patients suffering with other afflictions. "I'm not against the homosexual, we'll reach them, we'll treat them the same. Preferential treatment is wrong. AIDS has become a political disease" (E8). One pastor spoke out against allowing gays and lesbians to serve in the armed forces because "after all, George Washington opposed it" (E11). Concern was also expressed about the political clout of the gay community:

The NAMBLA organization, man-boy love association, that . . . listen, as perverse as they are, they're very, very influential. The homosexual community, now listen, they just recently were proved wrong in the fact that . . . our population is not one in ten homosexual, but one third in ten. So we have been given this line for so many years that 10 percent [are gay], . . . therefore they're so powerful politically. (E5)

It is fascinating that the pastors who expressed the most concern about issues of family and sexual morality were relatively uninvolved in politics. After all, these are issues that have mobilized hundreds of thousands of conservative Protestants for political action since 1980. The clergy I interviewed who embraced this set of issues in their agendas, however, were notable for their (reported) *lack* of direct political action, although it is true that fully half of the clergy who expressed concern about these issues were agenda setters. Perhaps large Christian Right interest groups such as the Christian Coalition are not always effective in their efforts to mobilize local clergy, at least in Milwaukee, because it was politically liberal clergy who were the most politically involved.

DISCRIMINATION

The third major category of issues with which these clergy were most concerned involves discrimination. The pastors' concern about discrimination appears to have stemmed from dissatisfaction about social divisions and the inequalities they perceived in the relative status of various social groups. Clergy who were troubled by discrimination based their discussions of society in terms of competing groups, but their specific conceptualizations of discrimination varied. Some pastors felt that they were themselves victims of discrimination because of their status as Christians, while others were concerned about discrimination against others. As table 5.5 illustrates, responses on the subject of discrimination

TABLE 5.5
Concerns about Discrimination

	Politically Disengaged	Agenda Setters	Political Leaders
Anti-Christian	5 (50%)	3 (30%)	2 (20%)
Race[a]	4 (20%)	7 (35%)	9 (45%)
Total	9 (30%)	10 (33%)	11 (37%)

Source: Compiled by author from interviews. Percentages are row percents.
[a] Racism; social justice; societal polarization.

fit into two clear categories: general discrimination against Christians and discrimination based on race. The table shows that clergy who said they were the victims of discrimination against Christians tended not to be very involved in politics. In an increasingly secular and pluralistic society, this is not an uncommon complaint, especially among evangelicals. As it turned out, most of the clergy who felt discriminated against were in fact evangelicals. It may be somewhat surprising, however, to see that these voices came from the ranks of the politically disengaged. It is curious that clergy who feel directly and personally wronged by American society and its political system were not involving themselves in political efforts to address these matters. Table 5.5 also shows that the struggle to combat racial discrimination is preponderantly a concern of the clergy who were politically involved. This particular finding is consistent with the argument that central city clergy are the most politically involved; some feel motivated to be involved because they see the effects of racial discrimination every day.

There were ten pastors who expressed concern about discrimination against Christians; they reported having personally experienced such discrimination. They believed that American society is hostile toward Christians, and that Christians are now paying the price for the secularization of the United States during the twentieth century. Some of them argued that increased pluralism in the twentieth century has squeezed Christians to the margins of society.[25] Now, according to one pastor, "You cannot speak negatively against any group—except Christians" (E6). In a slightly different context, one pastor expressed great concern about the Federal Communications Commission restricting religious broadcasting on television and radio. As he saw it, the FCC "will let another particular organization express their beliefs. But when it comes from a religious standpoint, then it's a no-no" (A1). Another saw irony in the fact that the Ten Commandments are inscribed on the wall of the United States Supreme Court building. "There has to be an ethical norm that our country runs by, . . . and that norm has to be a norm of morality, the Ten Commandments, but [the Court has] chosen to ignore them" (E14).

Several of the pastors echoed a sentiment that the United States is getting away from its "Christian roots" and embracing "humanism. That is the elevation of man. . . . To elevate man, you've got to bring God down" (E8). They all seemed to agree that at one time Christians made up "the moral fiber of the nation" (E11), but "now our national religion is whatever the government says it is" (E14). Perhaps the strongest indictment came from a pastor who insisted that the most serious problem in American society was "the vilification, the deliberate antagonization of Christians in this country . . . by the devil," despite the fact that "I don't believe this was ever a Christian country.... The founding fathers were steeped in the Christian culture of Europe, and that's what they brought over" (E3). In his view, the First Amendment has been misinterpreted so that "now the courts and the rest of the government won't let religious groups even be on equal footing with all the other groups" (E3).

Still, there were a few voices of dissent in the group. One commented that cultural pluralism in the United States brings about "challenges with opportunities" (E9). Christians, in his opinion, "try too hard to hold on to a homogeneous society" (E9). An even stronger argument against the notion that Christians have been the victims of discrimination came from a pastor who expressed his uneasiness with

> A tendency to ... have in mind what I think is a mythical golden era of the U. S., ... the concept of well, we started as a Christian nation and if one were to paint a picture of that, that ends up being essentially a white male Christian Protestant nation. And there's a discomfort with the fact that the nation doesn't look like that, and I would maintain it never looked like that. (M13)

The pastors also expressed concern about discrimination against minority groups. Seventeen of them were profoundly worried about American racism. Three more were concerned about social fragmentation into "haves and have nots" (M16). All of their worries dealt with discrimination against African Americans, with one exception. One pastor argued that "we seem to love Native Americans very much—like we do our zoos. We don't treat them like people, but like novelties" (M5).

It is particularly noteworthy that white clergy addressed the issue of racism much more freely than black clergy. This may have been due in part to the fact that their interviewer was Caucasian. Two African American pastors, however, did take a very hard line on racism by calling for reparations from the United States government. As one said,

> Japanese [Americans] were reparated, based on those who [were held in World War II internment camps]. But we have descendants of slaves. We're the only people in this country that have been wrongly brought here. We're the only ones who are not immigrants.... [Nothing will be resolved] until that is addressed in a dignified and formal manner. (A11)

Black and white clergy alike lamented the fact that racism exists at all: "We're going into the twenty-first century, and we still have this black and white issue, ... and the issue's more prevalent in the Milwaukee area" (A4). One was saddened by the fact that we are "removed from Dr. King and the civil rights thing, and so many people have assumed ... that we have progressed much farther down the road, and now ... there

76   FILLED WITH SPIRIT AND POWER

are some deeply ingrained racial issues that still need to be dealt with" (M11). He also observed that integration has not led to social homogenization:

> I think that the real change . . . is still the issue of being multicultural and being able to affirm not just people with a different skin tone, but to affirm different worldviews, different cultural ways of living. And saying that we can live together in the same house is not only the issue of being tolerant to do it but seeing a real strength and enrichment. (M11)

Another pastor made the related argument that "there has to be some very intentional working at integration, or at least learning what pluralism is, so that we develop a mutual respect" (M1).

In general, agenda setters and political leaders were more likely than the disengaged to be concerned about racial discrimination. The disengaged, on the other hand, were most concerned about discrimination against Christians. Outrage over discrimination on the basis of race is a logical component of a socially liberal belief system that could lead its possessors to work for social change in central city neighborhoods.

NONLOCAL ISSUES

Finally, there were some clergy who focused on issues concerning people and concepts that were several steps removed from Milwaukee. Nine pastors interpreted "issues" to mean "institutions," including the media, President Bill Clinton, Congress, and the litigiousness of American society. Nine others were troubled by war and genocide abroad, international trade issues such as the North American Free Trade Agreement (NAFTA), and the state of the environment. Table 5.6 displays the frequencies with which the pastors discussed these "non-local" issues.

TABLE 5.6
Concerns about Nonlocal Issues

	Politically Disengaged	Agenda Setters	Political Leaders
Institutions[a]	2 (22%)	6 (67%)	1 (11%)
International[b]	0	6 (67%)	3 (33%)
Total	2 (11%)	12 (67%)	4 (22%)

Source: Compiled by author from interviews. Percentages are row percents.
[a] Bill Clinton as president; litigiousness; mass media; representation.
[b] Environment; foreign affairs; NAFTA and trade.

Of the nine pastors who specifically expressed dissatisfaction with the institutions of the American government, a few had specific complaints about particular political elites. One said of Wisconsin's Governor Tommy Thompson: "He's a nerd. If you are poor . . . you don't fare very well" (A5). Others criticized President Clinton and expressed frustration that the American people elected him. As one pastor saw it, "For the first time in our nation we have a president who is openly espousing public policy that is contrary to God's word" (E14). Another argued that Clinton was unable to be a competent international leader: "He lacks moral courage, and he lacks ethical courage" (M3). A Southern Baptist pastor called Clinton "a charlatan. He has no business in our denomination. . . . He is acting like a non-Christian" (E3). The prominent policy role played by First Lady Hillary Rodham Clinton troubled him too, as "nobody elected her" (E3).

One pastor observed that "the people in Congress who are not running again are not voting the way they usually vote, and their colleagues are mad at them. . . . People don't vote their conscience unless they are not worrying about reelection" (E2). He reported having a "somewhat jaundiced view" of government because political officials fail to recognize the fact that "government is divinely ordained. . . . God's authority is delegated" (E2) to political officials. Two others complained that American society has become too litigious and identified lack of responsibility as the most important cause of this problem: "Life has been commodified. People sense that the world doesn't care, . . . [and] they're tempted not to care about others. People become less responsible, worrying more about rights than duties" (M8).

Nine pastors included issues of war, international trade, and the environment among their deepest worries. Their concerns ranged from "the slide of the dollar" (A6) to genocide in Rwanda and Bosnia-Herzegovina. "I feel that the dirtiest words in the world today are ethnic nationalism" (M5), said one. Another pastor, who was quite knowledgeable about international relations, expressed fear that the United States could be drawn into armed conflict in such places as North Korea and Cuba. As he saw it, "The days of isolationism are gone" (M3). A counterpoint was provided by a pastor who was principally concerned with economic issues and crime. He mentioned that he had been deeply involved in movements for world peace and disarmament during the 1980s, but in his current situation serving a central city congregation, "that stuff just feels one step removed from the immediate realities that we face" (M6). Finally, one pastor spoke from a unique perspective because of his extensive international travel. In his opinion, the United States ought to develop "a more coherent sense of what its role is in the world, because it is so incredibly endowed. . . . Now the biggest American import to me appears to be a pop culture that is neither useful nor helpful to people in other countries" (E2).

While a handful of the pastors were globally minded in their approach to politics, nonlocal issues were not high on many of their agendas. The bulk of overall concern was with domestic, and usually local, issues. Clergy who focused on nonlocal issues were preponderantly agenda setters, which is not surprising because they are focused on setting key issues before their congregations for their consideration. It therefore stands to reason that they would be aware of the "issues of the day."

LOOKING AHEAD

Tremendous diversity characterized these pastors' substantive political agendas. Generally speaking, they mentioned four general types of political issues: (1) people's immediate life circumstances, (2) family and sexual morality, (3) discrimination, and (4) nonlocal issues. As a group, they were most frequently concerned with the life circumstances of others. They also expressed concern about a wide variety of other issues, but issues involving economic welfare, physical well-being, education, and safety constituted the issue area of deepest concern.

These political agendas varied with involvement levels. Clergy classified as political leaders were the most concerned of all about issues of immediate life circumstance, while many of the politically disengaged clergy worried instead about discrimination against Christians. Furthermore, issues of morality and family values, as well as nonlocal issues, were mentioned most often by pastors classified as agenda setters.

These results are interesting for three reasons. First, while it is not surprising that some clergy revealed concerns about discrimination against Christians, the fact that they were politically disengaged is noteworthy. Evidently they were not moved to translate their personal grievance against American society into conventional political action. Perhaps the issue was just one of theoretical concern for them. They may not yet have identified any specific incident compelling enough to encourage them to become politically involved. Second, it is curious that the clergy who were most concerned about issues of morality and family values were not more politically involved. The Christian Right has placed these issues at the center of its agenda for a number of years. One might expect that some of the clergy who identified with this agenda would be deeply involved in politics, but this was not the case. Third, recall that the *New York Times*/CBS News poll for June–July 1994 showed that the American public felt that "the most important problems facing this country today" were health care and health insurance, crime and violence, unemployment, the economy, and foreign policy. All but one of these issues may be classified in the category of the immediate life circumstances of others, about which, of course, the clergy expressed the most worry.

Overall, then, the clergy's political agendas more clearly reflected the most pressing concerns of the American public in general than the events and issues most heavily reported in the media. It is impossible to know whether things would have been different had the O. J. Simpson murder case not been dominating the national news. In any case, the agenda-setting effect of the media seems not to have had a significant impact on any of the clergy.

Political leaders were more concerned with issues of the immediate life circumstances of others than their less politically involved counterparts. They also appeared to be quite worried about racial discrimination in Milwaukee. These findings bolster the argument that clergy who serve in distressed central city neighborhoods were most politically involved. Certainly it was they who were most concerned with issues of the immediate life circumstances of their fellow Milwaukeeans. Scholars of group identification have shown that the social groups people identify with most strongly affect they ways in which they evaluate political issues.[26] The issues the pastors mentioned probably reflect the interests of the groups they serve. Just as being a member of a certain social group has important ramifications for political attitudes and involvement, so too does serving as the leader of a certain type of congregation.

The most important remaining question is whether there are identifiable differences among the overall ideological orientations of the clergy on the basis of their political involvement. In order to assess this possibility, I asked the pastors to reflect upon three specific issues: abortion, crime and violence, and "family values." It is to their views on these issues that I now turn in the next three chapters.

CHAPTER 6

Abortion

Chapter 5 displayed the wide variety of issues that occupied the political agendas of the forty-six pastors. This variety, as well as the systematic nature of its apparent relationship with the pastors' levels of political involvement, naturally leads to a further question about the clergy's political belief systems. Chapters 6, 7, and 8 explore the comparative ideological orientations of these clergy with respect to their levels of political involvement in more detail.

Sidney Verba and Norman Nie have observed that "the close link between various sociological characteristics and participation is paralleled by a link between political preferences and participation."[1] There may be some relationship between the degree to which the pastors become involved in politics and their ideological leanings. James Guth and his colleagues present intriguing data that show relationships between political activism and ideology in their recent work, and the classic works on clergy in politics are based on the premise that liberal clergy were mobilized for civil rights activism.[2] I will not argue, though, that different political attitudes *cause* variation in political involvement. Scholars have differed in their assessments of whether there are meaningful differences, in the aggregate, between the political attitudes of citizens who participate in politics and those who do not.[3] Nonetheless, it is important to investigate the relationship between the ideological leanings of these forty-six clergy and their levels of political involvement.

It may be that clergy who become involved politically are simply more attracted to the political realm because they have more intense policy preferences than their colleagues who avoid politics.[4] Alternatively, clergy serving in a specific sort of political context—namely depressed central city neighborhoods—may feel more compelled than others to extend their influence from the pulpit into the realm of politics. It is reasonable to expect that clergy who are the most politically involved will be likely to express the most liberal attitudes when asked to reflect on specific cultural/social issues.

In investigating the pastors' ideological leanings, I relied on their reactions to the question "What comes to mind when you think about" the issues of (1) abortion, (2) crime and violence, and (3) "family values." Their responses to these questions will not lead me to comment technically on the amount of ideological "constraint" they may have displayed in their belief systems.[5] It is important to bear in mind that my discussion of the pastors' attitudes is only a cursory glance at their ideological orientations. Furthermore, scholars have shown that there are often only modest correlations between abstract ideologies and issue-specific opinions.[6] William Jacoby, though, has suggested that it is possible to characterize the degree of ideological content in people's political orientations in a somewhat more straightforward manner. He argues that certain issues are just easier than others for people to conceptualize along ideological lines.[7]

Therefore I asked the pastors about issues with which I expected them to have some familiarity. Abortion, crime and violence, and family values were central to political debates of the 1990s in which religious groups were involved. This chapter is a consideration of the pastors' views on the first of these issues: abortion. Chapter 7 addresses crime and violence, while chapter 8 deals with family values.

BACKGROUND

The debate over abortion was arguably the most emotional political struggle of the end of the twentieth century in the United States. Abortion has been a point of controversy among scholars of medicine, ethics, politics, and public policy since the nineteenth century.[8] But never in American history was abortion in a position of such political centrality as it was in the late twentieth century. Particularly in the wake of the U.S. Supreme Court's 1973 decision in *Roe v. Wade*,[9] many Americans divided into factions around the issue of abortion. The conflict among these groups has on occasion erupted in violence. In fact, the noted sociologist of religion James Davison Hunter has called abortion one of "the knottiest moral and political dilemmas of the larger culture war"[10] that he has perceived in modern American society.

Among the many explanations for the emergence of abortion as a central element of modern American political discourse is the relatively recent reentry by conservative Protestant groups into the political fray. Stopping abortion is central to the agendas of many organizations that claim to represent or identify with this so-called "Christian Right." For example, in its *Contract with the American Family*, the Christian Coalition said it was looking "forward to the day when the humanity and right to life of the unborn child [are] recognized by all people of good will, and [are] once again reflected in our laws and social norms."[11]

Many scholars have traced the paths of abortion activists. One of their most frequently employed compasses has been religion, or more specifically, the religious beliefs and affiliations of these activists. In her study of abortion attitudes, Kristin Luker depicts the power of religion in the personal lives of pro-life activists and the relative lack thereof in the lives of their pro-choice opponents.[12] Further detail was provided by James Guth and his colleagues, who report that the positions abortion activists of both stripes hold on the issue are related to their denominational affiliation and their religious doctrine and practices; fundamentalism and religious orthodoxy both predict opposition to abortion, while affiliation with the mainline branch of Protestantism predicts support for abortion.[13] This, coupled with a report that relatively large numbers of evangelical Protestants reside in states where pro-life sentiment is high,[14] suggests that being a conservative Protestant translates into opposition to abortion.

Given that people who attend church frequently have been found to oppose abortion more adamantly than people who worship less frequently, it is reasonable to expect that anti-abortion clergy may play an important role in shaping their congregations' attitudes about abortion, and possibly even in mobilizing them for pro-life activism.[15] Indeed, the argument has been made that "Churches are convincing people that human life begins at conception . . . and this belief influences abortion decisions independent of ideological beliefs."[16] But is this true in all churches? A major study of public opinion about abortion revealed that conservative Protestants are overwhelmingly pro-life, while mainline Protestants are more sympathetic to a pro-choice position. Also, compared with their white counterparts, African American Protestants possess very strong pro-life attitudes.[17]

So what, then, is the role of clergy as purveyors of attitudes about abortion? Do evangelical and African American clergy attempt to mobilize their congregations for pro-life activism? African American clergy, after all, have the potential to be a formidable mobilizing force for the pro-life movement, especially in light of their strong track record in past mobilization efforts.[18] And what of mainline Protestant clergy? Many mainline churches risk losing members if their clergy are too adamant about pressing a pro-choice agenda.[19] Are they, as Ted Jelen has argued, "likely to regard the expression of political attitudes as personal opinions and . . . fearful that such personal use of the pulpit [is] . . . an abuse of their authority"?[20] Or do they reflect Luker's finding that mainline clergy have long been actively pro-choice, even to the extent of encouraging their congregations to participate in such things as "problem pregnancy counseling," which in some cases has led to the facilitation of abortions?[21] Alternatively, are traditional denominational divisions even relevant to the question of the relationship between the political involvement of Protestant clergy and their framing of abortion? It may be that an interplay between denominational affiliation and the socioeconomic characteristics of the neighborhoods where pastors' churches are located are more clearly related to their opinions about abortion.

CLERGY VIEWS

During the summer of 1992, the eyes of the nation were fixed first on Buffalo, New York, then Wichita, Kansas, and finally on Milwaukee,[22] as these cities played host to highly emotional and widely reported clashes between opponents and supporters of abortion. In Milwaukee, these clashes took place outside several clinics where abortions were performed. The protests were organized by a group called Missionaries to the Preborn, which was founded in September of 1990 by Matthew Trewhella of Milwaukee and Joseph Foreman of Atlanta. The group, which Trewhella described as "a Christian mission targeting the preborn," had offices in Milwaukee, Atlanta, and Wichita by the summer of 1992.[23] It was during that same summer that record numbers of abortion opponents (320 in the first week of protesting alone) were arrested for sitting and lying down in the entrance ways of Milwaukee area abortion clinics.[24] It was noteworthy that numerous children were among those arrested. The children's parents were subsequently charged with contributing to the delinquency of minors for allowing their children to participate in the protests. One Milwaukee County official suggested at the time that "Protesters appear to be putting children on the front lines because they believe the children will not be dealt with as firmly as adults by law enforcement personnel."[25]

It was against this backdrop that I gave the pastors two opportunities to discuss the issue of abortion. Some brought it up when they were asked to identify the issues they found most troubling in this day and age; later in the interview I asked those who did not do so to discuss "what comes to mind" when they thought about abortion. Of the forty-six pastors, eighteen introduced the topic of abortion as one of their issues of greatest concern; the rest made no mention of abortion before being prompted.

The pastors made four distinct types of comments about abortion, although on occasion their responses crossed between or among types. These response types varied most in the political implications of their content. The first type of response was entirely nonpolitical; it encompasses simple definitions of abortion and discussions of personal views on the issue. A second, and more broadly political, type of response involved more general criticism of the terms of the abortion debate.

Explicitly political content emerged in a third set of responses, which dealt with the government's proper role in the policy area. Finally, there were those who discussed their own involvement in abortion protests—or defended their lack thereof. Each of these four response types may be seen as containing a different, and increasing, degree of political content. Within all four substantive contexts, both "pro-life" and "pro-choice" views were expressed.

Definitions and Positions

While Jelen found that clergy were unwilling to reveal their positions on abortion,[26] the pastors I interviewed were anything but reticent about their views. There is no good reason why clergy, being like ordinary citizens in most respects, should not hold and express positions on the issue, although some pastors may have felt inhibited by institutional norms about doing so. Having an opinion is one thing, while setting it into political motion is quite another.

As such, providing definitions and positions constituted the least political of the four response types. By simply expressing their opinions, these clergy were not necessarily politicizing the issue or even referring to the political debate that surrounds it. Thirty-four of the pastors discussed such definitions and positions at some point. Sixteen of them expressed the general opinion that "abortion is murder," while five argued that abortion is wrong except in specific circumstances. Eleven said they were "pro-choice," but offered certain qualifications to this stance. Finally, two discussed their lack of coherent opinions about the issue.

"Pro-life" sentiment was expressed frequently. One pastor said quite simply that "the Bible says thou shalt not kill" (A1). His view was shared by many others: "We believe that whenever a child is conceived, that's life, and we have to uphold what the Bible says about it" (A7). The deep significance that some of the pastors saw in this issue was highlighted by one who stated that "I see it as the taking of an innocent life, and I believe that it is the one issue that will bring God's judgment upon this land" (E4).

Indeed, abortion may be, in the view of at least one of the pastors, "an expectable consequence of teaching people that they are animals, and I think that the general lowering of respect for human life makes it possible for women to consider killing within them what is really a human being" (E7). Abortion may be the result of a social perversion of the biological effect of sexual intercourse and the corresponding decline of the family unit, according to two clergy. "What comes to mind for me is destruction of the family unit. . . . God has given us the opportunity to help him in creation, to procreate, . . . and that means not having abortions" (E16). This theme was reiterated even more forcefully by a pastor who asserted that "man and woman were put together for procreation. . . . The abortion problem has evolved out of a misunderstanding of the purpose of sex. . . . What I think about abortion is that Satan has us all running around debating about issues that will . . . ultimately destroy mankind" (A3).

Of course some pastors qualified their opposition to abortion situationally. As one argued, "I think that in general abortion is wrong. I believe it is taking human life. But I see where there are certain circumstances where it is acceptable as the lesser of two evils. . . . I mean when the mother's life is in actual danger . . . [or] if they're able to demonstrate that the baby has no brain" (M3). He continued by pointing out that "the problem with my argument [is that] less than 3 percent of all abortions would be acceptable, and that's based on Planned Parenthood's own figures" (M3). Others cited cases of rape and incest or suggested that abortion should be used "only as a last resort" (A13).

A casual observer might expect clergy to express uniformly pro-life views. Indeed, much media coverage of clergy who are involved in some way with the struggle over abortion often portrays them as violently opposed to it. While the pro-life position was certainly well represented among the pastors I interviewed, there was also some support for the view that women should have the right to choose an abortion.

The strongest articulation of this pro-choice position came from a pastor who argued that "because we have had the ability and the knowledge to do it, it's just one more form of population control, and ought to be used wisely and well. . . . I certainly am pro-choice. . . . I love children too much to think of what would be happening to them if they did come" (M2). Another agreed, saying about himself and his colleague that "we clergy here are simply pro-choice" (M7). Just as some pro-life pastors offered qualifications to their stance, so too did the pro-choice clergy. "I think it's a woman's choice, but thoughtful people will disagree" (M8), said one. Others qualified their statements along a variety of specific lines. As one stated, "I am not in favor of abortions past the first trimester. Then you really do get into potential murder" (M16). Being pro-choice, of course, does not always mean being in favor of abortion at all times and under all circumstances. "I am not pro-abortion in the sense that I want abortions, but I certainly think that we must have legal abortions" (M4). Finally, one pastor recounted how he has "shifted a lot on the issue. . . . When [my spouse] got pregnant and I was reading like crazy, it was just so exciting. . . . I realized that I just hadn't taken a real close look. . . . It's very hard, but I am pro-choice" (M16).

It is interesting to note that only two of the forty-six pastors chose not to stake out a clear position on the issue of abortion. One had simply not resolved the issue for himself yet. "I know it's wrong to commit murder, . . . but I'm not really clear on the point where life really starts. . . . I'm just not totally sure" (A4). Another pastor, a woman, expressed a wholly different perspective: "I don't think anyone in my church knows where I stand. . . . They think that because I'm a woman, that I must be a feminist, so I must be against pro-life, but it's just not that simple" (M9).

Criticism of the Debate

Some of the pastors moved beyond discussing their own opinions regarding the abortion issue by criticizing the terms and participants in the debate, which is arguably a broader and more politicized approach than revealing one's own position on the issue. Twenty of the pastors chose to discuss the broad terms and effects of the abortion debate at some point during their interviews.

Of these twenty pastors, eight offered a general criticism of the terms of either the abortion debate itself or particular participants in it. One common complaint involved the labels that are used to describe various factions in the debate over abortion. One pastor shared that

> in my mind, the very terms pro-choice and pro-life are very inadequate because everybody I've met is pro-life if it's their own [child], and everybody I've met is [also] pro-choice when it comes to their own choices. And so unfortunately the issue becomes sloganized . . . and there's an inadequacy of thinking through the issues. (E2)

Another pastor complained that the way the abortion issue is presented by the media draws attention away from "the real issues. . . . We're getting talk of women's rights, but not men's rights, . . . and they also don't ever talk about what happens to women after they get abortions and all the psychological problems that can result" (E11). The media aroused similar dissatisfaction, because "we see the abortion clinic on TV, but we don't see the life. You don't see the real issue. They need to show *The Silent Scream*[27] on TV" (E12).

When debate over an issue is characterized by as much polarization as is the abortion debate, supporters of each side fire criticism at their opponents. The pro-choice movement was the target of one pastor's ire: "I've talked to a lot of people from the pro-choice side, and I really have some questions about their total agenda. . . . I think there are other things that they're not talking about, and [they] are using abortion as a convenient emotional hook to hang things on" (M3). Two other pastors expressed distaste for people engaged in the politicized opposition to abortion. As one said, "I'm about life, but I'm not associated with the pro-life movement. I think they're extreme" (A11). This position was clearly shared by another pastor who stated that "the criticisms I would have of the so-called pro-life movement is that it picks out a narrow slice of an issue, and isn't very holistic . . . because I don't see the Bible as being something where you can turn to chapter and verse and [find] the answer about what to do about abortion" (M13).

A somewhat different mode of criticizing the abortion debate and its participants was to identify groups that could be involved, but are not, and to lament this fact. Two pastors, for example, were adamant that the church itself must play a role in facilitating dialogue about the issue. As one said, "I don't think that as a church we should avoid conflict, so I believe we need to talk about all these things" (M11). Another suggestion about the proper place of certain groups in the abortion debate, albeit unrelated to the role of the church, was that "men should keep their mouths shut. It's none of their damn business until they pay their child support" (M15).

The social group that the pastors discussed most frequently in this context, interestingly, was the African American community. Comments about and criticisms of the position and role of African Americans in the abortion debate came almost exclusively from black clergy themselves. They shared a fear that abortion harms the black community disproportionately, and they wondered whether African Americans ought to mobilize against it. One pastor introduced the topic of abortion in the black community obliquely, noting that "one of those destroyed lives could be that bright black person who would have made a difference" (A12). This sentiment was also evident in another pastor's discussion of her

> Ancestors in slavery times, knowing that they were pregnant, . . . used to go out into the fields and the physical pressure of the work would cause them to abort their fetuses and keep on working. . . . This was natural. Nowadays there shouldn't be any unnatural abortions, especially among my people. (A3)

The concrete meaning of such sentiments is crystallized by the observation that

> because people don't have access across the board, we see a whole lot of disproportionate cases of abortion among African Americans and other minorities because we don't have the access. . . . You are intimidated by trying to bring up a child, and you just don't have the resources. (A11)

A white female pastor concurred: "Oppressed people experience genocide, and that is why so-called racial minorities in this country tend to be anti-abortion" (M15). Finally, the African American pastor of a multiracial congregation revealed that while in principle he and the members of his church supported the goals of groups like Missionaries to the Preborn, "we cannot involve ourselves with [them] because they are racist, too focused on the white agenda" (A10).

The Government's Role

There is a qualitative difference between expressing one's own opinion about an issue and criticizing the broader social discourse of which that opinion is a part. Clergy who engaged in such criticism were perhaps viewing the issue of abortion through a somewhat wider lens than those who dwelled on definitions and personal opinions. The next step in the politicization of discussions of abortion involves introducing the role of the government. Clergy who commented on the appropriate role of the government in the abortion debate shifted the discussion to the appropriateness of government regulation of abortion and possible inconsistencies in the policy area itself. Twenty-one pastors discussed the role of government in the abortion debate, and they did so in three distinct ways. First, some argued that government should not regulate abortion. Some saw inconsistencies in the policy area itself. Still others argued specifically that abortion should not be a political issue at all.

The most common view by far was "that government ought to just leave it alone, not get involved in it. . . . It's an incredible invasion of privacy for anyone to make that decision for another person" (M6). Nine pastors made the argument that the government should play a limited role in the regulation of abortion (particularly at the federal level). The right to abortion, which is rooted in the disputed right to privacy that forms the basis of *Roe* v. *Wade*, was the specific concern of one pastor. He declared that "it's wrong to portray it like it's the same thing as the right to clean air. . . . I don't think it's that basic of a right, but it needs to be available" (M4). Despite this fact, and despite widely perceived legal shortcomings in the *Roe* framework, another felt that "as a country I think we've got to stick with the conclusions that were arrived at in *Roe* v. *Wade*" (M14). The pragmatic side of this position was highlighted by a pastor who argued that "to prohibit it is really not very useful. It's going to happen anyway, for the rich, and [if outlawed] it's going to mean further suffering for the poor" (M5). Another pastor provided a real-life illustration: "[Abortion] is a horrible thing, but there are cases where not having an abortion is even more horrid. I see that in the neighborhood, when a single mother with four kids who are being physically abused gets pregnant" (M1). In general, these clergy shared the sentiment that "I don't think it was designed for government to regulate what is a spiritual, ethical concern" (A11).

Five others focused on inconsistencies they perceived in abortion policy. Their criticisms took on both anti-abortion and pro-abortion themes. One raised the dilemma of "why, when a pregnant lady is on her way to the abortion clinic, and she says it's not a life, and is at that time involved in an accident that kills the fetus, [then] she can sue" (A1). Another pastor stated that "it seems ironic to me that people do so much to preserve animals, and human babies are unprotected.... It's a terrible dichotomy that they can be that concerned about the hippo and the eagle and all that, when they ought to be concerned about the human" (A6). An international parallel to the American abortion controversy was offered by a well-traveled pastor, who pointed out that "if you go to China today as I did not long ago, and talk to a young Chinese, he was distraught by the fact that they're only allowed one child. Well, that's government in the womb, ... and the issue of responsibility is not being given full weight" (E2).

Criticisms of policy were not limited to abortion opponents; two pro-choice clergy also raised objections about inconsistencies they perceived. One wondered why "some of the same people that would say we need to have legislation to make abortion absolutely illegal would at the same time say we need to build bigger bombs ... and cut off women and children who need aid" (M13). In a similar vein of thought, the other pastor asked "if the government is going to say you have to have this child, if we're not going to pay for poor women's abortions, are they going to help raise that child" (M16)?

A few of the pastors felt abortion was not a political issue at all. "At this church we do not see [abortion] as a political issue, we see it as a moral issue" (E6). Some pastors asserted that government has no business at all in this policy area. One pointed out that "spiritual revival, not government, is the answer. Politicians haven't made much of a change despite many years of pro-life presidents" (E1). In practice, of course, it would take much more than a "pro-life president" to outlaw abortion, but that was not this pastor's point. While some pastors said abortion should not be regulated, others argued that this lack of regulation has de facto moral implications that have the effect of law. "You cannot say you don't legislate morality. You do legislate morality, and what does that do, it affects your ethics, it affects your economics, it affects everything" (E5). The most elaborate commentary of this variety came from a pastor who presented himself as an adamant foe of abortion and argued that "our present administration has a political agenda to appease a certain segment of our society that wants abortions, and they feel it's a sign of power, or women's rights, or something, that a woman needs to have this choice, this power over her own body, to have an abortion" (E4). He continued by stating that "changing the attitudes of the American people ... is not a political job, that is the job of the churches" (E4).

The Propriety of Protest

Clergy who introduced the topic of the appropriate role of government in the debate over abortion definitely thought about this issue in political terms. Still, this does not mean that they are politically involved in the struggle over abortion. Instead it implies that when they thought about abortion, political institutions and the policies they enact sprang to mind. Finally, some pastors focused on either the general acceptability of direct protest or the actions they and their congregations had taken. In all, sixteen of the pastors discussed protesting, and nine of them offered accounts of specific actions in which they had been involved.

Many of those who were concerned about the propriety of protesting against abortion stressed that protesters should avoid breaking the law at all costs. In fact, the strength of these pastors' collective commitment to political order was remarkable. One pastor emphasized the limits of freedom of expression: "There are those that have the right to oppose abortion clinics, but your liberty only goes to a certain point. . . . You don't kill the doctor; you don't have that liberty" (A2). Another pastor added that "I would be extremely reluctant to break any law, and I profoundly deplore any violent acts. Violence as a means to an end becomes an end" (E7). Similarly, "[trying] to solve an issue by violence is wrong. . . . They have the right to demonstrate but not to destroy property" (M8). An anecdote highlights this point: "I'm not for those protests; they're breaking the law. I can't join a group like that. I get a lot of mail to get involved with those groups, but I don't think you have to break the law to make your wishes known" (A9). Only one pastor even suggested that violence might be warranted to stem the tide of abortions. He made a passing reference to the fact that his congregation does "not apologize for any form of anti-abortion protest, including violence, but we are not violent. We don't chain ourselves to any cars" (A10). Even he, however, did not make reference to the most violent form of abortion protest: murdering abortion providers.

Other pastors were most intent on searching for peaceful, legal alternatives to protest. This was because, as one said, "When you get out there and picket, you're just yelling, and you're picketing the symptom. You're not really trying to fix the cause of the problem" (E16). Instead of protesting, "we need to go to where people are hurting and spend time helping them, and then this problem [of abortion] may be lessened" (A6). Exploring such alternatives to protest is important because

> I wouldn't march at an abortion clinic. I would not teach my congregation to do it, but I tell them there are other ways, there are letters to

be written to your congressman.... Besides, with demonstrating, half your congregation ends up in jail, and you along with them, and this paints a bad picture to those standing outside of religion. (A1)

Rejecting protest does not come without cost, however. As one pastor lamented, "Some people feel that because we don't go out and stand before clinics, [we're] not interested in what's going on. That's not true" (A9). Another pastor outlined his embrace of the principle of separation between church and state quite clearly: "I have been solicited, and sometimes derided, for not participating. The reason I have not participated is because I feel that to do so would be an encroachment on another person's rights, and I would be interfering with the state" (A13).

Finally, nine pastors described their own efforts in the abortion debate in some detail. While their activities represented the full spectrum of positions on the issue, all of them stopped short of participating in, or even endorsing, violence. Noteworthy efforts by the prolife side included counseling pregnant women rather than blocking them from abortion clinics. "We are helping [our denomination] to develop a referral and resource network for pregnant women that will set up individual churches as 'places of refuge'" (E10). Another pastor said his congregation observes a "Right to Life Sunday" each year (E6). The pastor whose church has been most active in the abortion debate reported that "Historically, going back to the '70s, ... we've been involved in the issue of life. We helped start two particular agencies in town that are currently in existence, particularly the Crisis Pregnancy Center[28] ... and a chapter of an adoption agency from Chicago" (E13).

Not all of the pastors were pro-life, however, and some reported a significant amount of involvement on behalf of women seeking abortions. One stated that "there have been those who have needed an abortion and I've gone with them to the clinic" (M11). Another reported undertaking a much more controversial action on behalf of women seeking abortions.

> I was in a situation [in the early 1970s] where I had a benefactor of a private fund, quite sizable, ... for various social action of a fairly liberal nature. We bought abortions too. We had thirteen-year-olds sent as far as New York, pre-*Roe*.... The issue was how can we salvage life with dignity and hope and a future for these people, and if abortion's the way, well, then let's do it. (M5)

None of these clergy may accurately be described as a foot soldier in the war over abortion. None had ever been arrested for abortion protests, although some had participated in them sporadically. Many did, however, involve themselves in the abortion debate in a more indirect way. Perhaps what is most interesting here is the frequency with which the pastors indicated that action other than protest was the only answer to the abortion question.

ANALYSIS

It is now important to consider the relationships between the ideological content of the pastors' remarks and their levels of political involvement. First, the degree to which the pastors found the abortion issue salient may be assessed through a simple dichotomy. Clergy who introduced the topic on their own may be thought to find the issue highly salient, while those who did not discuss it without prompting may find it less so. Notice that none of the pastors suggested that abortion was *not* an issue worthy of public debate. Some just mentioned it on their own, while others had to be asked. Table 6.1 shows that pastors classified as political leaders were less likely to find abortion highly salient than the other two groups of clergy. This pattern is statistically significant (*gamma* = 0.41; *chi-square* = 8.31; *p* = 0.01).

But do the most politically active clergy display the most liberal ideological orientations? There is only limited evidence that political leaders were most consistently pro-choice. While the disengaged and agenda setters were more likely to be pro-life than pro-choice, fewer than half of the political leaders were pro-choice. As table 6.2 reveals, though, this relationship is not statistically significant.

This result suggests that the political involvement of clergy must be motivated by issues other than abortion. After all, pastors who did employ a political framework in discussing the issue insisted that they were searching for *alternatives* to protest. As it turns out, the pastors' abortion opinions were firmly rooted in the theological orientations of the denominational traditions in which they serve, or what James Guth and his colleagues have called "social theology."[29] Abortion opinion (the

TABLE 6.1
Salience of Abortion

	Politically Disengaged	Agenda Setters	Political Leaders
Salient	7 (44%)	10 (59%)	1 (8%)
Not Salient	9 (56%)	7 (41%)	12 (92%)

Source: Compiled by author from interviews. Percentages are column percents.
Gamma = 0.41; *chi-square* = 8.31; *p* = 0.01; *N* = 46.

pro-life/pro-choice dichotomy) was significantly associated with denomination. Table 6.3 illustrates that the pastors' abortion positions broke down almost perfectly by their denominational groupings (*gamma* = –0.52; *chi-square* = 36.48; *p* = 0.00). All but two mainline clergy were pro-choice, while only one African American pastor shared this opinion.

Finally, a note about the setting of the study is in order. The role of Milwaukee's political context in shaping the attitudes of its clergy about abortion is important to consider, but nearly impossible to measure. The fact that widely publicized abortion protests took place in Milwaukee two years before the interviews were conducted may be significant, not only because they made pastors aware and informed about the issue, but also because they may have structured their own political responses to it. Matthew Trewhella, the Milwaukee pastor who co-founded Missionaries to the Preborn, has stated that his identity as a clergy person played an important role in his decision to become involved in the abortion debate.[30] For this reason, clergy (particularly white evangelicals) may plausibly have been expected to identify with him and his group. Trewhella's already controversial public image suffered even more dam-

TABLE 6.2
Positions on Abortion

	Politically Disengaged	*Agenda Setters*	*Political Leaders*
Pro-life	10 (63%)	11 (65%)	5 (39%)
Pro-choice	5 (31%)	4 (23%)	6 (46%)
Unclear	1 (6%)	2 (12%)	2 (15%)

Source: Compiled by author from interviews. Percentages are column percents. *Gamma* = 0.26; *chi-square* = 2.79; *p* = 0.59; *N* = 46.

TABLE 6.3
Abortion Positions by Denomination

	Mainline	*Evangelical*	*African American*
Pro-life	1 (6%)	15 (94%)	10 (71%)
Pro-choice	14 (88%)	0	1 (7%)
Unclear	1 (6%)	1 (6%)	3 (22%)

Source: Compiled by author from interviews. Percentages are column percents. *Gamma* = –0.52; *chi-square* = 36.48; *p* = 0.00; *N* = 46.

age in 1994, however, when he began making remarks that were widely interpreted as support for the murders of abortion providers.[31] Trewhella's extreme views may have had a chilling effect on the potential political involvement of Milwaukee's clergy in the arena of abortion. On the other hand, it is important to remember that political "context is an information channel, an intervening mechanism, rather than an independent agent in politics."[32] At the very least, though, Milwaukee's clergy may have been dissuaded from becoming involved in abortion protests because of the tremendous controversy that swirled around such activity in their city. This may be one of many possible explanations for the curious absence of a relationship between abortion opinions and political involvement among Milwaukee's clergy.

LOOKING AHEAD

Despite differences in their viewpoints and approaches to the issue, these pastors agreed that abortion should occupy an important place on the American political agenda. None of them dismissed it as meaningless or irrelevant. At the same time, and not surprisingly, the pastors employed a variety of different approaches in discussing the issue. Their approaches were not clearly related to their levels of political involvement, however. It is still interesting to note, though, that most political leaders did not assign a high priority to abortion.

What all of this provides is an increasingly sharp picture of the politics of the most politically involved clergy. While they did not dispute the importance of abortion as an issue, they did not make it a priority. The next issue, which will be taken up in chapter 7, is crime and violence. While abortion tells us relatively little about the political choices clergy make, perhaps the immediacy of crime—particularly in an urban setting—will.

CHAPTER 7

Crime and Violence

To establish a sense of the forty-six pastors' ideological orientations, it is crucial to investigate their views on key issues of the day. In the 1990s, these issues included abortion, crime and violence, and "family values." Chapter 6 is an exploration of the clergy's views on abortion. Because most of the clergy expressed pro-life viewpoints on this matter, though, it is difficult to speculate about their overall ideological orientations on the basis of their views on abortion alone. Especially because chapter 5 shows that plenty of these clergy are much more concerned about issues of immediate life circumstances than they are about moral and family issues, there must be better indicators of these pastors' ideologies than abortion. It is for that reason that I now turn to their views on a key issue of immediate life circumstance: crime and violence.

BACKGROUND

While doing the research for this book, I visited a wide variety of neighborhoods in the metropolitan Milwaukee area. They differed tremendously in their socioeconomic status and their crime rates. During one of my last interviews, a terrified woman came rushing into the church office after having her purse stolen at gun point. The police were called, the woman was calmed, and the pastor lamented that "of all the years we've been located here, since 1968, . . . this is the first time that we have had a violent act right here on the church premises" (A13).

This is not to say that there were few violent crimes committed in Milwaukee during the summer of 1994. Perhaps the most important story of crime and violence in Milwaukee in the period between 1992 and 1994, though, involved the dramatic disparity between Milwaukeeans' perceptions about the severity of crime and actual crime rates in the city. A *Milwaukee Journal* survey conducted at the end of 1993 revealed that "most people in the Milwaukee area . . . were optimistic about the year with one exception, violent crime."[1] In 1991, 24 percent of Milwaukee area residents reported a decline in their personal feelings of safety, and 43 percent reported the same thing in the 1993 study.[2] Fully 89 percent of Milwaukee area respondents in 1993 said that crime in their city had gotten worse.[3] This may be attributed to the fact that Milwaukee's homicide rate doubled from 1980 to 1993, which (according to one national reporter) led the city to respond "with more fear, bigger dead bolts, and more angry debate about gun control and the breakdown of families."[4] The rise of gangs, coupled with an influx of crack cocaine and weapons, led Milwaukee County Sheriff Richard Artison to say of the perpetrators of violent crime: "It used to be your money or your life. Now they'll shoot you anyway."[5] Similarly, Milwaukee Public Schools' Superintendent Howard Fuller, who in 1993 presided over the implementation of a program of random weapons searches in high schools and middle schools, regretted that in a meeting with elementary school students "the very first question was about what to do when someone starts shooting! We spent the whole time talking about how to hit the floor and hide under a desk. Have we gone mad?"[6]

A variety of studies, however, suggested that crime rates in Milwaukee actually decreased from 1992 to the beginning of 1994. "In contrast to the apparent public perception that crime [was] on the rise," the rate of violent crime in Milwaukee fell by 4.9 percent from 1992 to 1993, and the total crime rate dropped 9.4 percent.[7] The frequencies of aggravated assault and murder, however, increased by 5.5 percent and 7.5 percent, respectively.[8]

Milwaukee Police Captain Tony Brzonkala attempted to focus the local media's attention on the decline in crime rates.

> The crime rate has decreased in the city of Milwaukee. That is the third year in a row, . . . and it is below the 1988 levels. Milwaukee, as we understand it, is the fourth-safest city of our size. . . . This community will not be satisfied until crime is reduced or until this community does not feel any fear any longer of being victimized.[9]

These views were put into motion in the form of several specific 1994 policies and proposals. During the summer months, the Milwaukee Police Department's "Summer Initiative 1994," a $50,000 gun buyback program, went into effect.[10] In the November general election, however, a much-debated and highly publicized proposal to ban handguns in Milwaukee failed by a two-to-one margin.[11] Observers attributed the defeat of the proposal to over $250,000 in publicity by the National Rifle Association.[12]

Crime rates did not continue to decline in 1994. According to data provided by Wisconsin's Office of Justice Assistance,[13] the total crime rate for Milwaukee County rose by 1.7 percent from 1993 to 1994, and the rate of violent crime (murder, rape, robbery, and aggravated assault) rose by a startling 9.1 percent. The county's rate of property offenses also rose by 0.9 percent. Within the actual city of Milwaukee, increases in 1994 crime rates from their 1993 levels closely reflected the trends at the county level. Total crime increased by 1.8 percent, while violent offenses were up by 9.1 percent, and property offenses rose 0.8 percent. Perhaps the pastors were already sensing this increase in violent crime in mid-1994.

It is interesting to compare the cumulative crime rates in the city of Milwaukee with those in the specific suburbs where I conducted some of the interviews for this study. The trends for the crime rates in these suburbs are quite different than those for the city itself. Total crime decreased in these suburbs by 4.9 percent from 1993 to 1994, and property crimes were down 5.6 percent. However, violent crime in the suburbs rose by a staggering 18.9 percent. Table 7.1 summarizes these data.

CLERGY VIEWS

It is not surprising that many Milwaukee clergy were interested in fighting crime. The specific involvement of the Milwaukee Innercity Congregations Allied for Hope (MICAH) in crime-fighting initiatives was particularly noteworthy.[14] Many of the efforts of clergy like the MICAH pastors have focused on protecting the rights of criminally accused central city residents. During the summer of 1994, in fact, one of MICAH's principal new efforts focused on preventing police brutality. Conservative Protestant groups, by contrast, have tended to be more concerned with *victims'* rights. For example, in its *Contract with the American Family* the Christian Coalition argues that "convicts should be required to work, study, pass random drug testing while in prison, and be required to pay restitution to their victims subsequent to release."[15] Such obvious differences give rise to incompatible views about how religious people ought to deal with the problem of crime and violence in modern society. Scholars have sometimes mistakenly interpreted this divergence to mean that the intensity of one's religious belief will predict toughness on crime.[16] Kathlyn Gaubatz has clarified that it is actually people who espouse less traditional, more liberal religious beliefs who are the least likely to call for harsh criminal penalties to solve the problem of crime.[17] Other studies have shown that people in the poorest neighborhoods are most likely to say that crime is a serious problem.[18] There are, however, few differences between the degree to which white and black people judge criminals punitively.[19] The ways people judge criminals vary depending on the environment in which they live.[20] Therefore the pastors who were most politically involved—those who serve in central city neighborhoods—should be expected to espouse the most liberal attitudes about crime.

TABLE 7.1
Milwaukee Area Crime Rates, 1992–1994

	Total Offenses[a]	Percent Change[b]	Violent Offenses[a]	Percent Change[b]	Property Offenses[a]	Percent Change[b]
City of Milwaukee (1994)	8,243	+1.8	1,043	+9.1	7,200	+0.8
City of Milwaukee (1993)	8,090	–9.4	955	–4.9	7,135	–9.9
City of Milwaukee (1992)	7,462	–3.0	722	+1.6	6,740	–3.6
Milwaukee suburbs[c] (1994)	3,478	–4.9	120	+18.9	3,359	–5.6
Milwaukee suburbs[c] (1993)	3,695	–6.1	106	–15.4	3,593	–5.8
Milwaukee suburbs[c] (1992)	3,981	+3.0	122	–16.5	3,859	+3.8
Milwaukee County (1994)	6,869	+1.7	736	+9.1	6,133	+0.9
Milwaukee County (1993)	6,766	–9.1	676	–6.1	6,090	–9.4
Milwaukee County (1992)	8,928	–3.1	1,005	–1.6	7,923	–3.2

Source: Wisconsin Crime and Arrests 1992, 1993, 1994 (Madison, Wisc.: Office of Justice Assistance Statistical Center).
[a] Number of offenses per 100,000 people.
[b] Percent change = ([1994 rate – 1993 rate] × 100) / (1993 rate).
[c] Only suburbs in which interviews were conducted are included.

The remarks the pastors made about crime and violence were rooted in the fact that they live each day in the reality described by the crime statistics reported above. As was the case with abortion, some clergy presented their views on crime and violence when asked to identify the issues that concerned them most, while others were later prompted by the question "What comes to mind when you think about crime and violence?" Nine pastors mentioned crime and violence among the issues that concerned them most. It is somewhat surprising that more clergy did not mention crime as one of the issues that concerned them most. In a study by Shanto Iyengar, for example, 34 percent of subjects said crime was among the most important issues facing the nation.[21] Only 20 percent of these clergy said the same.

While it is important to remember that all forty-six clergy agreed on the general importance of the issue of crime and violence, the specific ways in which they discussed the issue varied. Nonetheless, their responses were alike in one important respect. All but a few chose to comment on the *causes* of crime and violence rather than suggesting possible *solutions* to the problem. The angles from which the pastors discussed crime and violence corresponded to categories utilized by social psychologists and political scientists who study "responsibility attribution." They have argued that people assign responsibility either to those whom they believe *cause* the problem, or to those whom they believe ought to *solve* the problem.[22] Iyengar identifies three principal targets of responsibility attribution for crime: (1) criminals themselves, (2) societal conditions, and (3) inadequate punitive policies.

The Milwaukee pastors' views on the problem of crime and violence may be organized along similar lines. They took three distinct approaches to the issue. Twenty-four of them discussed *societal* causes of crime and violence, including unemployment, the political establishment, racism, and the media. Iyengar might say that they used "societal cause" frames. Thirty-four pastors responded by saying that the perpetrators of crime themselves must be blamed; they identified *personal* flaws in criminals as the root of the problem. Some of these thirty-four pastors were more critical than others, complaining about social pathologies outside their own communities, a lack of social discipline, and laziness. The rest pointed to issues such as dependency on drugs, feelings of inferiority due to social polarization, and an environment that increases children's chances of being exposed to and involved in crime. Finally, nine of the pastors offered *solutions* to the problem of crime and violence. Six of them argued that religion can end criminal activity, and that perpetrators of crime should be encouraged to dedicate their lives to Jesus Christ. The remaining three offered other solutions.

Societal Causes of Crime

The twenty-four clergy who discussed societal causes of crime and violence focused on several specific factors that lie outside of the control of criminals. These include unemployment, the political establishment, racism, and the media. Eight of them framed crime as a ramification of a lack of good jobs. As one said, "When people are unemployed, there's an increase in crime and violence. And another thing, people say they don't want to work. That's not necessarily true. . . . Job training would do a lot to curb crime" (A12). Another pastor shared this view, stating quite simply that "I think the heart of it is economics" (M13). The lack of good jobs may result in a lack of meaningful involvement in society for some people. This idea is particularly clear in the commentary of one pastor who said "I think jobs are key. If people don't have a future, . . . they get desperate and they'll do violent things. I think we have an underclass in this country that is desperate and that doesn't see any future. . . . I think they've never been able to see that hard work pays off" (M7). Similarly, another pastor stated that "today we have a system in which if you work at the wages offered, for many of the jobs they get, they're better off on welfare" (M8).

Blaming the political establishment for crime and violence in America was also a common theme in the clergy's comments. Twelve pastors believed that the causes of the problem were rooted in the institutions and policies of the American government. Their comments came in two distinct varieties. Three of them levied general criticism of the political establishment, while the remaining nine specifically targeted the legal and law enforcement systems. As one pastor said, "I don't trust the government to solve the problem of crime and violence, because . . . they're just inept" (E1). More specifically, another pastor argued, "One problem is that the government is not very willing to ban handguns" (A9). Finally, one expressed his belief that the political system did not deserve all of the blame it sometimes receives. He stated that "the temptations of politicians, in trying to meet the needs of a constituency, is to offer quick and dramatic solutions. . . . The oversimplified answer [to identify the cause of crime] is to say Ronald Reagan's policies, but much of the issue came before him and has continued well after" (M8).

The legal and law enforcement systems, though, were much more frequently targeted as the causes of crime and violence. One said quite simply, "Mind you, our court systems are kind of screwed up" (E16). As another said, "We as a society don't care so much about truth and justice as we do about playing games. . . . I'm not looking for vigilante justice or cops having free reign. . . . I think the legal system is just going to have to come back to where they can enforce the laws" (E6). Only one pastor made an argument that included some discussion of the historical roots of government's supposed inability to deal with crime and violence. "It's the police's hands being tied by a few of the judges who will not give up the vision of the Great Society" (M3).

A substantively different viewpoint was offered by a woman pastor: "The problem as far as I'm concerned has to do with our whole justice system and the fallacy that a punitive reaction is all that works. It doesn't fix anything" (M15). As a counterpoint, consider the statement of one of her peers: "I think we need to enforce more thoroughly the laws that we have. . . . We need to speed up the [justice] system, and if that means more policemen and more judges and more prisons, unfortunately maybe that's what we need" (M14). Finally, one pastor equated the justice system—and crime itself—with a government he perceives to be racist at root. In his words, "People amplify the crime and violence issues, but it is just a part of the political system. The jail system is part of the political system because it employs whites" (A2).

The pastors frequently echoed this theme of racism, especially in arguing that crime and violence are the inevitable results of a society that is profoundly racist. In all, ten pastors offered racism as an explanation for crime and violence in America. Of these ten, half were themselves African American. Some connected the problem of racism to economic injustice: "I think the heart of it is economics, and tied in with economics would be racial, ethnic exclusionary practices" (M13). Another argued that "I think the crime and the violence are a result of anger. There is an incredible anger among particularly black men. . . . It comes out of a systemic long-term oppression" (M1). This problem may be particularly prevalent in Milwaukee, according to a pastor who suggested that "especially here in Milwaukee, which is such a segregated city, I think the roots are economic and racist" (E10). Three pastors went so far as to argue explicitly that there is a conspiracy against African Americans in this country. As one stated, "These little black boys going around with these beepers and bags, they are not going to South America for drugs. This has been brought in through a well organized, well thought out plan, . . . and it is a method of enslaving; . . . the modern day slavery is mental oppression" (A2). A similar argument was that

> The crime and violence focused on is in the African American community. It holds from my understanding that less than 20 percent of all the violence is committed by African Americans. . . . I even know some black people who are embezzling from credit unions and banks, . . . but none of that ever reaches the media. The only types that do get in the media are low level crimes, . . . while at the same time, skin heads' and nazis' crime rate is higher than the black community, but they are glo-

rified by talk shows.... You hear crime introduced in the media and you hear the north side, ... that this is where the crime is. That means the black folks (A3).

A different perspective, however, was offered by two pastors who were critical of African Americans. As one suggested, "I feel that black families as a whole have just lost all their interest in ... raising their children" (A8). In a related vein, "In the black community, ... I think the absence of positive male role models has been a major factor. I do not think it is an accident that most violent crime is by black males" (E3).

Some pastors blamed crime and violence on the media and the entertainment industry. One pastor attributed crime to "the violence purveyed in our society. We feed off it in our movies, our books" (E9). Similarly, says another, "I really think TV and the media have a lot to do with it.... I think video games are also a problem.... If something's in your way, blast it. Those video games don't show you any consequences" (M9). Consider too this interesting international contrast:

> In Tanzania, even in the cities, there's really not much violence, even though poverty is terrible, so you can't equate poverty with the creation of violence, but [rather] the combination of poverty and a media culture that baits and markets a certain lifestyle as the only one where you can have a decent self-image. (M6)

To a person, this first group of clergy attributed blame for the problem of crime and violence to societal factors that lie beyond the control of the perpetrators of crime. While the characteristics of the neighborhoods where their churches are located are not related to the way they frame crime and violence, mainline clergy made up more than half of the group who attribute blame for crime to societal causes. This provides support for the notion that issue positions are, as Guth and his colleagues have argued, structured by social theology.[23]

Personal Causes of Crime

Most of the Milwaukee clergy attributed blame for crime and violence to the perpetrators of criminal and violent acts. Some stressed the proliferation of drugs, social polarization, and children being raised in poor environments. Others were even more critical of the personal choices and social pathologies they believed to be the causes of crime and violence in America; they focused on a lack of discipline and laziness in American society. They also tended to discuss crime and violence in abstract terms and seemed to feel that the problems of crime and violence lay outside of their own neighborhoods.

On the subject of drugs, one pastor said, "There's no doubt in my mind that drugs are a part of it. . . . Drugs make them violent, and they are violent to get more drugs" (E3). Another noted that "there's a lot of money to be made from drugs" (E10). One pastor said crime was the result of drug abuse: "When they turn to drugs, the problems start mounting, and in order to try and solve the problems, they resort to crime" (A1).

Six pastors looked to the more general notion of social polarization, which they felt some people use as an excuse for engaging in criminal behavior. One pastor observed that "as people have less and less, there's nothing to protect, and others that do have more, they ought to be sharing it with us or we're going to take it anyway. I think in this way part of it is the struggle to become more of an equalized society" (M2). Another shared this sentiment in observing that crime and violence stem from the existence of "haves and have nots. I think it is a very simple issue. . . . You have a continuing human condition where some have and some don't have, and those who don't have take from those who have, or who they perceive to have" (E3). Such social divisions may also have ramifications that reach beyond the problem of crime and violence.

> Every crime damages more than just victims, but it damages us all incrementally by ratcheting up our fear, our decreasing desire to trust any other human being, having to view every other person in our community with suspicion. . . . You end up with only the poor and the elderly and the people who prey on the weak left in the central city, and that is just killing cities. (E7)

Eleven other pastors complained about a lack of positive, nurturing environments for children. As one observed, "Children need to learn respect in the home, . . . [and if they do not,] they're not going to respect anyone else's property when they get out on their own" (E4). Another pastor was thinking in particular about Milwaukee's young people during the summer months when he rued the "lack of anything meaningful for the young people to do now that it's the summertime" (A6). Several wondered "What values do we teach our children? . . . If they're brought up in a neighborhood of crime, they see that criminal kind of lifestyle in the home, so that's all they know" (A14). Similarly, said one, "I think that you can find people growing up in a certain social environment where their chances of being involved in crime later on are very, very high indeed" (E2). One pastor stressed the often hard lot of Milwaukee's youth. In his opinion,

> Milwaukee is a crummy place to be a kid. I know there's wonderful people in our inner city, but by and large we see more and more decay. . . . Kids who are locked into that system, . . . because they're victimized by crime and neglect, they're going to be violent and neglectful and abusive themselves. (E9)

The most frequently mentioned cause of crime, however, was a perceived lack of discipline and punishment in society. One pastor revealed his firm belief that "people just have no respect for property or for life. I think a lot of them don't have a conscience" (E1). A similar argument was provided by a pastor who said "I think one important problem is the lack of swift and proper punishment for criminals. . . . I imagine if we implemented caning in this country, much of the graffiti would disappear" (E4). Some felt this lack of discipline was rooted in the upbringing of children. Said one pastor:

> They send all of these children off to psychiatrists. These children are never punished. It's said they're undisciplined. Every time they come back, they've got something, like attention deficit disorder. It's always placing the problem on this disease or that disorder, never upon the person, . . . and so we become victim-oriented and everyone's a victim, except the true victims of crime. (E8)

Another pastor recalled his own upbringing: "When I grew up, if I did something wrong, it didn't matter who they were, could be a perfect stranger, they'd whip my natural behind. . . . Nowadays, you say anything to a seven-year-old, you get shot" (A10). By way of contrast, though, not all pastors agreed that discipline means the same thing: "There's this notion that somehow whipping a kid is acceptable, that somehow physical punishment is a help. This is simply not true" (M6).

Some pastors argued that perpetrators of crime and violence are simply lazy. One pastor said criminals "don't want to work. They don't want to have jobs, just welfare, . . . and there's no respect for human life and property. It's if I want it, I take it" (M3). In the same vein, another pastor stated that "lots of times when people steal stuff, they steal it for themselves, even if it's to the point where they're going to steal it and sell it to get the money for themselves. . . . Some people are too lazy to work for it. They don't have a good work ethic, . . . or they feel the world owes them" (E16).

Four others characterized Milwaukee's near north side, which is heavily populated by African Americans and severely economically disadvantaged, as a frightening bastion of crime and violence. As one stated, "The near north side of Milwaukee seems to be where most of it comes from. . . . The crimes that seem to be happening here, the people are coming from the near north side into our community. They break in and steal, and then they leave. Crime comes and goes with them" (M3). Some fear that their neighborhoods are "transitioning," and that the "pathologies" of the near north side will creep into their lives. "Across the street there are people getting mugged, and this used to be considered one of the better areas, but it's starting the transition a little bit" (E1).

A substantial proportion of the pastors, then, blamed nothing and no one for crime other than criminals themselves. It is interesting to note at this point that all but one of the pastors who assigned blame for crime to criminals themselves served congregations located outside of high-crime neighborhoods. Therefore it is reasonable to guess that they received little of their information about crime and violence from daily first-hand dealings with it. More than half of them were evangelicals.

How to Curb Crime

Nine pastors went one step beyond discussing the causes of crime and violence by suggesting several ways in which it might be reduced. Six of them made arguments similar to this statement:

> You don't steal, you don't lie, you don't take a life, . . . if you live by God's principles. You'll find that there's no way you'll be involved in crime yourself. . . . If you can get the love of God into the hearts of people, you'll find they'll be transformed. . . . They'll stop doing that stuff. (E15)

Religion, in essence, was framed as the answer to the problem of crime and violence. "Once you start de-emphasizing the Ten Commandments, like thou shalt not steal, then guess what you're going to have? . . . We need to have God bring the Bible to the land" (E11).

Three pastors offered other specific proposals to end crime and violence. In the opinion of one, "I suspect we probably need to legalize drugs in order to get a handle on some of it" (M15). Another pastor said that "if it were up to me I would slap on heavy duty gun control" (M16). Finally, one proposed the most provocative plan of all to end crime and violence. He stated that

> the solution to every ghetto has been that the people have left. I'd have black people leave. They've got to go somewhere else. . . . I happen to think they would become more industrious and successful if they were out of the crippling atmosphere. . . . If we would just decide that we would, with giant bulldozers, just flatten a one hundred block area. . . . You've got to start somewhere. You take a black lady and her three little kids, single parent family collecting welfare; . . . it just strikes me that if that lady were to end up in Watertown, or in Sparta, there might be a lady next door to bring over a pie when she moved in. There might be a church that would say come on over, come to church with me. There might be a teacher who would have those three kids in a classroom where they were the only blacks, and they would get an education like everybody else. (M5)

It is interesting that so few pastors offered solutions to the problem of crime, and that the majority of those who did so did not offer specific policy proposals. Evangelicals chose to leave the solutions to crime and violence up to God. Mainline pastors were more likely to make more secular recommendations. It is also noteworthy that all of the pastors who made such suggestions served suburban congregations.

ANALYSIS

What relationship, if any, exists between the pastors' political involvement and their attitudes about crime and violence? In large part, the nature of this relationship ought to depend upon the political agendas that motivate clergy who are politically involved. As was the case with abortion, some pastors elected to mention crime and violence as one of the issues that concerned them most; those who did so may be said to have found crime and violence more salient than those who did not do so. Table 7.2 shows that more than half of the politically involved clergy mentioned crime and violence as one of the issues that concerned them most, while only one disengaged pastor and one agenda setter did the same. This stands in contrast to the abortion results presented in table 6.1, which show that political leaders did *not* find abortion to be a salient issue. Here, then, is more evidence that the political agendas of the most politically involved clergy were focused on bettering the immediate life circumstances of others.

I expected to show that the most politically involved clergy would have espoused the most liberal ideological outlooks. This hypothesis is rather difficult to evaluate in the context of the issue of crime and violence, especially in light of Iyengar's finding that responsibility attributions for crime and ideological leanings are weakly correlated.[24] Nonetheless, table 7.3 displays a summary of the frequencies of each response type by political-involvement category. The most interesting result is that political leaders are proportionately more likely to indict societal causes of crime and violence and less likely to suggest that personal factors are to blame. To the extent that responsibility attribution for crime measures ideological outlook, then, there is some evidence that the most politically involved clergy were not conservative. If they were, they would have joined the disengaged and the agenda setters in assigning personal blame to the perpetrators of crime. Blaming society at large, however, implies a focus on the rights of the criminally accused—and thus a more liberal ideological outlook.

LOOKING AHEAD

Taken together, Chapters 6 and 7 provide an increasingly sharp picture of the politics of the most politically involved clergy. Crime and violence

TABLE 7.2
Salience of Crime and Violence

	Politically Disengaged	Agenda Setters	Political Leaders
Salient	1 (6%)	1 (6%)	7 (54%)
Not Salient	15 (94%)	16 (94%)	6 (46%)

Source: Compiled by author from interviews. Percentages are column percents. *Gamma* = 0.78; *chi-square* = 13.53; *p* = 0.00; *N* = 46.

TABLE 7.3
Positions on Crime and Violence

	Politically Disengaged	Agenda Setters	Political Leaders
Societal causes	7 (29%)	7 (32%)	10 (56%)
Personal causes	14 (58%)	13 (59%)	7 (39%)
Solutions	3 (13%)	2 (9%)	1 (5%)

Source: Compiled by author from interviews. Percentages are column percents.

was particularly salient for political leaders as compared with the disengaged and agenda setters, and political leaders also appeared to shun the conservative "law and order" stance embraced by their less politically involved counterparts. Given that many of the most politically involved clergy served in the central city, it stands to reason that their political involvement would have been motivated by issues that speak to immediate survival needs of poor people.

Do politically involved clergy embrace liberal ideological outlooks? The classic literature on clergy in politics certainly suggests that they did so in the 1960s.[25] But is that still true today? To the limited extent that these pastors' attitudes about abortion and crime and violence reflect their ideologies, the answer to this question is yes. Clergy with conservative views on abortion and crime and violence were among the least politically involved. They tended to serve congregations located in relatively affluent neighborhoods, where congregation members would be likely to have access to a wide range of opportunities for political involvement in places other than their churches. Therefore, they may have had far less incentive to attempt to translate their institutional power from the religious realm into politics. Clergy serving in economically depressed neighborhoods, however, may be among the only community leaders with the resources to give political voice to the concerns of those in their neighborhoods. Therefore it makes good sense that politically involved clergy would have been less conservative, particularly with regard to the issue of crime and violence, with which they contend on a very regular basis. In chapter 8, I will further explore the pastors' ideological orientations through the lens of one final issue: "family values."

CHAPTER 8

Family Values

In chapters 6 and 7, I explored the forty-six pastors' orientations to two central issues of modern American political, cultural, and social debate: abortion and crime and violence. The pastors' views on these issues were diverse, and this diversity was related in meaningful ways to their political-involvement levels. The most politically involved clergy displayed liberal attitudes, especially about crime and violence. Notably, however, none of the pastors argued that either abortion or crime and violence was in any way an unimportant issue. No one suggested, for example, that either issue was a mere rhetorical device or a creation of the media.

The pastors were asked to discuss another issue about which they did *not* display consensus of any sort. That issue was the controversial notion of "family values." The pastors displayed different ideological orientations in their remarks about this issue, but they also disagreed about its *importance* in American political discourse. Many of the pastors believed that family values actually constituted a "nonissue": a matter that was in their view diverting public attention away from other, "more pressing" matters. It is reasonable to expect that when the clergy were asked to reflect on family values, those who were the most involved in politics would express the most liberal attitudes. Once again, it is important to bear in mind that this discussion of the pastors' attitudes marks only a cursory glance at their ideological orientations.[1]

To measure the pastors' views about the relative importance of family values in American political debate, I classified each pastor as either an "acceptor," an "ignorer," or a "rejecter" with regard to the issue. Acceptors argued that family values constituted an important element of American political debate. Ignorers provided comments that were devoid of explicit political content. Rejecters were those who felt that talk of family values constituted an illegitimate political debate that only serves to divert public attention away from other matters.

BACKGROUND

If you drive down the highways of America at election time, you may see prominently displayed homemade signs proudly proclaiming the need to "save our family values" by voting for specific candidates. With each passing federal, state, and local election since the early 1980s, the old signs fade and new ones appear touting the latest self-proclaimed defender of family values. Politicians and the media have bombarded American voters with messages about the nebulous concept of family values for many years. What are family values? How has this elusive concept evolved as a political symbol?

Symbolic debates, from which substantive issues arise, serve in part to drive the American policy agenda.[2] Participants in politics contribute to these debates by defining and shaping them. In fact, the absolute political power of various groups derives in part from their ability to define political issues in their own symbolic terms.[3] The more effectively a group is able to set the terms of a symbolic debate, the more success they will likely have in influencing public policy on the issues that arise from that debate. In general, it is reasonable to expect that people who believe they have a special stake in a specific policy area will attempt to shape the debate surrounding it. In fact, certain groups in society may come to "own" certain public problems.[4] If this is so, then such groups are allowed by other citizens to define the meaning and importance of the issues at stake, although this "is always conditional and potentially subject to challenge and change."[5]

One of the most powerful American political symbols during the second half of the twentieth century was the contested notion of "family values." The question of family decline has occupied a place on the American political agenda, as well as in the research programs of an array of scholars, for decades. More than any other symbolic debate, however, it is difficult to identify the specific groups of Americans who would have the most stake in preserving and defending "family values." This is a debate that has taken on myriad forms and in which a vast number of groups have expressed interest. There are three main camps in the overall debate. On the Left are radical reformers who push for "liberation" from oppressive family structures. On the Right are Christian conservatives and others active in what has been called the "profamily" movement. Somewhere in between are academics who study and comment on the state of the American family.[6]

Each of these groups has expressed different opinions about the argument that the American family is in decline. Many conservatives began to argue in the 1960s that the United States was being weakened by the decline of the traditional nuclear family, and that efforts should be made to renew its strength. Many liberals disagreed, arguing instead that "the American family" never had a simple shape.[7] Similarly, scholars have presented a confusingly mixed set of findings about whether the American family has even been in decline.[8] There have been significant disagreements over the years about whether the American family was ever a "strong" social institution in the first place. Some have argued, in fact, that the American family actually grew stronger as an institution during the late twentieth century than it had ever been before.[9] The complexity of this debate becomes eminently clear upon reflecting even for a moment on the huge variety of possible definitions of the terms "family," "values," and "decline."

In the early 1960s Nathan Glazer and Daniel Patrick Moynihan incited controversy by proposing that families that deviated from the traditional nuclear model, especially African American families, were ensconced in a "tangle of pathology."[10] Glazer and Moynihan expressed particular concern about single-mother families: their argument was that problems were more likely to crop up in families without a strong father figure. Over the years, liberals have attacked this argument, calling it (among other things) racist. The assertion that the absence of fathers from American homes poses a serious problem has nonetheless continued to find voice among academics. David Blankenhorn published an entire book about the impact of "fatherlessness" in American families in which he argues that "the most urgent domestic challenge facing the United States at the close of twentieth century is the re-creation of fatherhood as a vital social role for men."[11]

The enduring legacy of the original argument forwarded by Glazer and Moynihan is evident in the evolution of the political debates about the American family. Although it was not yet specifically labeled "the family values debate," the issue of family decline arose frequently on the Washington policy agenda during the 1970s. Senate hearings were held in 1973 on the topic of "American Families: Trends and Pressures,"[12] and in 1977, the Carnegie Council on Children published a report charging that "legislators rarely address the question of how best to support family life."[13] Later the Carter administration held a series of much-publicized White House Conferences on Families, which served to focus national attention on the growing debate over the family.[14] By the early 1980s, evangelical Christians galvanized by Jerry Falwell's Moral Majority were calling for a somewhat less tolerant approach to family policy. During the 97th Congress, the Moral Majority lobbied for Sen. Paul Laxalt's (R-Nevada) Family Protection Act, an omnibus measure that ultimately failed in the Senate. It contained provisions against abortion, gay rights, school desegregation, sex education, and teachers' unions, and it sought to institute or protect parental rights, prayer in public schools, and tuition tax credits.[15] More significantly, when the proposed Equal Rights Amendment (ERA) finally failed on June 30, 1982, the growing "pro-family" movement was said to have had a hand in its demise.[16]

The significance of the debate over the family during the 1980s was evident in the realm of political rhetoric as well as on the policy agenda. Politicians frequently alluded to family issues and appealed to voters' emotional attachments to the concept of family. In fact, State of the Union addresses reveal that "family values" rhetoric was popular with both presidents of the 1980s. Ronald Reagan and George Bush referred in their State of the Union addresses to such terms as "family values" and "children" significantly more often than any of their predecessors in the post–World War II era.[17] This suggests that despite the limited success of the pro-family movement in the realm of public policy, the debate was alive and well in symbolic political discourse.[18]

The terms and conduct of this debate have evolved and changed over time.[19] When evangelical Protestants first began raising concerns about family decline, many observers found their rhetoric stark and inflammatory. The Christian Right's early ire focused almost exclusively on attacking "secular forces" in society—and responding to rejoinders by the targets of such attacks. In 1982, for example, the evangelical Christian author Tim LaHaye argued that "the pro-family movement that speaks for at least eighty-five percent of the American people . . . [is being attacked by] many of the radical activist groups that seem to exercise an inordinate amount of influence over government."[20]

In the 1990s, the "family values" debate was transformed. Recently, Christian conservatives have focused much less attention on perceived attacks on the family by secular forces. Their agenda has expanded to include a much wider range of issues.[21] Nonetheless, the Christian Right may owe its continued political viability to the staying power of the family values debate.[22] At the same time, some evangelical Christian political leaders have expressed concern about the evolution of the debate out of fear that it has lost its meaning. In 1992, Gary Bauer, president of the Family Research Council, stated that "by itself, the label pro-family no longer means a thing. . . . Even people intent on changing the traditional family to alternative structures have tried to incorporate the label."[23]

Voices of the political Left and academia have also adjusted their messages regarding the debates over the American family in the 1990s. The Communitarian movement has placed the need for strong family units among its centerpieces. As the noted Communitarian Amitai Etzioni has argued, "Parents have a moral responsibility to the community to invest themselves in the proper upbringing of their children, and communities . . . [must] enable parents to so dedicate themselves."[24] Moreover, James Q. Wilson used his presidential address to the American Political Science Association to echo themes from his widely discussed work on "the moral sense." This moral sense, he has argued, is essential to the qualities that make people good citizens in democratic societies, and it is first developed and nurtured in children by their families.[25]

Despite its deep moral significance, the family values debate has been used as a political football. In his 1994 State of the Union address, Bill Clinton made nearly one hundred references to family and religious imagery.[26] Some observers criticize politicians for discussing family values because they feel politicians should not do so: "Who are they? What moral qualifications do they bring to the work of the spirit?"[27] Others are more critical of the symbolic nature of the message than of the messengers: "I never know who it is that they mean to convince. . . . The harder questions are political, not moral."[28] And so it goes: the campaign signs extolling family values may fade, but they do remain in place on the sides of American roads, carrying messages that grow deeper roots in the collective American political imagination with each passing election year.

CLERGY VIEWS

To characterize the pastors' attitudes about the family values debate, I asked them to discuss "what immediately comes to mind" when they thought about "family issues" or "family values." This question was prefaced by the statement "a lot of politicians have been talking recently about 'family issues' or 'family values' and various problems regarding the state of the American family." The pastors' responses fell into three broad categories. Sixteen of the pastors accepted the notion of family values as meaningful and important. They discussed it by suggesting a variety of causes for what they perceived to be the decline of the American family. They represented the conservative "pro-family" stance. Another seven pastors appeared to have neither interest in nor knowledge of the family values debate, and instead shared anecdotes about their own family lives. Finally, twenty-three others asserted that the family values debate was meaningless. This viewpoint is typical of the political Left.

Accepting the Debate as Legitimate

The sixteen pastors who fully accepted the family values debate as meaningful argued that the American family really was in decline. None of them defended "nontraditional" (non-nuclear) family arrangements, either. These "acceptors" framed the notion of family values by attributing blame for family decline instead of challenging the terms of the debate itself.[29] Acceptors assigned responsibility for the decline of family values to a wide variety of sources. Many said the problem was rooted in society's abandonment of the "one man, one woman" ideal of family. They also identified several social impulses that they believed to have taken hold in the absence of the paradigm of the nuclear family, specifically technology, materialism, and moral relativism. They criticized what they saw as a decline in social responsibility and discipline. They believed that family decline was perpetuated by the government, which they saw as playing the inappropriate role of *in loco parentis* to a society without moral standards.

Moreover, nearly all of those who accepted the terms of the family values debate defended the normative superiority of the nuclear model of family and expressed the belief that a moral crisis had been brought about by its decline. One typical statement illustrates this position with great conviction: "I know what family values are: one man committed to one woman, committed to each other, loving one another and putting each other . . . and their family first, and that being your family. And anything that takes away from that is wrong" (E12). Acceptors asserted that the nuclear, heterosexual model of family was prescribed by divine ordination. "I believe there's only two things ordained and one is the family and the other is the church, . . . and I'm talking traditional family, husband, wife, and children" (E15). The vital role of the family in child rearing was also given great attention. One pastor noted that "the Bible gives clear guidelines for raising children" (E4).

Acceptors vigorously engaged in blame assignment for the decline of American family values. Popular targets of their criticism were technology, materialism, and moral relativism. More than one pastor expressed concern about the increasing role of technology in American life and argued that it was tearing at the fabric of the family. "No one sits down and eats together no more. . . . Now there's microwaves. Anyone can come home, stick their food in the microwave, [and go] off to their room" (A4).

Acceptors also indicted the media and the entertainment industry for the decline of family values. They were apt to argue that if family values are not held up as a standard on television, they cannot be promoted in society at large: "I think that it's television. . . . There's a sense through the media of do what you feel, rather than do what's right" (A13). A lack of positive portrayals of African Americans in the media was noted by one pastor: "If the media played up families in the community, about the positive things, like they do the O. J. Simpson thing,[30] we'd have a great community. . . . TV is to me a gigantic mockery. . . . Ugh, it's terrible what they do on TV now" (A9). Some clergy also blamed the music industry, particularly forms of music that convey violent and sexually explicit themes. Of rap music, the same pastor said:

Some of that stuff is crazy. I'm sitting next to a guy in a car, and his music is blasting and saying "F" this and lick this and that, and it's terrible. They're getting all this stuff in their minds, and what happens is it causes men to treat women in a negative way, and it causes women to act rough. (A9)

Acceptors cast the United States as a nation of greedy consumers: "People want the material side of life, but they don't want to deal with the spiritual, and there's not a balance" (A9). This theme was echoed by another observation that "we spend too much time trying to make a living and too little making a life" (A14). Technology and greed, these pastors argued, had given rise to moral relativism, which many saw as the ultimate cause of family decline. "There is no morality," one pastor argued.

> Every individual now can choose one's own values, except that for some people values are as soon as I have enough money I'm going to buy a couple of bags of cocaine and I'm going to snort it down.... Societies cannot exist on that kind of personal narcissism.... [A]nd without the absolute moral code of the Bible, how can you tell them they're wrong? (E7)

Some acceptors include supernatural phenomena in their discussions of the forces they see as destroying family values. "The devil has the world system in his grasp" (E3), said one. Another suggested that "there are evil forces at work that would destroy the family" (E15), but he did not explicitly implicate the devil. Those who suggested such supernatural causes of family decline also argued that "it's going to take something like a revival or a spiritual awakening" (E1) to solve the problem.

Some assigned blame for the decline of family values to a widespread lack of responsibility among Americans. They spoke of slippage in Americans' willingness to assume responsibility for their own lives. One suggested that "earlier generations were more responsible than current ones.... People want anonymity now and do not want to make commitments" (E1). This was a common refrain, as was the notion that "people are not willing to take responsibility for their own actions. They want to blame someone else, and they teach their kids to do that too. Once you give up your responsibility, you can do anything without having any sort of consequences" (A10). If people are unwilling to accept responsibility for their own lives, they will by definition be rendered unable to assume responsibility in the context of a family. It is this absence of the ethic of responsibility, these pastors argued, that compromises the integrity of American society.

One solution offered by clergy who accepted the legitimacy of the family values debate was a return to a more disciplined society. Several pastors argued that American parents have lost control of their children. "I find that the children today don't fear anybody" (A14), said one. Others thought increased social consciousness about child abuse had compromised parents' ability to discipline their children.

> I'm sure there are some parents who abuse children, but I think that most parents have the good of their children at heart, . . . and I don't think their hands should be tied to the extent that they are afraid really to do what needs to be done. The crazy thing about it is that if parents don't do it and the kids grow up and get in trouble, the police will. (A12)

A similar and even more striking argument about the value of discipline was that "a parent ought to teach their children. . . . We take this child abuse thing so far out of context. Parents ought to be able to discipline their children, if that means *breaking a leg*, not maliciously, but in the line of discipline" (A14).

Furthermore, acceptors frequently pointed to the institutions and policies of the federal government as part of the problem with the American family. Specifically, they linked a demise in personal responsibility with the expansion of the federal government in the twentieth century. "I think one of the problems with families is that people have begun to look to the government as an entity that owes them something" (E1). Another pastor added that "I think that a lot of the laws on the books today . . . work against the family and not for it" (E5). Political elites themselves are blamed for this: "It doesn't help when . . . you get somebody into office, and their moral values aren't the standards that churches see" (A13). Acceptors also pointed to specific policy areas in assessing blame for the demise of the American family. Education policy troubled some; as one said, "Kids are not being taught what the Bible says at home or at school" (E16). Welfare policy was attacked even more stringently. "The government takes the role of the family. . . . We have to feed these children, so we come out with food stamps. What happens with welfare is that the government seeks to become a surrogate father, . . . and that's not the way God designed it" (E4). Another pastor portrayed public assistance as a vicious cycle that perpetuates irresponsibility:

> The welfare system has said it's easier for the woman to make it without the man than it is to be in the home and support them. So they say get rid of the man. So what does he do? It causes him to lie and to cheat. . . . Therefore you have children growing up in homes where they see the man is not useful, . . . and the man doesn't feel responsible any more. (E5)

Some acceptors focused specifically on a decline they perceived in family values among African Americans. Most who made this argument were themselves African American pastors.[31] One of them suggested that "when you destroy the seeds, you destroy nations, and there's a need for the African American family to remain together. It seems like . . . we have lost the family" (A11). Others cited the plight of African Americans in the central city. As one said, "We've got our kids growing up with no hope and no real self-esteem" (A7). Another pastor actually blamed the civil rights movement: "I really believe we took more time with political things than we did the children, and wanting to have a good time and everything, and now it has caused . . . the demise of the family structure, because look at the children. They're going crazy" (A9). The reverse may be true, however, according to an alternative conceptualization. African American families may in fact have given too much attention to their children in recent years. "A lot of times I feel that we as black folk kind of feel that 'I was denied some things in my coming up, and I want to see that my children have some of the things that I didn't have.' When we do that we tend to spoil our children" (A4). Just a handful of white pastors obliquely discussed "the inner city and its problems" (E16). One, however, was bold in arguing that "well, there isn't any marriage in the black community. In the white community at least they make the marriage. . . . I think it's a function of race" (E12).

The pastors who accepted the family values debate, therefore, were unanimous in their belief that the moral foundations of America have been compromised by the demise of the traditional family structure. They attributed blame to a wide variety of sources. None of them defended the position that the American family had merely changed, not declined. All of the views expressed by these clergy reflected the agenda of the conservative pro-family movement. It is especially interesting to hear the voices of African American pastors in this context, as they are not often considered to be part of the pro-family movement.

Ignoring the Debate

Seven pastors ignored the family values debate altogether. They expressed their thoughts on the topic of family values in nonpolitical terms. They appeared to have scarcely any familiarity with the political family values debate, and discussed instead reminiscences of their own family lives or how the church can save families. Those who ignored the political ramifications of the family values debate also commented on it less extensively than other clergy. One pastor said that to him, family values meant "that old family tradition where you come to the supper table and talk about the day's events, and then go to take a drive in the countryside" (A1). Several others delineated their perceptions of the appropriate role of the church in facilitating healthy family structures.

One said he strives to "teach families how to be peaceable toward each other and to respect one another" (M8). A second pastor was glad to help keep marriages together, but did not regret "the breakdown of truly bad marriages" (M2). Others were nostalgic for "the *Ozzie and Harriet* era. . . . In the 1950s it was only necessary for the man to work, but then people wanted to raise their standard of living, until now when it is almost essential to work two jobs" (E14). In general, though, these pastors did not address the political implications of the family values debate at all.

Rejecting the Debate as Meaningless

The final (and largest) group of clergy reacted to the issue of family values with great distaste. In fact, one pastor responded immediately to my mentioning the phrase "family values" with "gag me with a spoon" (M16). While no other pastors stated it in quite these terms, fully half of them approached the family values debate from a liberal perspective: their *position* on the issue of family values was that it is actually *not* an important issue at all. They criticized the debate itself, suggesting that it was "owned" by the conservative pro-family movement.[32] Many made the argument that it was a rhetorical invention of the political Right or an exclusionary political tool. Others asserted that "family values" was a meaningless catch phrase or a "cop-out" used by politicians to avoid facing "real issues." Some indicated that the way the issue is presented by the media creates false conflict, while others suggested that the family values discourse marginalizes churches and their work. Still others expressed the opinion that talk of "family values" is sexist and racist. What really set them apart from the acceptors, though, was the fact that their commentary revolved around criticizing the *terms* of the debate, while acceptors mainly discussed the actual decline of the family.

The most popular approach that these "rejecters" used to challenge the family values debate was to argue that it was an entirely imaginary, strategic creation of the political Right. Many pastors said that the purveyors of this discourse were rewriting history; as one pastor said, "I don't think we were ever in the *Ozzie and Harriet* phase that people idealize" (M1). As evidence of their belief that the Right had invented the notion of family decline, many pastors argued that America was never the society depicted in television shows of the 1950s. Some suggested that the Right honestly believed that family life was once idyllic, though: "They're grieving over something they think they had" (M12). In the wake of social change, one pastor argued, "We look to our imagined picture of what the family once was, which I don't believe it ever was, . . . thinking if we say this loud enough and often enough it will become true, and . . . we won't have to try risky ways of living and being family" (M15). Rejecters also believed that "family values" were exclusionary by their very nature: "The term bothers me. . . . It seems to be exclusive, and it diminishes people" (M9). These pastors strongly believed that the definition of family must extend beyond the nuclear model. Some suggested that the controversy devalues alternative family structures, particularly single-parent families.

Many rejecters perceived the family values discourse as a convenient rhetorical tool of the political Right. The linkage between conservatism and ownership of this concept was seen as almost conspiratorial by some. As one pastor argued, "If a person is very conservative, they will use [family values] as a wedge to drive people farther apart" (M11). Another said of the political Right and its use of family values rhetoric, "I know that they've got a secret set of definitions" (M7). This distaste extended for some pastors to a belief that the political Right had strategically co-opted organized religion. "You're talking about a group of white elitists, and it's a Republican agenda, and they hide behind the cloak of religion" (A2). This link to the Republican Party was emphasized by several pastors. As one said, "Reagan and Bush sure cashed in on it" (M4).

Many of the rejecters argued that the term "family values" was devoid of meaning. "It's a sound bite" (E9), said one pastor. "The term family values is something people use politically, some disingenuously" (E9). As another asked, "I wonder what they mean by [family values]. It's some kind of a knee jab, to get an emotional response. . . . It's a wastebasket kind of category" (M7). An interesting undercurrent of distrust for politicians was evident here, which would suggest support for the idea that those who reject the discourse also avoid political involvement. As one said of politicians, "They find those good phrases that really will stretch out and grab a lot of people because they will say 'yeah, I agree'" (E10).

A few of the pastors who discounted the family values debate expressed great concern that it was polarizing American society by creating false conflict. One argued that "everybody can sort of read into it what you want, and it is going to be a frustrating and pointless debate that keeps people apart, until you say what is family and what are values" (M10). Another believed that "what we have to do is really just more dialoging and listening to each other, and there the consensus develops, rather than going along political lines, because that's when people get in camps and start hating each other" (M11). Some pastors asserted that the discourse had the effect of marginalizing all churches and discounting the contributions they make to society. Because of the family values debate, they argued, churches had been co-opted by the political system; they felt organized religion had become just another voice in the pluralist cacophony of interest groups. "Churches lose their prophetic voice . . . and do not bring mission to the country. . . . When we become just a political voice we become indistinguishable from the other voices around" (E9).

Several rejecters accused the family values debate of being sexist. One pastor made the argument that talk of family values is "another way to get women out of the work force" (M16). The liberalization of divorce law was attacked by some proponents of the family values discourse as a major social problem and a cause of the decline of the American family. However, a few of the rejecters saw no-fault divorce as a positive development of the twentieth century that often benefits and liberates women from destructive relationships: "The talk of family values worries me more about dysfunctional family systems, how much secret keeping is a part of that system, and how we protect the offender, the oppressor, by keeping the family secret and by putting on an outward appearance of perfection" (M15). This pastor's opinion of the family values debate was that it is an affront to women and a threat to their liberation.

Finally, several pastors argued that the political use of the term "family values" was profoundly racist. "It does more damage than good because the African American family is no *Leave It to Beaver* family" (A2). Even more pointed was this criticism:

> Politicians in my neighborhood haven't the slightest idea about family values because they don't know anything about the people they represent. . . . The notion of the nuclear family is Eurocentric and ignores the African tradition of extended family, . . . and besides, in our community the males have systematically been removed from the home, and no one can convince me that this was not a prescribed agenda set in motion. (A3)

A number of others made reference to the African American tradition of extended family as well. In particular, one African American pastor recalled that "it used to be that we all met at Grandma and Grandpa's house for Sunday supper, and Mama and Daddy, brothers and sisters, aunts and uncles and cousins were all there. . . . We all took care of each other, we were one family" (A1). He was discouraged, however, because "now the politicians don't even think of that as legitimate, and they ignore the African American families" (A1). Because some rejecters felt that the purveyors of the family values debate undervalued traditional African American family configurations, they dismissed the importance of the debate and refused to join it.

One of the pastors who challenged the importance of the debate deserves special mention because he simultaneously made the argument that American family values could use strengthening. While he did not see value in the political debate itself, he leaned toward substantive agreement with its proponents. This interesting conundrum was most evident in his discussion of the discourse's shortcomings:

> I firmly believe that marriage and family is a divine institution, . . . but when I talk about family values, I don't talk about *traditional* family values, because if they want to use that term I want to know what tradition you're talking about, you know, the *Ozzie and Harriet* sort of thing? As far as I'm concerned the nuclear family probably has more to do with the industrial revolution than with biblical norms. If we talk about biblical family, I think we're talking extended family and that is not what most people mean by traditional family values. (E2)

ANALYSIS

Table 8.1 reveals that clergy who accepted "family values" and those who rejected it were almost equally represented in all three involvement categories. The only hint of a direct relationship between attitudes about family values and political involvement lies in the fact that the majority of pastors who ignored the debate were politically disengaged. Statistical analysis reveals that the relationship itself is not significant (*chi-square* = 3.92; p = 0.42).

This absence of a statistical relationship, however, does not mean that nothing interesting about the political involvement of clergy can be learned from their attitudes about family values. The literature on the family values debate makes much of the stark, dichotomous disagreement between what James Davison Hunter calls "the impulse toward orthodoxy and the impulse toward progressivism"[33] regarding the definition of the American family and the degree to which it may have

TABLE 8.1
Positions on Family Values

	Politically Disengaged	Agenda Setters	Political Leaders
Accept	5 (31%)	5 (29%)	6 (46%)
Ignore	4 (25%)	3 (18%)	0
Reject	7 (44%)	9 (53%)	7 (54%)

Source: Compiled by author from interviews. Percentages are column percents. *Cramér's V* = 0.21; *chi-square* = 3.92; p = 0.42; N = 46.

declined. Nowhere, however, are the differences among racial groups' approaches to the debate discussed. As it happens, the most interesting story to be told about clergy attitudes on family values is one of tremendous divergence between white and black pastors.

Despite talk among rejecters of the potentially racist nature of the family values debate, African American pastors held the *most* consistently conservative views about family values. This fact is illustrated in table 8.2. On the other hand, mainline clergy were almost uniform in rejecting conservative "family values" rhetoric. And there was more variety in the opinions of the evangelical clergy than a casual observer might expect. Only half of them were classified as acceptors. Fully 56 percent of African American pastors, however, expressed the conservative, "accepting" viewpoint on family values. Of these acceptors, five of eight were political leaders. It should be noted that the three African American pastors who expressed the more liberal position on family values were also the only ones who labeled the debate racist. This fact is particularly interesting because many of the white pastors expressed a similar complaint. Yet few black pastors themselves, who are leaders in the communities said to be discriminated against, shared this opinion.

Another important upshot of the relationship between pastors' attitudes about family values and their political involvement relates to their views on crime and violence. Blankenhorn made the provocative argument that "much of our national discussion of youth crime simply ignores the elephant in the room called fatherlessness."[34] Wilson has presented a related argument in his discussion of the correlation between increasing moral relativism and crime rates.[35] From these assertions it is reasonable to draw out a logical expectation that people who are concerned about crime ought also to be concerned about the decline of traditional family structures. Clergy who were most politically involved were also those who served in economically distressed neighborhoods. These pastors have thus far appeared to have had relatively liberal polit-

TABLE 8.2
Political Involvement, Family Values, and Denomination

	Mainline	*Evangelical*	*African American*
Accept	0	8 (50%)	8 (56%)
Ignore	2 (13%)	2 (13%)	3 (22%)
Reject	14 (87%)	6 (37%)	3 (22%)

Source: Compiled by author from interviews. Percentages are column percents. Gamma = –0.70; *chi-square* = 16.44; *p* = 0.00; *N* = 46.

ical outlooks. The results of this section, however, have shown that African American clergy who espoused a *conservative* approach to the family values debate were also among those who were most politically involved.

Two conclusions may be drawn from this finding. First, a simple ideological dichotomy is clearly insufficient for characterizing these clergy's political agendas. Second, perhaps African American clergy are unique in their ability to perceive connections between the discrete problems of crime and family decline. If so, they may be best equipped to lead the "interfaith council of religious leaders" that Blankenhorn has argued "could speak up and act up on behalf of marriage"[36] and other family values. Of course, Blankenhorn, like most other observers of religion, morality, politics, and society, does not explicitly mention African American clergy in this context. But it would seem that they are not to be ignored.

LOOKING AHEAD

In their remarks about abortion, crime and violence, and "family values," the forty-six pastors displayed a great deal of attitudinal diversity. This diversity is moderately related to the pastors' levels of political involvement. In particular, pastors classified as political leaders were very unlikely to express conservative attitudes about crime and violence. The findings of this chapter, however, have shown very little relationship between clergy's views on family values and their political involvement.

I expected to show that the clergy who were most politically involved would have exhibited the most liberal ideological orientations, but there was only very limited support for this conjecture. Therefore, it would appear (not surprisingly) that the ideological leanings of these clergy are difficult to assess. This is so despite the fact that I specifically asked the pastors about issues with which they might reasonably have been familiar. Perhaps more significantly, the last three chapters show that characterizing the choices pastors make about political involvement is more complicated than saying that those who are liberal become involved while those who are conservative do not.

The pastors' remarks about family values proved to be rather complex as they related to clergy's political involvement. While on the surface there appears to be little relationship between the pastors' views on this topic and their levels of political involvement, upon further examination an interesting fact emerges. African American clergy, particularly those classified as political leaders, frequently expressed conservative "pro-family" positions when asked to comment on family values. This combination of political views and involvement suggests that a simple ideological dichotomy is insufficient to characterize the pastors' political attitudes.

African American clergy may be in a unique position to bridge the gap between ideologues of the Left and the Right who hold seemingly incompatible positions on crime and violence and family values. White mainline and evangelical pastors do not see eye-to-eye on family values because they lack a common language for discussing the matter. Theoretically, African American clergy might be able to communicate with both of these groups and therefore to foster common understanding. If so, perhaps they could galvanize pastors who espouse different theological and ideological outlooks to perceive social problems from a common standpoint. On the other hand, perhaps the social significance of race would prevent this from happening.

CHAPTER 9

Filled with Spirit and Power

All of the pastors interviewed for this study regularly had to confront the possibility that they could become politically involved as one of their official roles as clergy. Only some of them, though, chose to do so. When they think about how they might best serve their congregations, some decide not to enter the political realm at all in their capacity as clergy. Others raise political issues for the consideration of their congregations without taking direct action themselves. Finally, some decide that they must personally lead their congregations in political action.

Forty-six interviews with Protestant clergy in the metropolitan area of Milwaukee, Wisconsin formed the basis for this book. It is important to bear in mind that all of these pastors shared a common identity as Protestant clergy serving congregations in the Milwaukee area. Thus, this book is not the story of *all* Protestant clergy in the United States. Nor is it even the story of *all* Protestant clergy in urban American settings. However, it is possible to learn a great deal from the factors that combine to shape these pastors' choices about political involvement. Personal resources, including views about the propriety of clergy political involvement, feelings of political efficacy, gender, and career stage exert an influence over the extent to which pastors become involved in politics. So too do the contextual resources inherent in different denominational traditions and church neighborhoods. Moreover, pastors' choices about political involvement also bear relationships to their substantive political agendas and their general ideological orientations.

Least involved in politics were the "politically disengaged." Sixteen pastors fell into this category because they chose not to involve themselves in any political efforts as part of their official roles as clergy. While many of them did report being involved in their communities in various social capacities, they did not consider any of their activities to be political. Seventeen pastors fell into the second category of political involvement. These "agenda setters" were pastors who set important issues of the day before their congregations, sometimes from the pulpit, sometimes by encouraging discussion groups. They did not, however, take the important step of personally venturing out into the community to lead their congregations into political endeavors. The third and final group of clergy were classified as "political leaders" because they did make the leap that agenda setters did not: they involved themselves personally in community political activism. Thirteen pastors fit this categorization; they were involved as political activists, and in a few cases as actual public officials, as part of their roles as clergy. To a person, the political leaders had difficulty conceiving of their professional lives in the absence of political involvement. It is important to keep in mind that "political involvement" here refers to the engagement by pastors in politics *as part of their institutional roles as clergy*. I define political involvement as those activities in the community that the pastors *themselves* labeled as political. Politics, then, was taken to encompass all of these pastors' own definitions of politics.

There are many personal and contextual factors that may explain pastors' political involvement. American clergy are sharply divided on whether or not they should be involved in politics, and whether political elites will listen to their political pronouncements. Pastors who approved in principle of political activism by clergy tended to be more politically involved than pastors who rejected the legitimacy of political engagement. Similarly, politically efficacious clergy were more involved in politics than their counterparts who lacked feelings of efficacy. Gender also matters: female clergy were less politically involved than their male colleagues because they found it more difficult to feel accepted in such leadership roles. Since I only interviewed four female pastors, this result must be interpreted with great caution. It does, however, show that further research on women clergy is warranted, particularly because more and more women are now entering the clergy profession.[1] Finally, pastors' career stages also have an effect on their political involvement. Younger, less established pastors, as well as those approaching retirement, were less politically involved than their colleagues at mid-career. Younger pastors were grappling with adjustments to a myriad of day-to-day operational procedures, while older pastors were slowing down as they approached retirement.

There are two central contextual resources that shape clergy political involvement: denominational tradition and church neighborhood socioeconomic status. One of the more interesting findings that emerges from this study is that evangelical clergy were less politically involved than their mainline and African American counterparts. This is rooted in the fact that evangelical clergy have historically focused less on the political realm than clergy in the other two denominational traditions. At the same time, it is not possible to conclude that being a mainline or African American pastor by itself makes one more apt to become politically involved. Furthermore, clergy serving in middle-to-upper-class or suburban neighborhoods were less likely to become politically involved than those in depressed neighborhoods of the central city. U.S. census data show that political leaders were quite likely to have been serving in neighborhoods with comparatively large percentages of people living below the poverty level, facing unemployment, and holding membership in racial minority groups. Pastors who work in such settings face an entirely different set of demands than those who work in more economically stable areas. Every day they confront visible struggles for survival, as the central city is disproportionately plagued by hunger, homelessness, drug abuse, and violent crime.

When they were asked to identify "the issue or set of issues that concerns you most in this day and age," the pastors mentioned four general types of issues. A plurality were most worried about the immediate life circumstances of members of their community. Others were troubled by issues involving family and sexual morality. Various forms of discrimination also concerned some pastors, and a handful expressed interest in nonlocal issues. Interestingly, clergy who were classified as political leaders most frequently expressed views reflecting concerns about the immediate survival needs of their neighbors. Despite the focus of politically involved evangelical groups, the clergy who were most concerned about issues of family and sexual morality (like abortion) were rarely classified as political leaders.

In order to examine the pastors' ideological leanings, I asked each of them to comment on three key cultural/social issues of the day: abortion, crime and violence, and "family values." All of the pastors agreed about the general importance of public debate concerning both abortion and crime and violence. The pastors' positions on abortion corresponded well with the denominational traditions within which they served rather than the degree to which they were politically involved. Again it is noteworthy that abortion protest was *not* one of the principal forms of political activism in which these clergy engaged, even in a city where the abortion issue is particularly politicized. Attitudes about crime and violence were more clearly related to the pastors' levels of political involvement. Clergy who were classified as political leaders were the least likely to articulate conservative responsibility attributions for the problem of crime and violence. They were more likely than their less politically involved counterparts to place the blame for crime and violence on personal attributes of criminals; instead, they tended to implicate societal causes of crime. Despite the diversity in their viewpoints on abortion and crime and violence, none argued that either issue was an insignificant element of the modern American political agenda. They displayed no such consensus, however, about the legitimacy of the debate over family values. An interesting relationship emerged between the expression of conservative "pro-family" positions and political involvement among African American clergy. Because politically involved African American clergy appear to have perceived a connection between crime and violence and family decline, they may be in a unique position to organize interfaith political movements of clergy.

PROTOTYPE CLERGY

So what, then, steers clergy down various paths when it comes to political involvement? In order to answer this question, consider the following prototypes of three pastors, each of whom chose a different path regarding political involvement. Let us explore for a moment the lives of a disengaged pastor fictitiously named Timothy Anderson, an agenda setter named Michael Darion, and a political leader named Thomas Wayne.

Timothy Anderson, of course, is not necessarily disinterested in or ill-informed about politics. He does, however, consciously choose not to include political involvement among the official roles he plays as a clergy member. He is an evangelical pastor. His general attitude toward political involvement by clergy is negative, and he does not have a strong sense of political efficacy. Reverend Anderson serves on the outskirts of Milwaukee, in a church located in a neighborhood with a per capita income in the range of $15,000 and with an unemployment rate well below 5 percent. His neighborhood also includes fewer than 5 percent who live below the poverty level and fewer than 15 percent who belong to racial minority groups. He is also in the early stages of his career as a pastor. Reverend Anderson's political agenda includes issues of family and sexual morality; he also expresses some concern about discrimination against Christians by society at large. When asked what comes to mind when he thinks about abortion, he simply defines his own position on the issue (he is pro-life). Regarding crime and violence, he attributes responsibility to criminals themselves rather than broader social forces. He also makes the point that the debate over family values is a waste of time. It is interesting to note that while politicians constantly launch appeals to the "Christian Right," clergy like Reverend Anderson, who serve evangelical churches and espouse a conservative political agenda, are not politically involved.

Rev. Michael Darion, our typical agenda setter, is a pastor who does not shy away from preaching about politics from the pulpit or encouraging the formation of discussion groups about political issues in his church. He does not, however, take the crucial step of personally involving himself in politics as the leader of his congregation. He serves a mainline congregation, but evangelical and African American pastors also often embrace agenda setting as their orientation to political involvement. Agenda setters like him are just as likely to feel that clergy should be engaged politically as to say they should not, but Reverend Darion also feels that pastors who do become deeply involved do not have much influence. His church is located in the suburbs, but agenda setters are equally likely to be found in the city. His church's neighborhood is relatively well-off economically, with a per capita income of around $17,000 and an unemployment rate below 5 percent. Only about 10 percent of the residents of his church's neighborhood live below the poverty level, and fewer than 10 percent belong to racial minority groups. Reverend Darion, who is at mid-career, has a substantive political agenda that includes issues involving the immediate life circumstances of others as well as family and sexual morality. Protesting springs to his mind when he is asked about the issue of abortion, and he attributes responsibility for crime and violence to forces outside of criminals' control. He is quite likely to argue that the debate about family values is important.

Rev. Thomas Wayne, the prototype of a political leader, cannot conceive of his role as a pastor in the absence of his involvement in the political realm. He is African American, but many who are as politically involved as he is serve in mainline churches. He believes strongly that clergy should be involved in politics, and that they can and do have an effect on elected officials and public policy. His church is situated in a central city neighborhood with a per capita income well below $10,000, where the unemployment rate is often above 20 percent. More than half the residents of this neighborhood live below the poverty level, and over 85 percent belong to a racial minority group. Like Reverend Darion, Reverend Wayne is at mid-career. The issues that concern him most are those involving the life circumstances of his neighbors and racial discrimination. When abortion is mentioned, he is likely either to consider various definitions of the issue or to discuss the topic of protesting. He is not inclined to attribute responsibility for the problem of crime and violence to criminals themselves. Rather, he blames broader societal forces. As an African American pastor, he expresses a conservative "pro-family" position on the family values debate.

Overall, then, clergy who choose a political path for themselves appear to be motivated by a liberal political agenda. They are much more concerned with bettering the life circumstances of their neighbors than they are about "moral" issues like abortion. Clergy who espouse more conservative political agendas tend to be wary of political involvement, despite the highly visible activities of the politically mobilized Christian Right. The single most important factor that distinguishes between those who follow a political path and those who are more hesitant to do so, however, is the socioeconomic status of the neighborhoods in which pastors' churches are situated. In fact, the "tale of two pastors" in chapter 1 illustrates that two pastors who might appear similar on paper often pursue divergent paths when it comes to political involvement. In fact, the two pastors profiled in that tale served in very different neighborhoods. The pastor who was disengaged served in one of Milwaukee's most affluent suburbs, while the one who was a political leader worked in the central city. Despite the similarity in their backgrounds, their political choices diverged because of the nature of the daily challenges they face.

REFLECTIONS

Among the most valuable resources for political participation are civic skills, and of all voluntary social organizations, churches are one of the most effective facilitators of the development of such skills.[2] Churches may play different roles in the development of congregational political involvement. "Skill-producing churches" are said to provide their congregations with opportunities to learn and exercise skills that might be beneficial to them should they choose to become involved in the political realm, while "politically mobilizing churches" directly expose their members to political messages and involve them in collective political action.[3]

Two important conclusions may therefore be drawn. First, even clergy who are politically disengaged may play a role in the political lives of the members of their congregations if they facilitate the attainment of civic skills through nonpolitical activities. Second, pastors play explicit political roles other than serving as significant political mobilizers (as in the case of African American clergy). They also have the potential to play a number of other more subtly political roles. Perhaps they are in fact unique among elites of nonpolitical social institutions in this regard. Even pastors who say they have no interest in politics or activism, then, cannot be discounted as potential agents of political socialization. The very fact that millions of Americans are exposed to clergy on a weekly basis means that the various ways in which pastors approach politics deserve careful attention. It is just as valuable to learn that pastors teach their flocks to shun politics as it is to witness clergy-led political protests.

It is important to revisit the relationship between the pastors' denominational traditions and the degree to which they were involved in politics, particularly because denomination and theology are the key explanatory variables stressed in previous studies of clergy in politics.

The evangelical clergy I interviewed were almost completely unwilling to act in an explicitly political capacity as part of their official roles. Given the immense amount of attention that has been focused on the political activities of the organized Christian Right since the early 1980s, it would have been reasonable to expect that evangelical clergy would be quite politically engaged. James Guth and his colleagues find that in recent years, the political interest and involvement of some evangelical clergy has been growing.[4] However, while a sizable proportion of the evangelical pastors I interviewed were classified as agenda setters, many others were disengaged. This finding is actually consistent with a variety of other previous studies.[5] What is the real story?

Many religious conservatives actually do not support the efforts of politically active religious organizations.[6] Perhaps evangelical clergy are overrepresented among these nonsupporters. Or maybe macro-level religious interest groups like the Christian Coalition do not feel the need to appeal to local clergy because of the strength of their direct grassroots outreach to laity. The power of one conservative Christian radio station in Milwaukee to cause divisions between clergy and laity was noted in chapter 2. On the other hand, in the early 1980s the Moral Majority profited from building a network of clergy who were sympathetic to their political agenda. It is unclear whether today's Christian Right organizations embrace a similar approach, or if they, like the Milwaukee radio station, prefer to do an end run around clergy. In any case, the evangelical clergy with whom I spoke were far less interested in politics than many of those surveyed over the years by James Guth and his colleagues.[7]

My most significant conclusion has to do with the fact that the clergy who were classified as political leaders were, without a doubt, those who served in the most economically distressed neighborhoods in Milwaukee. These pastors also displayed liberal political attitudes on crime and violence (they implicated societal causes of crime) and family values (they characterized the debate as an invention of the political Right). It is clergy who serve in poor central city neighborhoods who confront the most *need* for political leadership. Citizens who lack financial resources, particularly poor residents of central cities, have been shown to participate much more in politics when community leaders (such as clergy) mobilize them through voluntary organizations.[8] And in central city neighborhoods, there may be few other professionals present to undertake such mobilization efforts.[9]

Central city clergy find themselves in positions that allow them to translate their status as religious elites into the political realm. Pastors who serve congregations in more economically stable neighborhoods may simply have fewer demands upon them for their political leadership. This is because citizens who have access to a wide variety of sources of political stimuli come to rely less on any one source than those with fewer resources.[10] It therefore may be that it is simply incumbent upon pastors who serve in poor neighborhoods to enter the political realm. For clergy, political involvement must be a secondary pursuit.[11] They must first deal with the demands of their pastoral responsibilities, such as writing sermons, visiting the sick, and leading Bible study. Those pastors who make the substantial investment of time necessary for political activism must include those who feel most compelled, or called, to do so. Central city clergy may see their political activism not only as helpful, but *essential*. They may feel that they are among the only people in their neighborhood with the ability to address the crushing problem of poverty and its consequences.

Previous studies of religion and politics have not included much in the way of analysis of multiracial political coalitions of religious people. This may be because many scholars simply do not include discussion of African American churches in the first place. Others who do consider African Americans may simply be adopting the common assumption that the most segregated hour in the United States occurs on Sunday morning. The most profound manifestation of clergy political involvement I found in Milwaukee, however, came in the form of the Milwaukee Innercity Congregations Allied for Hope (MICAH), an ecumenical, multiracial coalition of religious people who claim to be working for social change in the central city. In MICAH, white mainline pastors (and Catholic priests, for that matter) work hand-in-hand with African American clergy to address the problems of poverty, unemployment, drug abuse, and crime. In a 1976 study of racial politics in Milwaukee, Peter Eisinger argued that "coalition between the races is unlikely, . . . because goals differ."[12] He also suggested, however, that white liberal clergy would be among the most likely candidates to make such multiracial coalitions viable, and that the black community would stand to benefit from them.[13] It is not within the scope of this study to assess the objective effectiveness of MICAH. From the reports of the clergy involved in this coalition, however, great success has resulted from their efforts, so it would seem that Eisinger's predictions may have been correct.

Even though this study is situated in one specific location (Milwaukee, Wisconsin), there are important general conclusions to be drawn. First and foremost is the support this study adds to the assertions made by scholars who have argued that it is crucial to consider political context in studies of political participation. As other scholars have shown, the "standard socioeconomic model" of political participation is not adequate to explain all of the factors that contribute to people's decisions about getting involved in politics.[14] It is not enough to consider people's socioeconomic status on an individual basis. Rather, the political resources that are available to different groups, and therefore to the community leaders with whom they interact, are perhaps the best predictors of all for who becomes involved in politics and who does not. The political contexts in which people live and work are also important predictors of political participation. Clergy who serve in poor neighborhoods simply face different circumstances than those who work in middle-class suburban congregations. This must also be true of elites in other nonpolitical voluntary social organizations.

Nowhere in the literature have I found any systematic studies of the factors that motivate clergy to translate their roles as religious leaders into the political realm. Scholars who have previously studied the political involvement of clergy have focused almost exclusively on the predictive role of pastors' denominational affiliations and theological orientations.[15] While I do not mean to argue for a moment that denomination and theology are unimportant, it is also fruitful to incorporate contextual discussions of the relationships that exist between religion and politics.[16]

In chapter 1, I suggested that it is important to consider what the average Protestant pastor might be doing on a typical weekday afternoon. Having come to the end of the investigation, it is important to revisit this consideration. Clearly some pastors will not be involved in political activities, but others will. A number of factors, as I have shown, combine to steer pastors down various paths when it comes to political involvement. Each of the forty-six pastors I interviewed was a unique individual, but clear patterns regarding political involvement appear upon investigation of their individual circumstances, goals, and preferences. While they may differ in their political involvement, though, the feelings of spirit and power that initially drew them to the ministry are clearly present in all of them.

APPENDIX

Methodology

This study is based on forty-six in-depth, semistructured personal interviews with Protestant clergy in the metropolitan area of Milwaukee, Wisconsin, conducted between June 10 and August 16, 1994. The ultimate substantive and theoretical direction of the study was inductively generated. It became clear during the research process that the most interesting story was the variety of political involvement of Milwaukee's clergy. In constructing a sample of forty-six Protestant clergy, I sought to interview equal numbers of mainline, evangelical, and African American pastors so as to capture the full spectrum of diversity within Protestantism in Milwaukee.[1]

To establish a list of potential interviewees, I telephoned regional denominational offices to obtain names of "clergy who are involved in social or political activities." To insure against interviewing only politically involved clergy, I supplemented the list with random choices from the Milwaukee telephone book. Potential interviewees were mailed introductory letters before I telephoned them to schedule interviews. I enjoyed a very high success rate in obtaining interviews: of the sixty-six pastors to whom I sent introductory letters, forty-six agreed to be interviewed, two refused, one failed to appear for the interview, and seventeen were not contacted a second time. Interviews were conducted in the church offices or homes of the clergy, and were tape recorded with written permission. The duration of the interviews ranged from forty-five minutes to over two hours. The semistructured interview protocol is presented below.

The case study approach, while providing rich detail, makes generalizability difficult. Protestant clergy in other urban areas may behave differently than the clergy in Milwaukee, because other cities have different political and religious traditions. Clergy in other cities operate within different political contexts. For this research question, interviewing is clearly the superior research method because of the depth of information that it affords. I chose to trade breadth for depth in this study.

Inherent in this research design, as in any other, were questions of both reliability and validity. In the absence of follow-up interviews, it is impossible to know whether the clergy would provide similar responses at another point in time. Validity is challenged by the fact that the design provides no way of checking whether the clergy presented honest representations of their political involvement. The design's dependence on self-reporting was, however, one of its strengths, because it implied that the responses were a valid representation of the clergy's *personal perceptions* of their own political involvement. The real question is, after all, about the choices individual pastors make regarding political involvement. Finally, I make no arguments about the *effectiveness* of these pastors in terms of political mobilization or socialization. The limits of the present study were defined by what the ministers related about their own involvement in politics. But there was much to be learned from their tales.

INTERVIEW QUESTIONS

1. I'd like to start by asking you to tell me a bit about yourself.
   - How long have you been serving this congregation? How long have you been in the ministry? Do you have plans to retire soon?
   - Tell me about your congregation—what's it like?
2. Does your congregation have a tradition of involvement in social or political causes? By this I mean the congregation as a group, not individual members. What specific social or political projects have you and your congregation been involved with lately?
3. What political issue or set of issues concerns you most as a clergy member in this day and age?
4. There are two specific issues I'd like your opinions on now.
   - What immediately comes to mind when you think about abortion?
   - What immediately comes to mind when you think about crime and violence?
5. Now I'd like to talk to you a bit about the American family. A lot of politicians have been talking recently about "family issues" or "family values" and various problems regarding the state of the American family. What immediately comes to mind when you think about "family issues" or "family values"?
6. In general, how involved do you think clergy ought to be in politics?
7. Do you think clergy have a lot of influence when it comes to politics?

NOTES

CHAPTER ONE. A TALE OF TWO PASTORS

1. Fictional names have been adopted to protect subjects' confidentiality.
2. This was also documented in the Milwaukee press. See Julio V. Cano, "MICAH Glad Bar's License Not Renewed," *The Milwaukee Sentinel* (June 30, 1994), A12.
3. Each of the forty-six pastors interviewed for this study has been assigned a code number. The letter M denotes pastors of mainline churches; E represents evangelical pastors; A refers to pastors of African American churches.
4. Erving Goffman, *The Presentation of Self in Everyday Life* (Garden City, N.Y.: Doubleday, 1959), 6.
5. Alexis de Tocqueville, *Democracy in America*, ed. Francis Bowen and Phillips Bradley (New York: Knopf, 1840/1945).
6. For discussion of this point, see Leo Pfeffer, *God, Caesar, and the Constitution: The Court as Referee of Church-State Confrontation* (Boston: Beacon, 1975) and Walter Berns, *The First Amendment and the Future of American Democracy* (New York: Basic Books, 1976).
7. On the role of African American churches in the civil rights movement, see Aldon D. Morris, *The Origins of the Civil Rights Movement: Black Communities Organizing for Change* (New York: Free Press, 1984). On mainline churches in the civil rights movement, see James F. Findlay, *Church People in the Struggle: The National Council of Churches and the Black Freedom Movement, 1950–1970* (New York: Oxford University Press, 1993). On churches and the women's movement, see Sara Evans, *Personal Politics: The Roots of Women's Liberation in the Civil Rights Movement and the New Left* (New York: Knopf, 1979).
8. On evangelicals and presidential elections, see Corwin Smidt, "Evangelicals and the 1984 Election," *American Politics Quarterly* 15 (1987): 419–444. On evangelicals and congressional elections, see John C. Green, James L. Guth, and Kevin Hill, "Faith and Election: The Christian Right in Congressional Campaigns, 1978–1988," *Journal of Politics* 55 (1993): 150–165.
9. See Allen D. Hertzke, *Echoes of Discontent: Jesse Jackson, Pat Robertson, and the Resurgence of Populism* (Washington, D.C.: Congressional Quarterly Press, 1993).
10. The original exposition of the theory is in James Davison Hunter, *Culture Wars: The Struggle to Define America* (New York: Basic Books, 1991). For an updated account, see James Davison Hunter, *Before the Shooting Begins: Searching for Democracy in America's Culture War* (New York: Free Press, 1994).

11. Harold E. Quinley, *The Prophetic Clergy: Social Activism among Protestant Ministers* (New York: Wiley, 1974); Jeffrey K. Hadden, *The Gathering Storm in the Churches* (Garden City, N.Y.: Doubleday, 1969); Rodney Stark, Bruce D. Foster, Charles Y. Glock, and Harold E. Quinley, *Wayward Shepherds: Prejudice and the Protestant Clergy* (New York: Harper & Row, 1971).

12. Ted G. Jelen, *The Political World of the Clergy* (Westport, Conn.: Praeger, 1993); James L. Guth, John C. Green, Corwin E. Smidt, Lyman A. Kellstedt, and Margaret M. Poloma, *The Bully Pulpit: The Politics of Protestant Clergy* (Lawrence: University Press of Kansas, 1997).

13. Kenneth D. Wald, Dennis E. Owen, and Samuel S. Hill Jr., "Churches as Political Communities," *American Political Science Review* 82 (1988): 531–548; Kenneth D. Wald, Dennis E. Owen, and Samuel S. Hill Jr., "Political Cohesion in Churches," *Journal of Politics* 52 (1990): 197–215. Also of interest on this topic are Clyde Wilcox, "The New Christian Right and the Mobilization of Evangelicals," in *Religion and Political Behavior in the United States*, ed. Ted G. Jelen (New York: Praeger, 1989), 139–156; Ted G. Jelen, *The Political Mobilization of Religious Beliefs* (New York: Praeger, 1991a).

14. James L. Guth, "Southern Baptist Clergy: Vanguard of the Christian Right," in *The New Christian Right: Mobilization and Legitimation*, ed. Robert C. Liebman and Robert Wuthnow (New York: Aldine, 1983), 117–130; James L. Guth, "The Political Mobilization of Southern Baptist Clergy, 1980–1992," in *Religion and the Culture Wars: Dispatches from the Front*, ed. John C. Green, James L. Guth, Lyman A. Kellstedt, and Corwin E. Smidt (Lanham, Md.: Rowman and Littlefield, 1996), 146–173.

15. Guth et al. (1997).

16. Jelen (1993). There are also a number of other good studies on the subject of clergy and politics.

On the mainline, see Quinley (1974); Audrey R. Chapman, *Faith, Power, and Politics: Political Ministry in Mainline Churches* (New York: Pilgrim, 1991); Findlay (1993); Andrew R. Murphy, "The Mainline Churches and Political Activism: The Continuing Impact of the Persian Gulf War," *Soundings* 76 (1993): 526–549.

On evangelicals, see Guth (1983, 1996); Kathleen Murphy Beatty and Oliver Walter, "A Group Theory of Religion and Politics: The Clergy as Group Leaders," *Western Political Quarterly* 42 (1989): 129–146.

On African American clergy, see Manning Marable, *How Capitalism Underdeveloped Black America: Problems in Race, Political Economy, and Society* (Boston: South End, 1983); Morris (1984); Adolph L. Reed Jr., *The Jesse Jackson Phenomenon: The Crisis of Purpose in Afro-American Politics* (New Haven, Conn.: Yale University Press, 1986); and particularly C. Eric Lincoln and Lawrence H. Mamiya, *The Black Church in the African American Experience* (Durham, N.C.: Duke University Press, 1990).

The involvement of Catholic clergy in politics has also been well documented. See Thomas J. Reese, *Archbishop: Inside the Power Structure of the American Catholic Church* (New York: Harper & Row, 1989); Timothy A. Byrnes, *Catholic Bishops in American Politics* (Princeton, N.J.: Princeton University Press, 1991).

17. Housing patterns in Milwaukee have been so racially divided that the city has been labeled "hypersegregated" by Douglas S. Massey and Nancy A. Denton, *American Apartheid: Segregation and the Making of the Underclass* (Cambridge, Mass.: Harvard University Press, 1993), 74–77.

18. It is important to note that because of Hispanic Americans' traditional identification with the Catholic Church, there are far fewer Protestant congregations on the south side than on the north side.

19. All historical information is drawn from H. Russell Austin, *The Milwaukee Story: The Making of an American City* (Milwaukee, Wisc.: The Milwaukee Journal Company, 1946); Robert W. Wells, *This Is Milwaukee* (Garden City, N.Y.: Doubleday, 1970); Peter K. Eisinger, *Patterns of Interracial Politics: Conflict and Cooperation in the City* (New York: Academic Press, 1976), chapter 2; Henry Maier, *The Mayor Who Made Milwaukee Famous: An Autobiography* (Lanham, Md.: Madison Books, 1993).

20. Eisinger (1976), 42–43.

21. Laura R. Woliver, *From Outrage to Action: The Politics of Grass-Roots Dissent* (Urbana: University of Illinois Press, 1993), chapter 4.

22. Ibid., 90.

23. Robert Wuthnow, *The Restructuring of American Religion: Society and Faith Since World War Two* (Princeton, N.J.: Princeton University Press, 1988), 23–24.

24. Robert Booth Fowler, *Unconventional Partners: Religion and Liberal Culture in the United States* (Grand Rapids, Mich.: Eerdmans, 1989), 83–98.

25. James L. Adams, *The Growing Church Lobby in Washington* (Grand Rapids, Mich.: Eerdmans, 1970).

26. Lincoln and Mamiya (1990), 228–229.

27. I am unable to identify these denominations more specifically because it could compromise the confidentiality of the interviews.

CHAPTER TWO. POLITICAL INVOLVEMENT

1. Sidney Verba and Norman H. Nie, *Participation in America: Political Democracy and Social Equality* (Chicago: University of Chicago Press, 1972), 2.

2. Samuel H. Barnes, Max Kaase, and Klaus R. Allerbeck, *Political Action: Mass Participation in Five Western Democracies* (Beverly Hills, Calif.: Sage, 1979).

3. Murray Edelman, *Politics as Symbolic Action: Mass Arousal and Quiescence* (New York: Academic Press, 1971).

4. Steven J. Rosenstone and John Mark Hansen, *Mobilization, Participation, and Democracy in America* (New York: Macmillan, 1993), 4.

5. See especially Sidney Verba, Kay Lehman Schlozman, and Henry E. Brady, *Voice and Equality: Civic Voluntarism in American Society* (Cambridge, Mass.: Harvard University Press, 1995). See also Henry E. Brady, Sidney Verba, and Kay Lehman Schlozman, "Beyond SES: A Resource Model of Political Participation," *American Political Science Review* 89 (1995): 271–294.

6. A clear exposition of this theme is made in Sidney Verba, Kay Lehman Schlozman, Henry Brady and Norman H. Nie, "Race, Ethnicity, and Political

Resources: Participation in the United States," *British Journal of Political Science* 23 (1993b): 453–497.

7. Brady et al. (1995), 271.

8. Verba et al. (1993b), 486–487.

9. V. O. Key Jr., *Public Opinion and American Democracy* (New York: Knopf, 1961), 189.

10. Sue E. S. Crawford, "Clergy at Work in the Secular City," Ph.D. diss., Indiana University, 1995.

11. It should be noted, however, that for years scholars have utilized similar sorts of typologies for illustrative purposes. For example, see Lester W. Milbrath, *Political Participation: How and Why Do People Get Involved in Politics?* (Chicago: Rand McNally, 1965), 9–13, and Verba and Nie (1972), 77–81.

12. Fictional names are used to protect subjects' anonymity.

13. C. Eric Lincoln and Lawrence H. Mamiya, *The Black Church in the African American Experience* (Durham, N.C.: Duke University Press, 1990), 12.

14. "105 Abortion Foes Arrested at Clinics," *The Los Angeles Times* (June 17, 1992), A20; "More Arrests in Milwaukee," *The New York Times* (June 19, 1992), D19.

15. Milwaukee Innercity Congregations Allied for Hope, *To Do What Is Just!* (Milwaukee, Wisc.: Milwaukee Innercity Congregations Allied for Hope, 1994), 12–13.

16. This goal in particular has made news in Milwaukee. See Julio V. Cano, "MICAH Issues Demands to Mayor: Church Group Seeks Improved Police-Community Relations," *The Milwaukee Sentinel* (May 25, 1994), A5.

17. This is also documented by John D. Hull, "Have We Gone Mad?" *Time* (December 20, 1993), 32.

18. Milwaukee Innercity Congregations Allied for Hope (1994), 23.

19. The scandal surrounding this realty company attracted significant attention. See Gretchen Schuldt, "HUD Urged to Drop Its City Appraiser: Two Aldermen Criticize Suhr Realty Inc.," *The Milwaukee Sentinel* (February 24, 1994), A5.

20. Jeffrey M. Berry, Kent E. Portney, and Ken Thomson, *The Rebirth of Urban Democracy* (Washington, D.C.: The Brookings Institution, 1993). A similar finding is reported by John Clayton Thomas, *Between Citizen and City* (Lawrence: University Press of Kansas, 1986).

21. In order to protect their anonymity, it is impossible for me to discuss their specific positions and activities.

22. Verba et al. (1993b), 486–487.

CHAPTER THREE. PERSONAL RESOURCES FOR POLITICAL INVOLVEMENT

1. Ted G. Jelen, *The Political World of the Clergy* (Westport, Conn.: Praeger, 1993), 23.

2. In fact, political participation may actually *lead to* feelings of political efficacy. See Steven E. Finkel, "Reciprocal Effects of Participation and Political

Efficacy: A Panel Analysis," *American Journal of Political Science* 29 (1985): 891–913.

3. Lester W. Milbrath, *Political Participation: How and Why Do People Get Involved in Politics?* (Chicago: Rand McNally, 1965), 59.

4. V. O. Key Jr., *Public Opinion and American Democracy* (New York: Knopf, 1961), 331; Sidney Verba and Norman H. Nie, *Participation in America: Political Democracy and Social Equality* (Chicago: University of Chicago Press, 1972), 97–101.

5. Arlene Kaplan Daniels, *Invisible Careers: Women Civic Leaders from the Volunteer World* (Chicago: University of Chicago Press, 1988); Anne Firor Scott, *Natural Allies: Women's Associations in American History* (Urbana: University of Illinois Press, 1992).

6. Kay Lehman Schlozman, Nancy Burns, and Sidney Verba, "Gender and the Pathways to Participation: The Role of Resources," *Journal of Politics* 56 (1994): 963–990; Kay Lehman Schlozman, Nancy Burns, Sidney Verba, and Jesse Donahue, "Gender and Citizen Participation: Is There a Different Voice?" *American Journal of Political Science* 39 (1995): 267–293.

7. Jackson W. Carroll, Barbara Hargrove, and Adair T. Lummis, *Women of the Cloth: A New Opportunity for the Churches* (New York: Harper & Row, 1981); Virginia Sapiro, *Women in American Society: An Introduction to Women's Studies*, 3d ed. (Mountain View, Calif.: Mayfield, 1994), 201–205; Frederick W. Schmidt Jr., *A Still Small Voice: Women, Ordination, and the Church* (Syracuse, N.Y.: Syracuse University Press, 1996).

8. Carroll et al. (1981).

9. Robert Wuthnow, *The Restructuring of American Religion: Society and Faith Since World War Two* (Princeton, N.J.: Princeton University Press, 1988), 225–235.

10. Martha Long Ice, *Clergy Women and Their Worldviews: Calling for a New Age* (New York: Praeger, 1987); Schmidt (1996).

11. Within the mainline, women adopt different strategies of dealing with the strictures of various denominations. See Schmidt (1996), 166–167.

12. For a fascinating description of the roles women play in Pentecostal churches, see Elaine J. Lawless, *Handmaidens of the Lord: Pentecostal Women Preachers and Traditional Religion* (Philadelphia: University of Pennsylvania Press, 1988).

13. C. Eric Lincoln and Lawrence H. Mamiya, *The Black Church in the African American Experience* (Durham, N.C.: Duke University Press, 1990), chapter 10.

14. Carrol et al. (1981).

15. James Davison Hunter and Kimon Howland Sargeant, "Religion and the Transformation of Public Culture," *Social Research* 60 (1993): 545–570; James L. Guth, John C. Green, Corwin E. Smidt, and Lyman A. Kellstedt, "Women Clergy and the Political Transformation of Mainline Protestantism," Paper presented at the Annual Meeting of the Social Science History Association, Atlanta, 1994; Barbara Finlay, "Future Ministers and Legal Abortion: Gender Comparisons among Protestant Seminary Students," *Women and Politics* 17 (1997): 1–15.

16. Verba and Nie (1972), 138–148; M. Kent Jennings, "Another Look at the Life Cycle and Political Participation," *American Journal of Political Science* 23 (1979): 755–771; M. Kent Jennings and Richard G. Niemi, *Generations and Politics: A Panel Study of Young Adults and Their Parents* (Princeton, N.J.: Princeton University Press, 1981); M. Kent Jennings and Gregory B. Markus, "Political Involvement in the Later Years: A Longitudinal Study," *American Journal of Political Science* 32 (1988): 302–316.

CHAPTER FOUR. CONTEXTUAL RESOURCES FOR POLITICAL INVOLVEMENT

1. Sue E. S. Crawford, "Clergy at Work in the Secular City," Ph.D. diss., Indiana University, 1995.

2. Sidney Verba and Norman H. Nie, *Participation in America: Political Democracy and Social Equality* (Chicago: University of Chicago Press, 1972).

3. Arthur H. Miller, Patricia Gurin, Gerald Gurin, and Oksana Malanchuk, "Group Consciousness and Political Participation," *American Journal of Political Science* 25 (1981): 494–511; Richard D. Shingles, "Black Consciousness and Political Participation: The Missing Link," *American Political Science Review* 75 (1981): 76–91.

4. Robert Huckfeldt, *Politics in Context: Assimilation and Conflict in Urban Neighborhoods* (New York: Agathon, 1986); Robert Huckfeldt and John Sprague, "Networks in Context," *American Political Science Review* 81 (1987): 1197–1216; Robert Huckfeldt, Eric Plutzer, and John Sprague, "Alternative Contexts of Political Behavior: Churches, Neighborhoods, and Individuals," *Journal of Politics* 55 (1993): 365–381; Robert Huckfeldt, Paul Allen Beck, Russell J. Dalton, and Jeffrey Levine, "Political Environments, Cohesive Social Groups, and the Communication of Public Opinion," *American Journal of Political Science* 39 (1995): 1025–1054. See also Christopher P. Gilbert, *The Impact of Churches on Political Behavior: An Empirical Study* (Westport, Conn.: Greenwood, 1993).

5. Henry E. Brady, Sidney Verba, and Kay Lehman Schlozman, "Beyond SES: A Resource Model of Political Participation," *American Political Science Review* 89 (1995): 271–294; Sidney Verba, Kay Lehman Schlozman, and Henry E. Brady, *Voice and Equality: Civic Voluntarism in American Society* (Cambridge, Mass.: Harvard University Press, 1995); Sidney Verba, Kay Lehman Schlozman, Henry Brady, and Norman H. Nie, "Race, Ethnicity, and Political Resources: Participation in the United States," *British Journal of Political Science* 23 (1993b): 453–496.

6. Charles Y. Glock and Rodney Stark, *Religion and Society in Tension* (Chicago: Rand McNally, 1965). A similar argument is set forth by Robert Wuthnow, *The Restructuring of American Religion: Society and Faith Since World War Two* (Princeton, N.J.: Princeton University Press, 1988). See also Wade Clark Roof and William McKinney, *American Mainline Religion: Its Changing Shape and Future* (New Brunswick, N.J.: Rutgers University Press, 1987).

7. Among the many studies on this subject, see Bradley R. Hertel and Michael Hughes, "Religious Affiliation, Attendance, and Support for 'Pro-Family' Issues in the United States," *Social Forces* 65 (1987): 858–882; Wuthnow (1988); James L. Guth, John C. Green, Lyman A. Kellstedt, and Corwin E. Smidt, "Faith and the Environment: Religious Beliefs and Attitudes on Environmental Policy," *American Journal of Political Science* 39 (1995): 364–382; James L. Guth, John C. Green, Corwin E. Smidt, Lyman A. Kellstedt, and Margaret M. Poloma, *The Bully Pulpit: The Politics of Protestant Clergy* (Lawrence: University Press of Kansas, 1997).

8. Guth et al. (1997).

9. See Norman Koller and Joseph Retzer, "The Sounds of Silence Revisited," *Sociological Analysis* 41 (1980): 155–161; Ted G. Jelen, *The Political World of the Clergy* (Westport, Conn.: Praeger, 1993), 63.

10. Harold E. Quinley, *The Prophetic Clergy: Social Activism among Protestant Ministers* (New York: Wiley, 1974); Jeffrey K. Hadden, *The Gathering Storm in the Churches* (Garden City, N.Y.: Doubleday, 1969); Rodney Stark, Bruce D. Foster, Charles Y. Glock, and Harold E. Quinley, *Wayward Shepherds: Prejudice and the Protestant Clergy* (New York: Harper & Row, 1971). See also James F. Findlay, *Church People in the Struggle: The National Council of Churches and the Black Freedom Movement, 1950–1970* (New York: Oxford University Press, 1993); James G. Hougland Jr. and James A. Christenson, "Religion and Politics: The Relationship of Religious Participation to Political Efficacy and Involvement," *Sociology and Social Research* 67 (1983): 405–420.

11. C. Eric Lincoln and Lawrence H. Mamiya, *The Black Church in the African American Experience* (Durham, N.C.: Duke University Press, 1990), chapter 8; Aldon D. Morris, *The Origins of the Civil Rights Movement: Black Communities Organizing for Change* (New York: Free Press, 1984), chapter 4.

12. Verba et al. (1993b), 472ff.

13. Verba and Nie (1972), 173; Shingles (1981), 76–91; Thomas M. Guterbock and Bruce London, "Race, Political Orientation, and Participation: An Empirical Test of Four Competing Theories," *American Sociological Review* 48 (1983): 439–453; Lawrence Bobo and Franklin D. Gilliam Jr., "Race, Sociopolitical Participation, and Black Empowerment," *American Political Science Review* 84 (1990): 377–393.

14. See David A. Roozen, William McKinley, and Jackson W. Carroll, *Varieties of Religious Presence: Mission in Public Life* (New York: Pilgrim, 1984).

15. See Guth et al. (1997).

16. This observation is drawn from the large body of work that examines the concept of political context. See Gilbert (1993); Huckfeldt, Plutzer, and Sprague (1993); Paul A. Djupe, "The Plural Church: Church Involvement and Political Behavior," Ph.D. diss., Washington University in St. Louis, 1997.

17. James L. Guth, "Southern Baptist Clergy: Vanguard of the Christian Right," in *The New Christian Right: Mobilization and Legitimation*, ed. Robert C. Liebman and Robert Wuthnow (New York: Aldine, 1983), 117–130. See also James Davison Hunter, *Evangelicalism: The Coming Generation* (Chicago: University of Chicago Press, 1987).

18. Nancy Tatom Ammerman, *Bible Believers: Fundamentalists in the Modern World* (New Brunswick, N.J.: Rutgers University Press, 1987). See also Ted G. Jelen, "Politicizing Group Identification: The Case of Fundamentalism," *Western Political Quarterly* 44 (1991b): 209-219.

19. Margaret Poloma, *The Charismatic Movement: Is There a New Pentecost?* (Boston: Twayne, 1982), 211-227. See also Margaret Poloma, *Assemblies of God at the Crossroads: Charisma and Institutional Dilemmas* (Knoxville: University of Tennessee Press, 1989); Corwin Smidt, "'Praise the Lord' Politics: A Comparative Analysis of the Social Characteristics and Political Views of American Evangelical and Charismatic Christians," *Sociological Analysis* 50 (1989): 53-72.

20. For a fine discussion of the mainline in the civil rights movement, see Findlay (1993).

21. Peter Skerry, "Christian Schools versus the I.R.S.," *The Public Interest* 61 (1980): 18-41.

22. In *Engel* v. *Vitale* 370 U.S. 421 (1962), the Court banned prayer in public schools. In *Roe* v. *Wade* 410 U.S. 113 (1973), the Court affirmed the legality of abortion.

23. Jerry Falwell, *Listen, America!* (Garden City, N.Y.: Doubleday, 1980), 102.

24. See Matthew C. Moen, *The Christian Right and Congress* (Tuscaloosa: University of Alabama Press, 1989), who has provided evidence that the Christian Right actually did have some measure of influence on Capitol Hill, particularly in the realm of agenda setting.

25. Jelen (1993), chapter 2.

26. On my latter point see especially Guth et al. (1997); the term "social theology" is theirs. See also Martin E. Marty, *Righteous Empire: The Protestant Experience in America* (New York: Dial, 1970); Wuthnow (1988); Lyman A. Kellstedt and John C. Green, "Knowing God's Many People: Denominational Preference and Political Behavior," in *Rediscovering the Religious Factor in American Politics*, ed. David C. Leege and Lyman A. Kellstedt (Armonk, N.Y.: M. E. Sharpe, 1993), 53-71; R. Stephen Warner, "Work in Progress: Toward a New Paradigm for the Sociological Study of Religion in the United States," *American Journal of Sociology* 98 (1993): 1044-1093.

27. On the history of the mainline, see Robert Booth Fowler, *Unconventional Partners: Religion and Liberal Culture in the United States* (Grand Rapids, Mich.: Eerdmans, 1989), chapter 6; Wuthnow (1988); Roof and McKinney (1987).

28. See Dean M. Kelley, *Why Conservative Churches Are Growing: A Study in Sociology of Religion* (New York: Harper & Row, 1972); Roof and McKinney (1987), chapter 2.

29. This argument has become quite popular. See Robert N. Bellah, Richard Madsen, William M. Sullivan, Ann Swidler, and Steven M. Tipton, *Habits of the Heart: Individualism and Commitment in American Life* (New York: Harper & Row, 1985).

30. The seminal work in this vein is Kelley (1972).

31. Roger Finke and Rodney Stark, *The Churching of America,*

1776–1990: Winners and Losers in Our Religious Economy (New Brunswick, N.J.: Rutgers University Press, 1992).

32. See Luke Eugene Ebersole, *Church Lobbying in the Nation's Capital* (New York: Macmillan, 1951); James L. Adams, *The Growing Church Lobby in Washington* (Grand Rapids, Mich.: Eerdmans, 1970); Allen D. Hertzke, *Representing God in Washington: The Role of Religious Lobbies in the American Polity* (Knoxville: University of Tennessee Press, 1988); Donald A. Luidens and Roger J. Nemeth, "After the Storm: Closing the Clergy-Laity Gap," *Review of Religious Research* 31 (1989): 183–195.

33. Jelen (1993), chapter 3.

34. Morris (1984), 4–12, 77–99.

35. See especially Guth et al. (1997).

36. William Julius Wilson, *The Truly Disadvantaged: The Inner City, the Underclass, and Public Policy* (Chicago: University of Chicago Press, 1987).

37. Cathy J. Cohen and Michael C. Dawson, "Neighborhood Poverty and African American Politics," *American Political Science Review* 87 (1993): 286–302; Wilson (1987).

38. Brady, Verba, and Schlozman (1995); Verba, Schlozman, and Brady (1995); Verba et al. (1993b).

39. Douglas S. Massey and Nancy A. Denton, *American Apartheid: Segregation and the Making of the Underclass* (Cambridge, Mass.: Harvard University Press, 1993).

40. Timothy Bledsoe, Susan Welch, Lee Sigelman, and Michael Combs, "Residential Context and Racial Solidarity among African Americans," *American Journal of Political Science* 39 (1995): 434–458.

41. Bobo and Gilliam (1990).

42. Bobo and Gilliam (1990); Cohen and Dawson (1993); Guterbock and London (1983); Verba et al. (1993b).

43. Cohen and Dawson (1993), 291.

44. Lincoln and Mamiya (1990); Morris (1984); Verba et al. (1993b).

45. It is also possible that in some instances clergy may choose to serve in economically disadvantaged neighborhoods because of their own political agendas.

46. Huckfeldt et al. (1995), 1050.

47. Hunter (1987); Jelen (1993); Koller and Retzer (1980).

48. Huckfeldt et al. (1995).

CHAPTER FIVE. SUBSTANTIVE POLITICAL AGENDAS

1. Elihu Katz, "The Two-Step Flow of Communication: An Up-to-Date Report on a Hypothesis," *Public Opinion Quarterly* 21 (1957): 67–78.

2. Robert Huckfeldt, Paul Allen Beck, Russell J. Dalton, and Jeffrey Levine, "Political Environments, Cohesive Social Groups, and the Communication of Public Opinion," *American Journal of Political Science* 39 (1995): 1048–1049.

3. Shanto Iyengar and Donald R. Kinder, *News That Matters: Television and American Opinion* (Chicago: University of Chicago Press, 1987), 16–33.

4. Ibid., 60.

5. Pamela Johnston Conover, "The Influence of Group Identifications on Political Perception and Evaluation," *Journal of Politics* 46 (1984): 760–785.

6. Iyengar and Kinder (1987), 42–46.

7. Data are derived from the *Vanderbilt University Television News Index and Abstracts*, June-July 1994 (Nashville, Tenn.: Vanderbilt Television News Archive).

8. *New York Times*/CBS News Poll (July 14–17, 1994).

9. The setting of this study in Milwaukee is important because responses may have been slightly different in another setting. Portland, Oregon, for example, is similar to Milwaukee in size and regional importance. Had I conducted this study in Portland, clergy may have provided at least some different responses. In the summer of 1994 in Portland, major local issues included scandals surrounding both U.S. Senator Bob Packwood and figure skater Tonya Harding. See "Packwood Hearings Face Delay," *The Oregonian* (July 2, 1994); "Packwood's Fund for Legal Defense Experiences Big Increase," *The Oregonian* (July 17, 1994).

Moreover, residents of the state of Wisconsin have been shown to be somewhat more conservative than people in other states. See Robert S. Erikson, John P. McIver, and Gerald C. Wright, "State Political Culture and Public Opinion," *American Political Science Review* 81 (1987): 797–813.

10. "Milwaukee Police Arrest Jeffrey L. Dahmer," *The Milwaukee Journal* (July 24, 1991), A1; "Parts of Many Bodies Found in a Milwaukee Apartment," *The New York Times* (July 24, 1991), A14.

11. "Churches Are Divided," *The Milwaukee Journal* (July 8, 1992), A2; "'Missionaries' Follow New Reasons to Rescue," *Christianity Today* (September 14, 1992), 58–60.

12. "Epidemic of Gastrointestinal Illness," *The Milwaukee Journal* (April 11, 1993), A3; "Fortunately, None Got into the Beer," *Newsweek* (April 19, 1993), 52.

13. Joe Williams, "O. J. Alibi Clouded by Nicolet Grad: City Native May Be Key Prosecution Witness," *The Milwaukee Sentinel* (June 22, 1994), 1A.

14. "The Man Who Brings the Owners Together," *The New York Times* (June 10, 1994), B11.

15. Sidney Verba and Norman H. Nie, *Participation in America: Political Democracy and Social Equality* (Chicago: University of Chicago Press, 1972), 271. Italics in original.

16. John R. Zaller, *The Nature and Origins of Mass Opinion* (New York: Cambridge University Press, 1992), chapters 2–3.

17. "Welfare Reform, Done Harshly," *The New York Times* (November 8, 1993), A18; Jason DeParle, "Way Out Front on a Hot Button Issue," *The New York Times* (October 20, 1994), A25.

18. Steve Schultze, "State Seeks Pot of Gold: Tribal Casinos Have It," *The Milwaukee Journal* (August 31, 1994), A1.

19. On this alleged "culture war," see especially James Davison Hunter, *Culture Wars: The Struggle to Define America* (New York: Basic Books, 1991).

20. John F. Witte, *Public Subsidies for Private Schools: Implications for*

Wisconsin's Reform Efforts (Madison, Wisc.: Wisconsin Center for Education Policy, 1991).

21. See Christopher J. Klicka, *The Right Choice: Home Schooling* (Gresham, Ore.: Noble, 1993).

22. See Arthur K. Ellis, *Research on Educational Innovations* (Princeton Junction, N.J.: Eye on Education, 1993).

23. This is documented in Laura R. Woliver, *From Outrage to Action: The Politics of Grass-Roots Dissent* (Urbana: University of Illinois Press, 1993), chapter 4.

24. Tom Held, "Dahmer Cops to Return to Force Today: Commission Reinstates Pair," *The Milwaukee Sentinel* (June 17, 1994), A1.

25. So too have many social commentators, such as Richard John Neuhaus, *The Naked Public Square: Religion and Democracy in America* (Grand Rapids, Mich.: Eerdmans, 1984).

26. Arthur H. Miller, Patricia Gurin, Gerald Gurin, and Oksana Malanchuk, "Group Consciousness and Political Participation," *American Journal of Political Science* 25 (1981): 494–511; Conover (1984).

CHAPTER SIX. ABORTION

1. Sidney Verba and Norman H. Nie, *Participation in America: Political Democracy and Social Equality* (Chicago: University of Chicago Press, 1972), 285.

2. James L. Guth, John C. Green, Corwin E. Smidt, Lyman A. Kellstedt, and Margaret M. Poloma, *The Bully Pulpit: The Politics of Protestant Clergy* (Lawrence: University Press of Kansas, 1997). See also Harold E. Quinley, *The Prophetic Clergy: Social Activism among Protestant Ministers* (New York: Wiley, 1974); Jeffrey K. Hadden, *The Gathering Storm in the Churches* (Garden City, N.Y.: Doubleday, 1969); Rodney Stark, Bruce D. Foster, Charles Y. Glock, and Harold E. Quinley, *Wayward Shepherds: Prejudice and the Protestant Clergy* (New York: Harper & Row, 1971).

3. Raymond E. Wolfinger and Steven J. Rosenstone, *Who Votes?* (New Haven, Conn.: Yale University Press, 1980); Cathy J. Cohen and Michael C. Dawson, "Neighborhood Poverty and African American Politics," *American Political Science Review* 87 (1993): 286–302; Sidney Verba, Kay Lehman Schlozman, Henry Brady, and Norman H. Nie, "Race, Ethnicity, and Political Resources: Participation in the United States," *British Journal of Political Science* 23 (1993b): 453–496.

4. This is the argument made by Lester Milbrath about political involvement in the American population at large. See Lester W. Milbrath, *Political Participation: How and Why Do People Get Involved in Politics?* (Chicago: Rand McNally, 1965), 44, 53.

5. This is the term used by Philip E. Converse, "The Nature of Belief Systems in Mass Publics," in *Ideology and Discontent*, ed. David Apter (New York: Free Press, 1964), 206–261.

6. Donald R. Kinder and David O. Sears, "Public Opinion and Political Behavior," in *Handbook of Social Psychology*, vol. 2, ed. Gardner Lindzey and

Elliot Aronson (New York: Random House, 1985); Henry E. Brady and Paul M. Sniderman, "Attitude Attribution: A Group Basis for Political Reasoning," *American Political Science Review* 79 (1985): 1061–1078.

7. William G. Jacoby, "The Structure of Ideological Thinking in the American Electorate," *American Journal of Political Science* 39 (1995): 314–335.

8. Kristin Luker, *Abortion and the Politics of Motherhood* (Berkeley: University of California Press, 1984), chapter 1.

9. 410 U.S. 113 (1973).

10. James Davison Hunter, *Before the Shooting Begins: Searching for Democracy in America's Culture War* (New York: Free Press, 1994), 13.

11. Christian Coalition, *Contract with the American Family* (Nashville, Tenn.: Moorings, 1995), 66.

12. Luker (1984), chapters 5–6.

13. James L. Guth, Corwin E. Smidt, Lyman A. Kellstedt, and John C. Green, "The Sources of Antiabortion Attitudes: The Case of Religious Political Activists," *American Politics Quarterly* 21 (1993): 65–80.

14. Robert E. O'Connor and Michael B. Berkman, "Religious Determinants of State Abortion Policy," *Social Science Quarterly* 76 (1995): 447–459.

15. See Jerome L. Himmelstein, "The Social Basis of Antifeminism," *Journal for the Scientific Study of Religion* 25 (1986): 1–15.

16. Joseph B. Tamney, Stephen D. Johnson, and Ronald Burton, "The Abortion Controversy: Conflicting Beliefs and Values in American Society and within Religious Subgroups," in *Abortion Politics in the United States and Canada*, ed. Ted G. Jelen and Marthe A. Chandler (Westport, Conn.: Praeger, 1994), 53.

17. Elizabeth Adell Cook, Ted G. Jelen, and Clyde Wilcox, *Between Two Absolutes: Public Opinion and the Politics of Abortion* (Boulder, Colo.: Westview, 1992), chapter 4.

18. As illustrations see Aldon D. Morris, *The Origins of the Civil Rights Movement: Black Communities Organizing for Change* (New York: Free Press, 1984), chapter 4; C. Eric Lincoln and Lawrence H. Mamiya, *The Black Church in the African American Experience* (Durham, N.C.: Duke University Press, 1990), chapter 8.

19. On this point and in general, see Faye D. Ginsburg, *Contested Lives: The Abortion Debate in an American Community* (Berkeley: University of California Press, 1989), 192–193.

20. Ted G. Jelen, "The Clergy and Abortion," *Review of Religious Research* 34 (1992a): 139.

21. Luker (1984), 122–123.

22. Jo Anne Weintraub, "Hundreds Join Ranks with Activists," *The Milwaukee Journal* (June 11, 1992), A12.

23. "The Two Sides," *The Milwaukee Sentinel* (June 17, 1992), A8.

24. "Saturday Protests Result in Record 144 Arrests in City," *The Milwaukee Journal* (June 21, 1992), A13.

25. "Parents May Be Cited in Arrests," *The Milwaukee Sentinel* (June 19, 1992), A1.

26. Jelen (1992a), passim.
27. *The Silent Scream* is a film that depicts the process of abortion.
28. "Crisis pregnancy centers" counsel pregnant women about alternatives to abortion.
29. Guth et al. (1997).
30. Ernst-Ulrich Franzen, "Trewhella Tells of Life's Turning Points," *The Milwaukee Sentinel* (October 17, 1994), A1.
31. Jo Anne Weintraub and Bob Helbig, "Church-run Militias Urged in Video," *The Milwaukee Journal* (August 17, 1994), A1.
32. Michael MacKuen and Courtney Brown, "Political Context and Attitude Change," *American Political Science Review* 81 (1987): 485.

CHAPTER SEVEN. CRIME AND VIOLENCE

1. Jeff Browne, "Crime Fears Clouding Outlook That's Upbeat for a Good '94," *The Milwaukee Journal* (January 2, 1994), B1.
2. Ibid.
3. Ibid.
4. John D. Hull, "Have We Gone Mad?" *Time* (December 20, 1993), 31.
5. Ibid.
6. Ibid.
7. Patrick Jasperese, "New Data Tell More of City's Crime Drop," *The Milwaukee Journal* (April 15, 1994), A1.
8. Mark Lisheron, "Violent Crime Bucks Trend, Falls in State," *The Milwaukee Journal* (August 2, 1994), A1.
9. "Crime Watches Should Not Let Up," *The Milwaukee Journal* (November 7, 1994), A1.
10. Mark Edmund, "Buy-back Kickoff Set for Weekend," *The Milwaukee Journal* (June 15, 1994), B3.
11. James Rowen, "Gun Bans Fail in Milwaukee, Kenosha," *The Milwaukee Journal* (November 9, 1994), A1.
12. Ibid.
13. *Wisconsin Crime and Arrests 1992* (Madison, Wisc.: Office of Justice Assistance, 1992); *Wisconsin Crime and Arrests 1993* (Madison, Wisc.: Office of Justice Assistance, 1993); *Wisconsin Crime and Arrests 1994* (Madison, Wisc.: Office of Justice Assistance, 1994).
14. See also Hull (1993), 32; Milwaukee Innercity Congregations Allied for Hope, *To Do What Is Just!* (Milwaukee, Wisc.: Milwaukee Innercity Congregations Allied for Hope, 1994).
15. Christian Coalition, *Contract with the American Family* (Nashville, Tenn.: Moorings, 1995), 121.
16. Graeme R. Newman and Carol Trilling, "Public Perceptions of Criminal Behavior: A Review of the Literature," *Criminal Justice and Behavior* 2 (1975): 230.
17. Kathlyn Taylor Gaubatz, *Crime in the Public Mind* (Ann Arbor: University of Michigan Press, 1995), 145–147.

18. Cathy J. Cohen and Michael C. Dawson, "Neighborhood Poverty and African American Politics," *American Political Science Review* 87 (1993): 286–302.

19. Steven F. Cohn, Steven E. Barkan, and William A. Halteman, "Punitive Attitudes Toward Criminals: Racial Consensus or Racial Conflict?" *Social Problems* 38 (1992): 287–296.

20. This point is made explicitly by Julian V. Roberts and Don Edwards, "Contextual Effects in Judgments of Crimes, Criminals, and the Purposes of Sentencing," *Journal of Applied Social Psychology* 19 (1989): 902–917.

21. Shanto Iyengar, *Is Anyone Responsible? How Television Frames Political Issues* (Chicago: University of Chicago Press, 1991), 45.

22. Ibid., 8. Iyengar provides a good overview of this topic.

23. James L. Guth, John C. Green, Corwin E. Smidt, Lyman A. Kellstedt, and Margaret M. Poloma, *The Bully Pulpit: The Politics of Protestant Clergy* (Lawrence: University Press of Kansas, 1997).

24. Iyengar (1991), 92–93.

25. Harold E. Quinley, *The Prophetic Clergy: Social Activism among Protestant Ministers* (New York: Wiley, 1974); Jeffrey K. Hadden, *The Gathering Storm in the Churches* (Garden City, N.Y.: Doubleday, 1969); Rodney Stark, Bruce D. Foster, Charles Y. Glock, and Harold E. Quinley, *Wayward Shepherds: Prejudice and the Protestant Clergy* (New York: Harper & Row, 1971).

CHAPTER EIGHT. FAMILY VALUES

1. For a more systematic look at the various components of pastoral ideologies, see James L. Guth, John C. Green, Corwin E. Smidt, Lyman A. Kellstedt, and Margaret M. Poloma, *The Bully Pulpit: The Politics of Protestant Clergy* (Lawrence: University Press of Kansas, 1997).

2. See Murray Edelman, *The Symbolic Uses of Politics* (Urbana: University of Illinois Press, 1964).

3. Roger W. Cobb and Charles E. Elder, *Participation in American Politics: The Dynamics of Agenda-Building*, 2d ed. (Baltimore, Md.: Johns Hopkins University Press, 1983).

4. Joseph Gusfield, *The Culture of Public Problems: Drinking-Driving and the Symbolic Order* (Chicago: University of Chicago Press, 1981), 10.

5. Cobb and Elder (1983), 182–183.

6. Brigitte Berger and Peter L. Berger, *The War over the Family: Capturing the Middle Ground* (Garden City, N.Y.: Doubleday, 1983), 20–21.

7. James Davison Hunter, *Culture Wars: The Struggle to Define America* (New York: Basic Books, 1991), chapter 7.

8. This point is made by David Popenoe, *Disturbing the Nest: Family Change and Decline in Modern Societies* (New York: Aldine, 1988), 281.

9. The argument that the family is not in decline is made by (among others) Theodore Caplow, Howard M. Bahr, Bruce A. Chadwick, Reuben Hill, and Margaret Holmes Wilson, *Middletown Families* (New York: Bantam, 1983),

320–330. For the counterargument, see Popenoe (1988), chapters 1, 12.

10. Nathan Glazer and Daniel Patrick Moynihan, *Beyond the Melting Pot* (Cambridge, Mass.: MIT Press, 1963), 24–85.

11. David Blankenhorn, *Fatherless America: Confronting Our Most Urgent Social Problem* (New York: Basic Books, 1995), 222.

12. Hunter (1991), 178.

13. Kenneth Kensiton and the Carnegie Council on Children, *All Our Children: The American Family under Pressure* (New York: Harcourt Brace Jovanovich, 1977), 76.

14. On these points see also Berger and Berger (1983), 18–19.

15. Matthew C. Moen, *The Christian Right and Congress* (Tuscaloosa: University of Alabama Press, 1989), 108; Hunter (1991), 178–180.

16. Jane J. Mansbridge, *Why We Lost the ERA* (Chicago: University of Chicago Press, 1986), 5.

17. Laura R. Olson, "Ronald Reagan's Rhetorical Appeal to the Christian Right," Paper presented at the Annual Meeting of the Midwest Political Science Association, Chicago, 1993.

18. Moen (1989) makes a similar argument.

19. See John Leo, "A New Values Vocabulary," *U.S. News & World Report* (October 3, 1994), 22.

20. Tim LaHaye, *The Battle for the Family* (Old Tappan, N.J.: Revell, 1982), 19.

21. See Ralph Reed, *Politically Incorrect: The Emerging Faith Factor in American Politics* (Dallas, Tex.: Word, 1994), chapter 6.

22. Jeffrey H. Birnbaum, "The Gospel According to Ralph," *Time* (May 15, 1995), 29–35.

23. Roy Beck, "Washington's Profamily Activists," *Christianity Today* (November 9, 1992), 21.

24. Amitai Etzioni, *The Spirit of Community: Rights, Responsibilities, and the Communitarian Agenda* (New York: Crown, 1993), 54.

25. James Q. Wilson, *The Moral Sense* (New York: Free Press, 1993), chapters 1, 7, 10; James Q. Wilson, "The Moral Sense," *American Political Science Review* 88 (1994): 1–11.

26. Laura R. Olson, "Bill Clinton's Strategic Use of Religious and Family Rhetoric: The Co-optation of Partisan Symbolism," Paper presented at the Annual Meeting of the Midwest Political Science Association, Chicago, 1997.

27. Charles Krauthammer, "Down with 'Family Values'," *Time* (October 17, 1994), 88.

28. Lewis H. Lapham, "Gospel Singing," *Harper's Magazine* (November 1994), 9.

29. This is interestingly consistent with an observation made by Shanto Iyengar that people often think about complex policy debates by assigning blame. See Shanto Iyengar, *Is Anyone Responsible? How Television Frames Political Issues* (Chicago: University of Chicago Press, 1991), 8.

30. At the time of the interview, the former professional football player O. J. Simpson had recently been charged with the murders of his ex-wife and her friend.

31. It should be noted at this point that of the pastors classified as acceptors, fully half are African American.

32. The "ownership" concept is discussed by Gusfield (1981), 10; Cobb and Elder (1983), 182–183.

33. Hunter (1991), 43.

34. Blankenhorn (1995), 29.

35. Wilson (1993), 9–11.

36. Blankenhorn (1995), 30.

CHAPTER NINE. FILLED WITH SPIRIT AND POWER

1. Paula D. Nesbitt, "Clergy Feminization: Controlled Labor or Transformative Change?" *Journal for the Scientific Study of Religion* 36 (1997): 585–598.

2. Sidney Verba, Kay Lehman Schlozman, Henry Brady, and Norman H. Nie, "Race, Ethnicity, and Political Resources: Participation in the United States," *British Journal of Political Science* 23 (1993b): 471–472.

3. Ibid., 486–487.

4. James L. Guth, John C. Green, Corwin E. Smidt, Lyman A. Kellstedt, and Margaret M. Poloma, *The Bully Pulpit: The Politics of Protestant Clergy* (Lawrence: University Press of Kansas, 1997).

5. See Norman Koller and Joseph Retzer, "The Sounds of Silence Revisited," *Sociological Analysis* 41 (1980): 155–161; Nancy Tatom Ammerman, *Bible Believers: Fundamentalists in the Modern World* (New Brunswick, N.J.: Rutgers University Press, 1987); James Davison Hunter, *Evangelicalism: The Coming Generation* (Chicago: University of Chicago Press, 1987); Robert Booth Fowler, "The Failure of the New Christian Right," Paper presented at the Ethics and Public Policy Center Conference on Evangelicals, Politics, and the Religious New Right, 1990; Ted G. Jelen, *The Political World of the Clergy* (Westport, Conn.: Praeger, 1993), chapter 2.

6. James L. Guth and John C. Green, "The Moralizing Minority: Christian Right Support Among Political Contributors," *Social Science Quarterly* 68 (1987): 598–610.

7. Guth et al. (1997).

8. See Lawrence Bobo and Franklin D. Gilliam Jr., "Race, Sociopolitical Participation, and Black Empowerment," *American Political Science Review* 84 (1990): 377–393; Cathy J. Cohen and Michael C. Dawson, "Neighborhood Poverty and African American Politics," *American Political Science Review* 87 (1993): 286–302; Verba et al. (1993b).

9. This argument is made by Sue E. S. Crawford, "Clergy at Work in the Secular City," Ph.D. diss., Indiana University, 1995.

10. Robert Huckfeldt, Paul Allen Beck, Russell J. Dalton, and Jeffrey Levine, "Political Environments, Cohesive Social Groups, and the Communication of Public Opinion," *American Journal of Political Science* 39 (1995): 1025–1054.

11. See Crawford (1995).

12. Peter K. Eisinger, *Patterns of Interracial Politics: Conflict and Cooperation in the City* (New York: Academic Press, 1976), 26.

13. Ibid., 164–166.

14. See Robert Huckfeldt, Eric Plutzer, and John Sprague, "Alternative Contexts of Political Behavior: Churches, Neighborhoods, and Individuals," *Journal of Politics* 55 (1993): 365–381; Verba et al. (1993b).

15. See especially Guth et al. (1997). See also Harold E. Quinley, *The Prophetic Clergy: Social Activism among Protestant Ministers* (New York: Wiley, 1974); James L. Guth, "Southern Baptist Clergy: Vanguard of the Christian Right," in *The New Christian Right: Mobilization and Legitimation*, ed. Robert C. Liebman and Robert Wuthnow (New York: Aldine, 1983), 117–130; James L. Guth, John C. Green, Corwin E. Smidt, and Margaret M. Poloma, "Pulpits and Politics: The Protestant Clergy in the 1988 Presidential Election," in *The Bible and the Ballot Box: Religion and Politics in the 1988 Election*, ed. James L. Guth and John C. Green (Boulder, Colo.: Westview, 1991), 73–93; Jelen (1993).

16. Of all previous studies of religion and politics that take context seriously, the most useful is Christopher P. Gilbert, *The Impact of Churches on Political Behavior: An Empirical Study* (Westport, Conn.: Greenwood, 1993). A clear call for more contextual research was made by David C. Leege, Joel A. Lieske, and Kenneth D. Wald, "Toward Cultural Theories of American Political Behavior: Religion, Ethnicity and Race, and Class Outlook," in *Political Science: Looking to the Future*, vol. 3., ed. William J. Crotty (Evanston, Ill.: Northwestern University Press, 1991) 193–238.

APPENDIX

1. Metropolitan Milwaukee includes the city of Milwaukee as well as the suburbs of Bayside, Brookfield, Brown Deer, Cudahy, Elm Grove, Fox Point, Franklin, Glendale, Greendale, Greenfield, Hales Corners, Menomonee Falls, Muskego, New Berlin, Oak Creek, River Hills, St. Francis, Shorewood, South Milwaukee, Wauwatosa, West Allis, West Milwaukee, and Whitefish Bay.

REFERENCES

"105 Abortion Foes Arrested at Clinics." *The Los Angeles Times* (June 17, 1992), A20.

Abowitz, Deborah A. 1990. "Sociopolitical Participation and the Significance ofSocial Context: A Model of Competing Interests and Obligations." *Social Science Quarterly* 71: 543–566.

Adams, James L. 1970. *The Growing Church Lobby in Washington*. Grand Rapids, Mich.: Eerdmans.

Ammerman, Nancy Tatom. 1987. *Bible Believers: Fundamentalists in the Modern World*. New Brunswick, N.J.: Rutgers University Press.

Austin, H. Russell. 1946. *The Milwaukee Story: The Making of an American City*. Milwaukee, Wisc.: The Milwaukee Journal Company.

Barnes, Samuel H., Max Kaase, and Klaus R. Allerbeck. 1979. *Political Action: Mass Participation in Five Western Democracies*. Beverly Hills, Calif.: Sage.

Beatty, Kathleen Murphy, and Oliver Walter. 1989. "A Group Theory of Religion and Politics: The Clergy as Group Leaders." *Western Political Quarterly* 42: 129–146.

Beck, Roy. 1992. "Washington's Profamily Activists." *Christianity Today* (November 9), 21.

Bellah, Robert N., Richard Madsen, William M. Sullivan, Ann Swidler, and Steven M. Tipton. 1985. *Habits of the Heart: Individualism and Commitment in American Life*. New York: Harper & Row.

Berelson, Bernard R., Paul F. Lazarsfeld, and William N. McPhee. 1954. *Voting: A Study of Opinion Formation in a Presidential Campaign*. Chicago: University of Chicago Press.

Berger, Brigitte, and Peter L. Berger. 1983. *The War over the Family: Capturing the Middle Ground*. Garden City, N.Y.: Anchor.

Berns, Walter. 1976. *The First Amendment and the Future of American Democracy*. New York: Basic Books.

Berry, Jeffrey M., Kent E. Portney, and Ken Thomson. 1993. *The Rebirth of Urban Democracy*. Washington, D.C.: The Brookings Institution.

Birnbaum, Jeffrey H. 1995. "The Gospel According to Ralph." *Time* (May 15), 29–35.

Blankenhorn, David. 1995. *Fatherless America: Confronting Our Most Urgent Social Problem*. New York: Basic Books.

Bledsoe, Timothy, Susan Welch, Lee Sigelman, and Michael Combs. 1995. "Residential Context and Racial Solidarity among African Americans." *American Journal of Political Science* 39: 434–458.

Bobo, Lawrence, and Franklin D. Gilliam Jr. 1990. "Race, Sociopolitical Participation, and Black Empowerment." *American Political Science Review* 84: 377–393.

Brady, Henry E., and Paul M. Sniderman. 1985. "Attitude Attribution: A Group Basis for Political Reasoning." *American Political Science Review* 79: 1061–1078.

Brady, Henry E., Sidney Verba, and Kay Lehman Schlozman. 1995. "Beyond SES: A Resource Model of Political Participation." *American Political Science Review* 89: 271–294.

Browne, Jeff. 1994. "Crime Fears Clouding Outlook That's Upbeat for a Good '94." *The Milwaukee Journal* (January 2), B1.

Browning, Rufus P., Dale Rogers Marshall, and David H. Tabb. 1984. *Protest Is Not Enough: The Struggle of Blacks and Hispanics for Equality in Urban Politics*. Berkeley: University of California Press.

Byrnes, Timothy A. 1991. *Catholic Bishops in American Politics*. Princeton, N.J.: Princeton University Press.

Campbell, Angus, Philip E. Converse, Warren E. Miller, and Donald E. Stokes. 1960. *The American Voter*. New York: Wiley.

Cano, Julio V. 1994a. "MICAH Glad Bar's License Not Renewed." *The Milwaukee Sentinel* (June 30), A12.

———. 1994b. "MICAH Issues Demands to Mayor: Church Group Seeks Improved Police-Community Relations." *The Milwaukee Sentinel* (May 25), A5.

Caplow, Theodore, Howard M. Bahr, Bruce A. Chadwick, Reuben Hill, and Margaret Holmes Wilson. 1982. *Middletown Families: Fifty Years of Change and Continuity*. Minneapolis: University of Minnesota Press.

Carroll, Jackson W., Barbara Hargrove, and Adair T. Lummis. 1981. *Women of the Cloth: A New Opportunity for the Churches*. New York: Harper & Row.

Chapman, Audrey R. 1991. *Faith, Power, and Politics: Political Ministry in Mainline Churches*. New York: Pilgrim.

Christian Coalition. 1995. *Contract with the American Family*. Nashville, Tenn.: Moorings.

"Churches Are Divided." *The Milwaukee Journal* (July 8, 1992), A2.

Cobb, Roger W., and Charles E. Elder. 1983. *Participation in American Politics: The Dynamics of Agenda-Building*. 2d ed. Baltimore, Md.: Johns Hopkins University Press.

Cohen, Cathy J., and Michael C. Dawson. 1993. "Neighborhood Poverty and African American Politics." *American Political Science Review* 87: 286–302.

Cohn, Steven F., Steven E. Barkan, and William A. Halteman. 1992. "Punitive Attitudes Toward Criminals: Racial Consensus or Racial Conflict?" *Social Problems* 38: 287–296.

Conover, Pamela Johnston. 1984. "The Influence of Group Identifications on Political Perception and Evaluation." *Journal of Politics* 46: 760–785.

Converse, Philip E. 1964. "The Nature of Belief Systems in Mass Publics." In *Ideology and Discontent*, ed. David Apter, 206–261. New York: Free Press.

Cook, Elizabeth Adell, Ted G. Jelen, and Clyde Wilcox. 1992. *Between Two Absolutes: Public Opinion and the Politics of Abortion.* Boulder, Colo.: Westview.

Crawford, Sue E. S. 1995. "Clergy at Work in the Secular City." Ph.D. diss., Indiana University.

"Crime Watches Should Not Let Up." *The Milwaukee Journal* (November 7, 1994), A1.

Daniels, Arlene Kaplan. 1988. *Invisible Careers: Women Civic Leaders from the Volunteer World.* Chicago: University of Chicago Press.

DeParle, Jason. 1994. "Way Out Front on a Hot Button Issue." *The New York Times* (October 20), A25.

Djupe, Paul A. 1997. "The Plural Church: Church Involvement and Political Behavior." Ph.D. diss., Washington University in St. Louis.

Ebersole, Luke Eugene. 1951. *Church Lobbying in the Nation's Capital.* New York: Macmillan.

Edelman, Murray. 1964. *The Symbolic Uses of Politics.* Urbana: University of Illinois Press.

———. 1971. *Politics as Symbolic Action: Mass Arousal and Quiescence.* New York: Academic Press.

Edmund, Mark. 1994. "Buy-back Kickoff Set for Weekend." *The Milwaukee Journal* (June 15), B3.

Eisinger, Peter K. 1976. *Patterns of Interracial Politics: Conflict and Cooperation in the City.* New York: Academic Press.

Ellis, Arthur K. 1993. *Research on Educational Innovations.* Princeton Junction, N.J.: Eye on Education.

"Epidemic of Gastrointestinal Illness." *The Milwaukee Journal* (April 11, 1993), A3.

Erikson, Robert S., John P. McIver, and Gerald C. Wright. 1987. "State Political Culture and Public Opinion." *American Political Science Review* 81: 797–813.

Etzioni, Amitai. 1993. *The Spirit of Community: Rights, Responsibilities, and the Communitarian Agenda.* New York: Crown.

Evans, Sara. 1979. *Personal Politics: The Roots of Women's Liberation in the Civil Rights Movement and the New Left.* New York: Knopf.

Falwell, Jerry. 1980. *Listen, America!* Garden City, N.Y.: Doubleday.

Findlay, James F. 1993. *Church People in the Struggle: The National Council of Churches and the Black Freedom Movement, 1950–1970.* New York: Oxford University Press.

Finke, Roger, and Rodney Stark. 1992. *The Churching of America, 1776–1990: Winners and Losers in Our Religious Economy.* New Brunswick, N.J.: Rutgers University Press.

Finkel, Steven E. 1985. "Reciprocal Effects of Participation and Political Efficacy: A Panel Analysis." *American Journal of Political Science* 29: 891–913.

Finlay, Barbara. 1997. "Future Ministers and Legal Abortion: Gender Comparisons among Protestant Seminary Students." *Women and Politics* 17: 1–15.

"Fortunately, None Got into the Beer." *Newsweek* (April 19, 1993), 52.

Fowler, Robert Booth. 1985. *Religion and Politics in America.* Metuchen, N.J.: Scarecrow.

———. 1989. *Unconventional Partners: Religion and Liberal Culture in the United States*. Grand Rapids, Mich.: Eerdmans.

———. 1990. "The Failure of the New Christian Right." Paper presented at the Ethics and Public Policy Center Conference on Evangelicals, Politics, and the Religious New Right.

Franzen, Ernst-Ulrich. 1994. "Trewhella Tells of Life's Turning Points." *The Milwaukee Sentinel* (October 17), A1.

Gaubatz, Kathlyn Taylor. 1995. *Crime in the Public Mind*. Ann Arbor, Mich.: University of Michigan Press.

Gilbert, Christopher P. 1993. *The Impact of Churches on Political Behavior: An Empirical Study*. Westport, Conn.: Greenwood.

Ginsburg, Faye. 1989. *Contested Lives: The Abortion Debate in an American Community*. Berkeley: University of California Press.

Glazer, Nathan, and Daniel Patrick Moynihan. 1963. *Beyond the Melting Pot*. Cambridge, Mass.: MIT Press.

Glock, Charles Y., and Rodney Stark. 1965. *Religion and Society in Tension*. Chicago: Rand McNally.

Goffman, Erving. 1959. *The Presentation of Self in Everyday Life*. Garden City, N.Y.: Doubleday.

Green, John C., James L. Guth, and Kevin Hill. 1993. "Faith and Election: The Christian Right in Congressional Campaigns, 1978–1988." *Journal of Politics* 55: 80–91.

Gusfield, Joseph. 1981. *The Culture of Public Problems: Drinking-Driving and the Symbolic Order*. Chicago: University of Chicago Press.

Guterbock, Thomas M., and Bruce London. 1983. "Race, Political Orientation, and Participation: An Empirical Test of Four Competing Theories." *American Sociological Review* 48: 439–453.

Guth, James L. 1983. "Southern Baptist Clergy: Vanguard of the Christian Right." In *The New Christian Right: Mobilization and Legitimation*, ed. Robert C. Liebman and Robert Wuthnow, 117–130. New York: Aldine.

———. 1996. "The Political Mobilization of Southern Baptist Clergy, 1980–1992." In *Religion and the Culture Wars: Dispatches from the Front*, ed. John C. Green, James L. Guth, Lyman A. Kellstedt, and Corwin E. Smidt, 146–173. Lanham, Md.: Rowman and Littlefield.

Guth, James L., and John C. Green. 1987. "The Moralizing Minority: Christian Right Support Among Political Contributors." *Social Science Quarterly* 68: 598–610.

Guth, James L., John C. Green, Lyman A. Kellstedt, and Corwin E. Smidt. 1995. "Faith and the Environment: Religious Beliefs and Attitudes on Environmental Policy." *American Journal of Political Science* 39: 364–382.

Guth, James L. John C. Green, Corwin E. Smidt, and Lyman A. Kellstedt. 1994. "Women Clergy and the Political Transformation of Mainline Protestantism." Paper presented at the Annual Meeting of the Social Science History Association, Atlanta.

Guth, James L., John C. Green, Corwin E. Smidt, Lyman A. Kellstedt, and Margaret M. Poloma. 1997. *The Bully Pulpit: The Politics of Protestant Clergy*. Lawrence: University Press of Kansas.

Guth, James L., John C. Green, Corwin E. Smidt, and Margaret M. Poloma. 1991. "Pulpits and Politics: The Protestant Clergy in the 1988 Presidential Election." In *The Bible and the Ballot Box: Religion and Politics in the 1988 Election*, ed. James L. Guth and John C. Green, 73–93. Boulder, Colo.: Westview.

Guth, James L., Corwin E. Smidt, Lyman A. Kellstedt, and John C. Green. 1993. "The Sources of Antiabortion Attitudes: The Case of Religious Political Activists." *American Politics Quarterly* 21: 65–80.

Hadden, Jeffrey K. 1969. *The Gathering Storm in the Churches*. Garden City, N.Y.: Doubleday.

Hallum, Anne M. 1991. "From Candidates to Agenda Setters: Protestant Leaders and the 1988 Presidential Campaign." In *The Bible and the Ballot Box: Religion and Politics in the 1988 Election*, ed. James L. Guth and John C. Green, 31–41. Boulder, Colo.: Westview.

Hanna, Mary T. 1991. "Divided, Distracted, and Disengaged: Catholic Leaders and the 1988 Presidential Campaign." In *The Bible and the Ballot Box: Religion and Politics in the 1988 Election*, ed. James L. Guth and John C. Green, 42–54. Boulder, Colo.: Westview.

Held, Tom. 1994. "Dahmer Cops to Return to Force Today: Commission Reinstates Pair." *The Milwaukee Sentinel* (June 17), A1.

Hertel, Bradley R., and Michael Hughes. 1987. "Religious Affiliation, Attendance, and Support for 'Pro-Family' Issues in the United States." *Social Forces* 65: 858–882.

Hertzke, Allen D. 1988. *Representing God in Washington: The Role of Religious Lobbies in the American Polity*. Knoxville: University of Tennessee Press.

———. 1993. *Echoes of Discontent: Jesse Jackson, Pat Robertson, and the Resurgence of Populism*. Washington, D.C.: Congressional Quarterly Press.

Himmelstein, Jerome L. 1986. "The Social Basis of Antifeminism." *Journal for the Scientific Study of Religion* 25: 1–15.

Hougland, James G., Jr., and James A. Christenson. 1983. "Religion and Politics: The Relationship of Religious Participation to Political Efficacy and Involvement." *Sociology and Social Research* 67: 405–420.

Huckfeldt, Robert. 1986. *Politics in Context: Assimilation and Conflict in Urban Neighborhoods*. New York: Agathon.

Huckfeldt, Robert, Paul Allen Beck, Russell J. Dalton, and Jeffrey Levine. 1995. "Political Environments, Cohesive Social Groups, and the Communication of Public Opinion." *American Journal of Political Science* 39: 1025–1054.

Huckfeldt, Robert, Eric Plutzer, and John Sprague. 1993. "Alternative Contexts of Political Behavior: Churches, Neighborhoods, and Individuals." *Journal of Politics* 55: 365–381.

Huckfeldt, Robert, and John Sprague. 1987. "Networks in Context." *American Political Science Review* 81: 1197–1216.

Hull, John D. 1993. "Have We Gone Mad?" *Time* (December 20), 31–32.

Hunter, James Davison. 1987. *Evangelicalism: The Coming Generation*. Chicago: University of Chicago Press.

———. 1991. *Culture Wars: The Struggle to Define America*. New York: Basic Books.

———. 1994. *Before the Shooting Begins: Searching for Democracy in America's Culture War*. New York: Free Press.
Hunter, James Davison, and Kimon Howland Sargeant. 1993. "Religion and the Transformation of Public Culture." *Social Research* 60: 545–570.
Ice, Martha Long. 1987. *Clergy Women and Their Worldviews: Calling for a New Age*. New York: Praeger.
Inglehart, Ronald. 1990. *Culture Shift in Advanced Industrial Society*. Princeton, N.J.: Princeton University Press.
Iyengar, Shanto. 1991. *Is Anyone Responsible? How Television Frames Political Issues*. Chicago: University of Chicago Press.
Iyengar, Shanto, and Donald R. Kinder. 1987. *News That Matters: Television and American Opinion*. Chicago: University of Chicago Press.
Jacoby, William G. 1995. "The Structure of Ideological Thinking in the American Electorate." *American Journal of Political Science* 39: 314–335.
Jasperese, Patrick. 1994. "New Data Tell More of City's Crime Drop." *The Milwaukee Journal* (April 15), A1.
Jelen, Ted G. 1991a. *The Political Mobilization of Religious Beliefs*. New York: Praeger.
———. 1991b. "Politicizing Group Identification: The Case of Fundamentalism." *Western Political Quarterly* 44: 209–219.
———. 1992a. "The Clergy and Abortion." *Review of Religious Research* 34: 132–151.
———. 1992b. "Political Christianity: A Contextual Analysis." *American Journal of Political Science* 36: 692–714.
———. 1993. *The Political World of the Clergy*. Westport, Conn.: Praeger.
Jennings, M. Kent. 1979. "Another Look at the Life Cycle and Political Participation." *American Journal of Political Science* 23: 755–771.
Jennings, M. Kent, and Gregory B. Markus. 1988. "Political Involvement in the Later Years: A Longitudinal Study." *American Journal of Political Science* 32: 302–316.
Jennings, M. Kent, and Richard G. Niemi. 1981. *Generations and Politics: A Panel Study of Young Adults and Their Parents*. Princeton, N.J.: Princeton University Press.
Katz, Elihu. 1957. "The Two-Step Flow of Communication: An Up-To-Date Report on a Hypothesis." *Public Opinion Quarterly* 21: 67–78.
Kelley, Dean M. 1972. *Why Conservative Churches Are Growing: A Study in Sociology of Religion*. New York: Harper & Row.
Kellstedt, Lyman A., and John C. Green. 1993. "Knowing God's Many People: Denominational Preference and Political Behavior." In *Rediscovering the Religious Factor in American Politics*, ed. David C. Leege and Lyman A. Kellstedt, 53–71. Armonk, N.Y.: M. E. Sharpe.
Kenny, Christopher B. 1992. "Political Participation and Effects from the Social Environment." *American Journal of Political Science* 36: 259–267.
Kensiton, Kenneth, and the Carnegie Council on Children. 1977. *All Our Children: The American Family under Pressure*. New York: Harcourt Brace Jovanovich.
Key, V. O., Jr. 1961. *Public Opinion and American Democracy*. New York: Knopf.

Kinder, Donald R., and David O. Sears. 1985. "Public Opinion and Political Behavior." In *Handbook of Social Psychology*, vol. 2, ed. Gardner Lindzey and Elliot Aronson. New York: Random House.

Klicka, Christopher J. 1993. *The Right Choice: Home Schooling*. Gresham, Ore.: Noble.

Koller, Norman, and Joseph Retzer. 1980. "The Sounds of Silence Revisited." *Sociological Analysis* 41: 155–161.

Korb, Lawrence J. 1993. "The President and the Military at Odds." *The Brookings Review* 11: 5.

Krauthammer, Charles. 1994. "Down with 'Family Values'." *Time* (October 17), 88.

Kuklinski, James H., Robert C. Luskin, and John Bolland. 1991. "Where Is the Schema? Going Beyond the 'S' Word in Political Psychology." *American Political Science Review* 85: 1341–1356.

LaHaye, Tim. 1982. *The Battle for the Family*. Old Tappan, N.J.: Revell.

Lapham, Lewis H. 1994. "Gospel Singing." *Harper's Magazine* (November), 8–9.

Lawless, Elaine J. 1988. *Handmaidens of the Lord: Pentecostal Women Preachers and Traditional Religion*. Philadelphia: University of Pennsylvania Press.

Lazarsfeld, Paul F., Bernard R. Berelson, and Hazel Gaudet. 1948. *The People's Choice: How the Voter Makes Up His Mind in a Presidential Campaign*. New York: Columbia University Press.

Leege, David C., Joel A. Lieske, and Kenneth D. Wald. 1991. "Toward Cultural Theories of American Political Behavior: Religion, Ethnicity and Race, and Class Outlook." In *Political Science: Looking to the Future*, vol. 3., ed. William J. Crotty, 193–238. Evanston, Ill.: Northwestern University Press.

Leighley, Jan E. 1995. "Attitudes, Opportunities and Incentives: A Field Essay on Political Participation." *Political Research Quarterly* 48: 181–209.

Leo, John. 1994. "A New Values Vocabulary." *U.S. News & World Report* (October 3), 22.

Lienesch, Michael. 1993. *Redeeming America: Piety and Politics in the New Christian Right*. Chapel Hill: University of North Carolina Press.

Lincoln, C. Eric, and Lawrence H. Mamiya. 1990. *The Black Church in the African American Experience*. Durham, N.C.: Duke University Press.

Lisheron, Mark. 1994. "Violent Crime Bucks Trend, Falls in State." *The Milwaukee Journal* (August 2), A1.

Lodge, Milton, Kathleen N. McGraw, Pamela Johnston Conover, Stanley Feldman, and Arthur H. Miller. 1991. "Where Is the Schema? Critiques." *American Political Science Review* 85: 1357–1380.

Luidens, Donald A., and Roger J. Nemeth. 1989. "After the Storm: Closing the Clergy-Laity Gap." *Review of Religious Research* 31: 183–195.

Luker, Kristin. 1984. *Abortion and the Politics of Motherhood*. Berkeley: University of California Press.

MacKuen, Michael, and Courtney Brown. 1987. "Political Context and Attitude Change." *American Political Science Review* 81: 471–490.

Maier, Henry. 1993. *The Mayor Who Made Milwaukee Famous: An Autobiography*. Lanham, Md.: Madison Books.

"The Man Who Brings the Owners Together." *The New York Times* (June 10, 1994), B11.
Mansbridge, Jane J. 1986. *Why We Lost the ERA*. Chicago: University of Chicago Press.
Marable, Manning. 1983. *How Capitalism Underdeveloped Black America: Problems in Race, Political Economy, and Society*. Boston: South End.
Marty, Martin E. 1970. *Righteous Empire: The Protestant Experience in America*. New York: Dial.
Massey, Douglas S., and Nancy A. Denton. 1993. *American Apartheid: Segregation and the Making of the Underclass*. Cambridge, Mass.: Harvard University Press.
Milbrath, Lester W. 1965. *Political Participation: How and Why Do People Get Involved in Politics?* Chicago: Rand McNally.
Miller, Arthur H., Patricia Gurin, Gerald Gurin, and Oksana Malanchuk. 1981. "Group Consciousness and Political Participation." *American Journal of Political Science* 25: 494–511.
Milwaukee Innercity Congregations Allied for Hope. 1994. *To Do What Is Just!* Milwaukee, Wisc.: Milwaukee Innercity Congregations Allied for Hope.
"Milwaukee Police Arrest Jeffrey L. Dahmer." *The Milwaukee Journal* (July 24, 1991), A1.
"'Missionaries' Follow New Reasons to Rescue." *Christianity Today* (September 14, 1992), 58–60.
Moen, Matthew C. 1989. *The Christian Right and Congress*. Tuscaloosa: University of Alabama Press.
"More Arrests in Milwaukee." *The New York Times* (June 19, 1992), D19.
Morris, Aldon D. 1984. *The Origins of the Civil Rights Movement: Black Communities Organizing for Change*. New York: Free Press.
Murphy, Andrew R. 1993. "The Mainline Churches and Political Activism: The Continuing Impact of the Persian Gulf War." *Soundings* 76: 526–549.
Nesbitt, Paula D. 1997. "Clergy Feminization: Controlled Labor or Transformative Change?" *Journal for the Scientific Study of Religion* 36: 585–598.
Neuhaus, Richard John. 1984. *The Naked Public Square: Religion and Democracy in America*. Grand Rapids, Mich.: Eerdmans.
Neustadt, Richard E. 1960/1990. *Presidential Power and the Modern Presidents*. New York: Free Press.
New York Times/CBS News Poll. July 14–17, 1994.
Newman, Graeme R., and Carol Trilling. 1975. "Public Perceptions of Criminal Behavior: A Review of the Literature." *Criminal Justice and Behavior* 2: 217–236.
O'Connor, Robert E., and Michael B. Berkman. 1995. "Religious Determinants of State Abortion Policy." *Social Science Quarterly* 76: 447–459.
Olson, Laura R. 1993. "Ronald Reagan's Rhetorical Appeal to the Christian Right." Paper presented at the Annual Meeting of the Midwest Political Science Association, Chicago.
———. 1997. "Bill Clinton's Strategic Use of Religious and Family Rhetoric: The Co-optation of Partisan Symbolism." Paper presented at the Annual Meeting of the Midwest Political Science Association, Chicago.

"Packwood Hearings Face Delay." *The Oregonian* (July 2, 1994).

"Packwood's Fund for Legal Defense Experiences Big Increase." *The Oregonian* (July 17, 1994).

"Parents May Be Cited In Arrests." *The Milwaukee Sentinel* (June 19, 1992), A1.

"Parts of Many Bodies Found in a Milwaukee Apartment." *The New York Times* (July 24, 1991), A14.

Pfeffer, Leo. 1975. *God, Caesar, and the Constitution: The Court as Referee of Church-State Confrontation.* Boston: Beacon.

Poloma, Margaret. 1982. *The Charismatic Movement: Is There a New Pentecost?* Boston: Twayne.

———. 1989. *The Assemblies of God at the Crossroads: Charisma and Institutional Dilemmas.* Knoxville: University of Tennessee Press.

Popenoe, David. 1988. *Disturbing the Nest: Family Change and Decline in Modern Societies.* New York: Aldine.

Quinley, Harold E. 1974. *The Prophetic Clergy: Social Activism among Protestant Ministers.* New York: Wiley.

Reed, Adolph L., Jr. 1986. *The Jesse Jackson Phenomenon: The Crisis of Purpose in Afro-American Politics.* New Haven, Conn.: Yale University Press.

Reed, Ralph. 1994. *Politically Incorrect: The Emerging Faith Factor in American Politics.* Dallas, Tex.: Word.

Reese, Thomas J. 1989. *Archbishop: Inside the Power Structure of the American Catholic Church.* New York: Harper & Row.

Reichley, A. James. 1985. *Religion in American Public Life.* Washington, D.C.: The Brookings Institution.

Roberts, Julian V., and Don Edwards. 1989. "Contextual Effects in Judgments of Crimes, Criminals, and the Purposes of Sentencing." *Journal of Applied Social Psychology* 19: 902–917.

Roof, Wade Clark, and William McKinney. 1987. *American Mainline Religion: Its Changing Shape and Future.* New Brunswick, N.J.: Rutgers University Press.

Roozen, David A., William McKinley, and Jackson W. Carroll. 1984. *Varieties of Religious Presence: Mission in Public Life.* New York: Pilgrim.

Rosenstone, Steven J., and John Mark Hansen. 1993. *Mobilization, Participation, and Democracy in America.* New York: Macmillan.

Rowen, James. 1994. "Gun Bans Fail in Milwaukee, Kenosha." *The Milwaukee Journal* (November 9), A1.

Sapiro, Virginia. 1994. *Women in American Society: An Introduction to Women's Studies.* 3d ed. Mountain View, Calif.: Mayfield.

"Saturday Protests Result in Record 144 Arrests in City." *The Milwaukee Journal* (June 21, 1992), A13.

Schlozman, Kay Lehman, Nancy Burns, and Sidney Verba. 1994. "Gender and the Pathways to Participation: The Role of Resources." *Journal of Politics* 56: 963–990.

Schlozman, Kay Lehman, Nancy Burns, Sidney Verba, and Jesse Donahue. 1995. "Gender and Citizen Participation: Is There a Different Voice?" *American Journal of Political Science* 39: 267–293.

Schmidt, Frederick W., Jr. 1996. *A Still Small Voice: Women, Ordination, and the Church*. Syracuse, N.Y.: Syracuse University Press.

Schuldt, Gretchen. 1994. "HUD Urged to Drop Its City Appraiser: Two Aldermen Criticize Suhr Realty Inc." *The Milwaukee Sentinel* (February 24), A5.

Schultze, Steve. 1994. "State Seeks Pot of Gold: Tribal Casinos Have It." *The Milwaukee Journal* (August 31), A1.

Scott, Anne Firor. 1991. *Natural Allies: Women's Associations in American History*. Urbana: University of Illinois Press.

Shingles, Richard D. 1981. "Black Consciousness and Political Participation: The Missing Link." *American Political Science Review* 75: 76–91.

Skerry, Peter. 1980. "Christian Schools versus the I.R.S." *The Public Interest* 61: 18–41.

Smidt, Corwin. 1987. "Evangelicals and the 1984 Election." *American Politics Quarterly* 15: 419–444.

———. 1989. "'Praise the Lord' Politics: A Comparative Analysis of the Social Characteristics and Political Views of American Evangelical and Charismatic Christians." *Sociological Analysis* 50: 53–72.

Stark, Rodney, Bruce D. Foster, Charles Y. Glock, and Harold E. Quinley. 1971. *Wayward Shepherds: Prejudice and the Protestant Clergy*. New York: Harper & Row.

Tamney, Joseph B., Stephen D. Johnson, and Ronald Burton. 1994. "The Abortion Controversy: Conflicting Beliefs and Values in American Society and within Religious Subgroups." In *Abortion Politics in the United States and Canada: Studies in Public Opinion*, ed. Ted G. Jelen and Marthe A. Chandler, 41–56. Westport, Conn.: Praeger.

Thomas, John Clayton. 1986. *Between Citizen and City: Neighborhood Organizations and Urban Politics in Cincinnati*. Lawrence: University Press of Kansas.

de Tocqueville, Alexis. 1840/1945. *Democracy in America*, ed. Francis Bowen and Phillips Bradley. New York: Knopf.

"The Two Sides." *The Milwaukee Sentinel* (June 17, 1992), A8.

United States Bureau of the Census. *1990 Census of Population and Housing*.

Vanderbilt University Television News Index and Abstracts. June–July 1994. Nashville, Tenn.: Vanderbilt Television News Archive.

Verba, Sidney, and Norman H. Nie. 1972. *Participation in America: Political Democracy and Social Equality*. Chicago: University of Chicago Press.

Verba, Sidney, Kay Lehman Schlozman, and Henry E. Brady. 1995. *Voice and Equality: Civic Voluntarism in American Society*. Cambridge, Mass.: Harvard University Press.

Verba, Sidney, Kay Lehman Schlozman, Henry Brady, and Norman H. Nie. 1993a. "Citizen Activity: Who Participates? What Do They Say?" *American Political Science Review* 87: 303–318.

———. 1993b. "Race, Ethnicity and Political Resources: Participation in the United States." *British Journal of Political Science* 23: 453–496.

Wald, Kenneth D. 1992. *Religion and Politics in the United States*. 2d ed. Washington, D.C.: Congressional Quarterly Press.

Wald, Kenneth D., Dennis E. Owen, and Samuel S. Hill Jr. 1988. "Churches as Political Communities." *American Political Science Review* 82: 531–548.

———. 1990. "Political Cohesion in Churches." *Journal of Politics* 52: 197–215.
Warner, R. Stephen. 1993. "Work in Progress: Toward a New Paradigm for the Sociological Study of Religion in the United States." *American Journal of Sociology* 98: 1044–1093.
Weintraub, Jo Anne. 1992. "Hundreds Join Ranks with Activists." *The Milwaukee Journal* (June 11), A12.
Weintraub, Jo Anne, and Bob Helbig. 1994. "Church-run Militias Urged in Video." *The Milwaukee Journal* (August 17), A1.
"Welfare Reform, Done Harshly." *The New York Times* (November 8, 1993), A18.
Wells, Robert W. 1970. *This Is Milwaukee*. Garden City, N.Y.: Doubleday.
Wilcox, Clyde. 1989. "The New Christian Right and the Mobilization of Evangelicals." In *Religion and Political Behavior in the United States*, ed. Ted G. Jelen, 139–156. New York: Praeger.
———. 1992. *God's Warriors: The Christian Right in Twentieth-Century America*. Baltimore, Md.: Johns Hopkins University Press.
Williams, Joe. 1994. "O. J. Alibi Clouded by Nicolet Grad: City Native May Be Key Prosecution Witness." *The Milwaukee Sentinel* (June 22), A1.
Wilson, James Q. 1993. *The Moral Sense*. New York: Free Press.
———. 1994. "The Moral Sense." *American Political Science Review* 88: 1–11.
Wilson, William Julius. 1987. *The Truly Disadvantaged: The Inner City, the Underclass, and Public Policy*. Chicago: University of Chicago Press.
———. 1991. "Public Policy Research and *The Truly Disadvantaged*." In *The Urban Underclass*, ed. Christopher Jencks and Paul E. Peterson, 3–42. Washington, D.C.: The Brookings Institution.
Wisconsin Crime and Arrests 1992. Madison, Wisc.: Office of Justice Assistance.
Wisconsin Crime and Arrests 1993. Madison, Wisc.: Office of Justice Assistance.
Wisconsin Crime and Arrests 1994. Madison, Wisc.: Office of Justice Assistance.
Witte, John F. 1991. *Public Subsidies for Private Schools: Implications for Wisconsin's Reform Efforts*. Madison, Wisc.: Wisconsin Center for Education Policy.
Wolfinger, Raymond E., and Steven J. Rosenstone. 1980. *Who Votes?* New Haven, Conn.: Yale University Press.
Woliver, Laura R. 1993. *From Outrage to Action: The Politics of Grass-Roots Dissent*. Urbana: University of Illinois Press.
Wuthnow, Robert. 1988. *The Restructuring of American Religion: Society and Faith Since World War Two*. Princeton, N.J.: Princeton University Press.
Zaller, John R. 1992. *The Nature and Origins of Mass Opinion*. New York: Cambridge University Press.
Zuckerman, Mortimer B. 1993. "Clinton's Shaky Start." *U.S. News & World Report* (February 22), 70.
Zwier, Robert. 1989. "Coalition Strategies of Religious Interest Groups." In *Religion and Political Behavior in the United States*, ed. Ted G. Jelen, 171–186. New York: Praeger.

INDEX

abortion, 11, 16, 21, 22–23, 48, 62, 64, 70, 71–72, 81–95, 97, 101, 113, 129–31
   and African Americans, 88
   salience of to clergy, 93
   and violence, 91–92, 94–95
   See also pro-choice sentiment; pro-life sentiment
Acquired Immune Deficiency Syndrome (AIDS), 70, 72
Acts, Book of, 32–33
African American Protestantism, 5, 8, 25, 32, 44, 46–47, 50–52, 128, 130, 132, 134, 137
   and abortion, 83, 88
   compared with white Protestantism, 50
   and family values, 124–26
   and women's ordination, 39
African Methodist Episcopal (AME) Church, 9, 46, 51
American Baptist Church, 8, 46
American Political Science Association, 114
Ammerman, Nancy, 47
Artison, Richard, 98
Assemblies of God, 8, 46
Atlanta, Georgia, 84

Baptist Church,
   See American Baptist Church; National Baptist Convention, U. S. A., Inc.; Southern Baptist Convention
Barrett, Tom, 28
Bauer, Gary, 114
Bellah, Robert, 50
"Beyond Racism," 27

Blankenhorn, David, 113, 124
Bosnia-Herzegovina, 64, 77
Brzonkala, Tony, 98
Buffalo, New York, 84
Bush, George, 114, 121

Carnegie Council on Children, 113
Carroll, Jackson, 38
Carter, Jimmy, 48, 113
Catholic Church,
   See Roman Catholic Church; Milwaukee, Wisconsin, Roman Catholic Church in
Central America, 19
Chicago, Illinois, 92
child abuse, 118
children, 68, 69, 71, 84, 88–90, 104–6, 113, 114, 116, 117–18, 124
China, 90
Christian Coalition, 8, 48, 73, 82, 99, 133
Christian Right, 4, 8, 45, 47–49, 59, 67, 70, 73, 78, 82, 99, 113–14, 130–31, 133
Church of God (Anderson, Indiana), 8, 46
Church of God in Christ (COGIC), 9, 46, 51
Church of the Nazarene, 8, 46
churches,
   central city, 17, 23, 76, 77, 79, 127
   membership challenges of, 16, 19, 20, 47, 49, 83
   multiracial, 9, 59, 88–89
   "politically mobilizing," 14, 29, 132

169

170 INDEX

churches *(continued)*
  "skill producing," 14, 29, 132
  in social movements, 4, 7
civic skills, 13, 14, 44, 53, 132
civil disobedience, 26, 27
civil rights activism, 2, 4, 7, 9, 25, 47, 51, 75, 81, 83, 119
clergy,
  African American,
    See African American Protestantism
  as agenda setters, 15, 19–23, 61, 65, 70, 76, 78, 109, 127, 130–31, 133
  attitudes about propriety of political activity by, 9, 10, 31, 32–35, 38, 42, 91–93, 127–28, 130–31
  calling to politics of, 2–3, 13–29, 31, 34, 128, 134
  career stages of, 9, 10, 31, 32, 40–41, 127–28, 130–31
  central city, 3, 40, 45, 52–58, 61, 68, 70, 74, 76, 79, 81, 99, 109–10, 133
  endorsement of political candidates by, 23–24, 28, 34
  evangelical,
    See evangelical Protestantism
  feelings of political efficacy among, 9, 10, 26, 31, 35–38, 42, 127–28, 130–31
  female, 27, 38–40, 87, 128
  fundraising by, 16–17
  ideological orientations of, 81, 93, 97, 108–9, 111, 124–26, 127, 129
  incentives for political leadership by, 10–11, 45, 52–54, 58, 70, 73, 74, 78, 81, 109–10, 133–34
  in Indiana, 5
  mainline Protestant,
    See mainline Protestantism
  media coverage of, 2n. 2, 23, 25nn. 16–17, 37, 62n. 11, 86, 94 n. 30, 95 n. 31, 99n. 14
  as opinion leaders, 61
  as political leaders, 15, 23–28, 52–54, 58–59, 61, 65, 70, 76, 78, 79, 95, 108, 109, 111, 124–25, 128, 129, 133
  political activities of, 1–3, 7, 13–29, 91
  political issue agendas of, 11, 61–79, 108, 127, 130–31
  politically disengaged, 15, 16–19, 20, 61, 65, 76, 78, 109, 127, 130, 133
  as public officials, 23, 27–28
  relationship to political elites of, 2, 7, 20, 24, 27–28, 32, 35, 36
  reminding congregations to vote, 17
  secular jobs held by, 18, 42, 51
  self-selection into neighborhood contexts by, 54n. 45
  time constraints of, 3, 17–18, 27–28, 33, 42, 43, 51, 134
clergy-laity gap,
  See mainline Protestantism
Clinton, Bill, 67, 72, 76, 77, 90, 115
Clinton, Hillary Rodham, 77
clothing programs, 17
Cohen, Cathy, 53
Communitarianism, 114
Conference on Religion and Race, 7
Congress, United States, 68, 76, 77, 113
Crawford, Sue, 14, 43
crime and violence, 3, 11, 25, 27, 54, 62, 65, 68–69, 77, 78, 79, 92, 97–110, 111, 124–26, 129, 130–31, 133–34
  personal causes of, 101, 104–7, 108
  and race, 107–8
  rates of in Milwaukee, 97–99, 100
  salience of to clergy, 101, 108
  societal causes of, 101–4, 108
  solutions to, 101, 107–8
crisis pregnancy centers, 92
cryptosporidium, 62
Cuba, 77
culture war, 4, 67, 82, 121

D-Day anniversary, 62
Dahmer, Jeffrey, 62, 69
Daniel (prophet), 32
David (king), 32
Dawson, Michael, 53
death penalty, 69
Democratic Party, 2
denomination,
　political significance of, 9, 10, 19, 32, 42, 43, 44, 46–52, 58, 83–84, 94, 127–28, 132, 135
discipline, 105–6, 116, 117, 118
discrimination against Christians, 36–37, 64, 65, 71, 73–75, 77, 78, 130
drugs, 3, 19, 25, 54, 65, 68–69, 71, 98, 101, 103–5, 117, 129, 134

economic issues, 11, 25, 62, 64–70, 77, 78, 79, 102–3, 120
ecumenism, 25, 126, 130, 134
education, 25, 65, 68, 78, 113, 118
　See also home schooling; outcome-based education; school choice
Eisinger, Peter, 6, 134
El Salvador, 26
Engel v. *Vitale*, 48n. 22
environment, 11, 76, 77
Episcopal Church, 8, 46
Equal Rights Amendment, 113
Etzioni, Amitai, 114
Evangelical Free Church, 8, 46
Evangelical Lutheran Church in America, 8, 46
evangelical Protestantism, 4, 5n. 16, 8, 22, 32, 44, 46, 47–49, 59, 74, 107, 108, 128, 129, 130, 133, 137
　and abortion, 83, 94
　compared with mainline Protestantism, 49–50, 59, 108, 126
　and crime, 107
　and family values, 113–14, 126
　and poverty, 67
　and women's ordination, 39

evangelism, 16, 18, 44, 47
Exodus, Book of, 72

Falwell, Jerry, 4, 8, 48, 113
Family Protection Act, 113
Family Research Council, 114
family values, 11, 48, 64, 65, 66, 70–73, 78, 111–126, 129, 130–31, 133
　and race, 113, 118–19, 120, 122, 124–25
　as symbolic debate, 112–15
fatherlessness, 113, 118, 124
Fay, Michael, 69
Feingold, Russ, 28
First Amendment, 4, 75
foreign policy, 19, 62, 64, 65, 76–78, 79
Foreman, Joseph, 84
Fuller, Howard, 98
fundamentalism, 8, 21, 47, 49, 83

gambling, 11, 65, 66
gangs, 98
Gathering, The, 16–17
Gaubatz, Kathlyn, 99
gay rights,
　See homosexuality
gender, 9, 31, 38–40, 42, 71, 87, 90, 120, 122, 127–28
　and political participation, 38
　See also clergy, female; women
Glazer, Nathan, 113
Glock, Charles, 44
Goffman, Erving, 3
Groppi, James, 7, 20, 68
group consciousness, 43
gun control, 27, 65, 68, 70, 98, 102
guns, 69, 98
　See also gun control; weapons collection programs
Guth, James, 5, 44, 47, 49, 81, 83, 93, 104, 133

Hadden, Jeffrey, 4
Haiti, 62, 64
Hansen, John Mark, 13

health care reform, 62, 64, 65, 67, 79
Hezekiah (prophet), 32
home schooling, 68
homosexuality, 37, 70, 71, 72–73, 113
housing, 7, 20, 25, 65, 68
Huckfeldt, Robert, 43–44, 61
Hunter, James Davison, 81, 123

Iyengar, Shanto, 61–62, 101, 108, 115n. 29

Jackson, Jesse, 4
Jacoby, William, 82
Jelen, Ted, 5, 32, 49, 83, 85
job training programs, 27, 102
jobs,
    See unemployment
Juneau, Laurent Solomon, 6

Kaelin, Brian "Kato," 63
Katz, Elihu, 61
Key, V. O., 14
Kinder, Donald, 62
King, Dr. Martin Luther, 75

Lacy, Ernest, 7, 69
LaHaye, Tim, 114
Lake Michigan, 5
law enforcement, 69, 84, 97, 98, 102, 118
    See also Milwaukee, police force of
Laxalt, Paul, 113
Leahy, E. M., 7
Leave It To Beaver, 122
letter writing campaigns, 17, 19, 92
Lincoln, C. Eric, 21
litigiousness,
    in American society, 76, 77, 90
Luker, Kristin, 83
Lutheran Church-Missouri Synod, 8, 46
Lutheran Church,
    See Evangelical Lutheran Church in America; Lutheran Church-Missouri Synod; Wisconsin Evangelical Lutheran Synod

Maier, Henry, 7
mainline Protestantism, 5n. 16, 7–8, 25, 44, 46, 47, 49–50, 59, 128, 130–31, 134, 137
    and abortion, 83, 94
    clergy-laity gap among, 8, 50, 59
    compared with evangelical Protestantism, 49–50, 59, 108, 124
    and crime, 104, 108, 126
    and family values, 124–25
    and women's ordination, 39
Mamiya, Lawrence, 21
meal programs, 17
media, 62, 69, 74, 76, 78, 79, 101, 104, 111, 116
    and race, 116
    See also clergy, media coverage of; radio, Christian
Menomonee River, 5
Micah, Book of, 1
Milbrath, Lester, 38, 81n. 4
Milwaukee Brewers, 63
Milwaukee Innercity Congregations Allied for Hope (MICAH), 2, 24–28, 36, 51, 69, 99, 133
    effectiveness of, 27, 134
Milwaukee River, 6
Milwaukee, Wisconsin, 2, 5–7, 137n. 1
    abortion conflict in, 22, 62, 84, 94
    citizens' perceptions of crime in, 97–98
    crime in, 97–99, 100
    education in, 68, 98
    German heritage of, 6
    government of, 7, 24, 35, 62
    immigration to, 6
    local news stories in, 62–63
    police force of, 69, 84, 97, 98
    poverty in, 52–58, 65–70, 103
    race relations in, 5–6, 7, 75, 79, 103, 134
    racial segregation in, 5–6, 7, 20, 25, 53, 68, 103
    Roman Catholic Church in, 6–7, 134
    youth in, 105

Missionaries to the Preborn, 22, 84, 89, 94
Moral Majority, 8, 48, 113, 133
Moynihan, Daniel Patrick, 113

National Baptist Convention, U. S. A., Inc., 9, 46, 51
National Rifle Association, 98
Native Americans, 6, 66, 75
neighborhood organizations, 26–27
neighborhood socioeconomic status, 3, 4, 9–10, 11, 21, 40, 42, 43, 45, 52–59, 67–70, 79, 84, 97, 99, 101, 105–8, 109, 119, 124, 127–29, 130–32, 133–35
Newark, New Jersey, 7
Nie, Norman, 13, 63, 81
Norquist, John, 24, 35
North American Baptist Conference, 46
North American Free Trade Agreement (NAFTA), 76
North Korea, 62, 64, 77

Old Testament, 33, 50
Operation Rescue, 22
outcome-based education, 68
Ozzie and Harriet, 120, 123

Panama Canal Treaty, 48
Paul (apostle), 32, 39
Pentecostals, 8, 39n. 12, 47, 49
Planned Parenthood, 86
police,
    See law enforcement; Milwaukee, Wisconsin, police force of
political context, 5, 9, 10, 11, 14, 31, 43–59, 45n. 16, 84, 95, 101, 127, 129, 131–32, 134–35, 137
political efficacy, 35
    See also clergy, feelings of political efficacy among,
political involvement, 13–14, 44, 128
    contextual resources for, 43–59
    personal resources for, 31–42
political participation, 13–15
    and age, 41
    and gender, 38
    and ideology, 81–82
    and intensity of policy preferences, 81
    and political efficacy, 35n. 2
    and race, 44, 53
    and social class, 45, 53–54, 133
    standard socioeconomic model of, 43, 134
    See also political involvement
political refugees, 26
political socialization, 132
Poloma, Margaret, 47
Portland, Oregon, 62n. 9
poverty, 52–58, 65–70, 77, 89, 90, 99, 102–4, 106–7, 109, 129, 130–31, 133–34
Presbyterian Church (U. S. A.), 8, 46
pro-choice sentiment, 83, 85–89, 90, 91–95
    See also abortion
pro-family movement, 112–114, 115, 119–20, 126, 129, 131
Prohibition, 47
pro-life sentiment, 83, 85–89, 90, 91–95, 97
    See also abortion

Quinley, Harold, 4

race relations, 19, 50
    in Milwaukee, 5–6, 7, 75, 79, 103, 134
racism, 11, 27, 64, 65, 67, 73, 74, 75–76, 79, 102, 103, 131
    and crime, 103–5
radio, Christian, 22, 133
rap music, 116–17
Reagan, Ronald, 26, 102, 114, 121
Republican Party, 48, 121
research methods, 1–3, 41, 51–52, 55–57, 93, 123, 137–38
responsibility attribution, 101, 108
Right to Life Sunday, 92
Right wing, 11, 120–21, 133
Robertson, Marion "Pat," 4, 8, 47, 48
Roe v. Wade, 48n. 22, 82, 89, 92

174   INDEX

Roman Catholic Church, 6, 7, 134
Roozen, David, 45
Rosenstone, Steven, 13
Rwanda, 62, 64, 77

SALT II Treaty, 48
Schlozman, Kay Lehman, 38
school choice, 48n. 22, 68
school prayer, 70, 113
Selig, Allan H. "Bud," 63
separation of church and state, 4, 36, 92
The Silent Scream, 87
Simpson, O. J., 62, 63, 79, 116
Singapore, 69
slavery, 50, 75, 103
social class, 45, 52–58, 67–70, 89, 90, 102, 105–6, 128, 130–31
 and race, 53, 56
 See also neighborhood socioeconomic status; poverty
social gospel, 8, 49, 59, 110
social isolation, 53, 101, 104–5
social justice, 26, 103
 See also social gospel
social movements,
See churches, in social movements
social theology, 5, 24, 49, 81, 83, 93, 104
Southern Baptist Convention, 5, 8, 46, 47, 77
Sparta, Wisconsin, 107
spiritual renewal, 16, 37, 90, 101, 107, 117, 122
Sprague, John, 43–44
Stark, Rodney, 4, 44
State of the Union addresses, 114–15
suburbanization of business, 52, 55
Supreme Court, United States, 48, 74, 82

Tanzania, 104
tax issues, 48, 113
theology, 2, 5, 7, 10, 18, 21, 40, 44, 46–51, 58–59, 83, 99, 126, 132, 135
 See also social theology
Thompson, Tommy, 66, 77
de Tocqueville, Alexis, 4
Trewhella, Matthew, 84, 94
tutoring programs, 17

Underground Railroad, 6, 26
unemployment, 55, 62, 65, 66, 79, 102, 129, 130–31, 134
United Church of Christ, 8, 46
United Methodist Church, 8, 46
United States census, 53–57

Verba, Sidney, 13, 14, 29, 44, 63, 81
Vietnam War, 47

Wald, Kenneth, 5
Washington, George, 72
Watertown, Wisconsin, 107
Watts, California, 7
weapons collection programs, 27, 70, 98
welfare, 48, 65, 66, 90, 106, 107, 118
White House Conferences on Families, 113
Wichita, Kansas, 84
Wilson, James Q., 114, 124
Wisconsin,
 conservatism in, 62n. 9
Wisconsin Evangelical Lutheran Synod, 8, 46
Wisconsin Office of Justice Assistance, 98–99
Woliver, Laura, 7
women, 27, 38–40, 71, 72, 87, 90, 122
 See also clergy, female; gender